Pentaparadox

Pentaparadox

Overcoming Five Excuses For Rejecting the Christ

<<<<<<<<<<<<<<<<<<<<<<<<<<<<<<<<<<<<<<<<<<<<<<<<<<<<<<<<<<<<<<<<<<<<<<<<>>>

Book One

Photo on page 1: Ancient Armenian map, taken outside the Armenian Tavern in Old City Jerusalem

D M Browning, Publisher

ISBN 978-0-578-02682-4

This book is dedicated to my family and to all those pursuing Jesus of Nazareth.

Doug Browning, 2009

A NOTE TO THE READER

I am honored and excited to share some thoughts and observations on this great human experience we call life. One of the things that makes life so interesting is that we keep bumping into puzzling and challenging "paradoxes." These are situations, conditions, arguments, etc. that seem contradictory, at least on the surface, but also seem to have some validity.

Theoretically, paradoxes should not arise in the minds of truly rational people since contradictions speak (*dicere*) against (*contra*) their own logic. But paradoxes pop up all over the place, and they tend to be both problematic and stimulating—problematic because it is difficult or impossible to eliminate the inherent contradictions, and stimulating because we seek closure on things (such as contradictions) that make us uncomfortable.

Some of the most challenging and rewarding of life's paradoxes reflect the thoughts and beliefs of previous generations. *Pentaparadox: Book One* examines the divinity of Jesus Christ as one of five great paradoxes that stem from Biblical times. His divinity, of course, has been controversial and paradoxical since He first claimed it. Its development as a key feature of Western thought and culture is undeniable, though in recent history secular atheism has made increasingly strenuous efforts to dismiss it.

My objective in addressing Jesus' divinity (and the other four paradoxes in later writings) is not to solve them in the sense of achieving consensus about what they assert. It is to challenge the supposed contradictions that underlie them—their status as being paradoxical. For all their usefulness in stimulating thought and debate, paradoxes usually leave a lingering sense of doubt. They allow us to easily set them aside as interesting but not totally convincing.

Rather than setting aside these five great paradoxes I am suggesting that we must ultimately recognize that they are something greater: *mysteries*, i.e. aspects of reality that are not fully comprehensible to human consciousness in this life through normal means. The beauty of realizing this is that we can begin to dispel the notion that the great, so-called "paradoxes" of the Bible are inherently irrational and undeserving of our confidence and belief in them. By admitting that they are mysteries we place the focus on our limitations in comprehending reality rather than presuming that reality is somehow contradicting itself.

Since before Christ's time it has always *seemed* that God (in the monotheistic sense) could or would not take on the form of a human being. God and man were always considered totally distinct, and yet it was understood that God could relate and reify to man as He chose. Why then have so many presumed that the combination of the two (God as man) is a contradiction of reality, rather than a valid expression of it? What is it that mankind brings—or fails to bring—to the experience of reality that so readily labels Jesus' divinity as "paradoxical?" In asking these kinds of questions my hope is to open the reader's mind to a metaphysical reality beyond that with which we are so familiar and comfortable—beyond the one that dubs a Creator taking on human form as paradoxical or even impossible.

The subject matter of *Pentaparadox: Book One* reaches beyond what we may fully comprehend, but not beyond imagination. In many respects people's failure to appreciate the Bible is, I believe, a failure of imagination rather than one of analysis or interpretation. And in today's world, unfortunately, using one's imagination is often equated with being unscholarly or fictional. Sophisticated media pundits, for example, are quick to brand believers in Biblical history and prophecy as "over-imaginative," "radical" and even "dangerous."

Personally, I prefer to think mulling over and imagining the meaning of Biblical paradoxes as planning for the future. Like it or not some day this life will end, and ignoring the possibilities beyond that day seems unimaginative, superficial, and defensive. Critics of such planning are either genuinely convinced that there is no future existence beyond the grave or have simply succumbed to the mind (and imagination) numbing emptiness of materialistic secularism.

Admittedly I have no particular training or qualifications to help lend credence to what you are about to read. My educational credentials are reasonably good (psychology, language and business) but not especially relevant. I do have a passion to know Jesus, and I have been blessed with an analytical mind, the basic resources to pursue my interest, and the desire to share my findings.

Reading this book will not be like breezing through a Grisham novel. More likely it will seem a bit difficult at times, possibly a little radical in some respects, and you may completely disagree with parts of it. I would encourage you to have a Bible handy as you read, and to set aside some time to meditate on scriptural passages as you proceed. Whatever your reactions and conclusions may be, I am delighted that you are taking the time and making the effort to consider my musings. I look forward to your comments and feedback on the web at: *dbrning7@yahoo.com.*

ACKNOWLEDGEMENTS

My wife, daughter and son deserve a special note of thanks for their contributions to this book. Patricia, my wife, has been a patient listener and collaborator in developing many of the ideas put forth here. Elizabeth Richmond Browning, my daughter, has graciously allowed me the use of her wonderful photography, and has provided stylistic and editorial advice along the way. My son Michael drew the gorgeous pencil-on-paper rendition of Jesus on the cover.

CONTENTS

Overview of Pentaparadox

In some respects it seems almost futile to probe the truths of the Bible. Its historic and theological scope is vast and multi-layered, mysterious and at times seemingly contradictory. How can one best approach what believers call "the word of God" with any hope of gaining real insight into its primary subject matter, God Himself? Scholars, skeptics, and simple humble folk have grappled with this challenge for millennia.

There is probably no single best or most inspired way to come to grips with Biblical Scripture and the truth it contains. It is quite clear, however, that humility is one of the prerequisites. Without it one forgets that no mere human—Augustine, Luther, Wesley, Billy Graham, etc.—has ever gained a complete and integrated grasp of the Bible's contents. To stand on the shoulders of past thinkers and believers in one's own search for enlightenment is an enormous advantage and great encouragement. It is also humbling.

Along with an attitude of humility, any spiritually fruitful search of Scripture requires trust in the Spirit of God for direction and strength. This trust or faith in the very object of inquiry is foreign to other approaches at truth discovery. Like scientific truth seeking, it acknowledges laws, forces, or systems that define reality. Simultaneously, however, it recognizes that the reality cannot be understood *in toto*. Trust in the laws of the universe—and ultimately God—implies dependence upon Him, and the corresponding inability to ever completely know Him. To *fully* understand would provide total control and thereby obviate God. In the views espoused here, the human tendency to replace a personal God with conceptual constructs is, at best, illusory.

Paradox Defined

Given this framework, I set out to ponder, analyze and gain insight and spiritual appreciation for five elemental aspects of the Christian belief system: (1) the DIVINITY of Christ; (2) the operation of human WILL in relation to the Creator; (3) the nature of HELL; (4) the ATONEMENT of Christ; and (5) the SECOND COMING of Christ. Each of these areas of interest presents a major paradox, a term that describes two basic situations.

"Swords into Plowshares," Haganah Museum, Tel Aviv

Paradox type A is a seemingly self contradictory statement that may be true, and paradox type B is a statement contrary to accepted opinion that may be true. Both types describe assertions that tend to be controversial and challenge conventional wisdom. Paradoxes, by their nature, usually allow for easy dismissal. Their apparent self-contradiction or lack of acceptance can provide ready excuses for rejecting any inherent truth.

The "Penta" in Pentaparadox

There are, I must admit, almost unlimited Bible subjects and study themes that may serve as valid means of organization and exposition. The five mentioned above had particular personal significance. Over the past several years they rose up from the pages of Scripture as topics that seemed confusing, mysterious, sometimes threatening, and at the same time full of promise and even joy.

It became increasingly apparent that I needed clarity in each of these areas—a more complete intellectual understanding and synthesis that could help build faith. It also became apparent that non-believers often struggle with one or more of these same topics. Frequently they lose interest in the need or possibility of salvation for lack of clarity on the same issues that challenged me. One's responses to what I have come to call *Pentaparadox*, five interrelated paradoxes, can drive a person to or from the arms of Christ.

Paradox (1) DIVINITY: Jesus, the focal point of Christianity, was fully man and Jesus was and is fully God. It seems contradictory that a Creator God could "be" or would take on the form of His creation.

Who is this man that we should care so greatly about what He said and did? Who is this "anointed one" from the land of Galilee? Why, in the minds of believers, does He tower above humankind? These questions (and central type A paradox) point to the bare essence of Christianity—a name, a man, a person so grand in character that He defines every aspect of the universe—all its dimensions, its purpose, its very existence. Ironically, it is this now-unseen person and not our physical surroundings that gives true relevance and meaning to the human experience.

His name in the Greek is "the Lord saves," Jesus. And as is so often the case in scriptural text, name reflects essence even to the point of being a complete substitute for the namesake. Jesus is Lord and Jesus saves. The name is clear. Confusion and contention arise over its sheer force and audacity—that a man can be absolute Lord and that his Lordship extends to eternal salvation.

Absent faith this name easily becomes a donnybrook, and for many an unbridgeable chasm. Witness Surah V-72 of the Qur'an. "Certainly they disbelieve who say: Surely Allah, He is the Messiah, son of Marium; and the Messiah said: O Children of Israel! Serve Allah, my Lord and your Lord. Surely whoever associates (others) with Allah, then Allah has forbidden to him the garden, and his abode is the fire; and there shall be no helpers for the unjust."[1] This passage, and by my count forty-eight others within the Qur'an, completely abjure the Lordship of the man named Jesus. The objection is not his manhood but his "association with" (his assumption of) Allah (divinity).

Rejection of the possibility of a divine being assuming the form and strictures of humanity is not unique to Islam. Orthodox Judaism claimed One God and no "association" of God and man for many centuries prior to Muhammad's rise to power. Even polytheistic pagan cultures were circumspect in combining divine and human attributes. King Gilgamesh of Sumeria, for example—who was believed to be the offspring of a goddess mother and human father—never achieved immortality.[2]

Any notion of The One God manifesting as a human being within His own creation is simply astounding. It is almost—I say *almost*—unbelievable. The unique truth of Jesus as God manifest is, however, cause for great joy, not consternation. It is this Jesus, this Christ who has redefined human existence and its ultimate design and potential. Jesus and those who put their faith in Him do not have to reconcile themselves to mankind. At some point all mankind must reconcile itself to the words, acts and personhood of this man named Jesus.

This text, *Pentaparadox: Book One*, contemplates Jesus' divinity and makes some initial attempts to relate it to the other four paradoxes mentioned below. Subsequent writings will cover paradoxes two trough five more completely and attempt to demonstrate interrelationships between them.

Paradox (2) WILL: Every person is responsible for his own actions and every man's eternal destiny was known to God before the dawn of time. It seems contradictory that man could bear responsibility for (and input into) his own destiny if God knew with certainty what each person's outcome would be before creating him or her.

Near the very end of the Bible (Rev 22:17) John the beloved and the revelator implores us: "The Spirit and the bride say 'Come!' And let him who hears say 'Come!' Whoever is thirsty, let him come; and whoever wishes, let him take the free gift of the water of life." Quotes such as this along with numerous others in both the Old and New Testaments point to an intimate and special relationship—an intimate and special interaction—between God and man.

This truth, that a Creator would condescend to interact with His creation, is beyond the pale of human consciousness. Who can fully appreciate that a God who spoke the universe into existence would ask His creation to join Him in eternal life? Listen to me, man, John is saying, if you wish it...if you desire it...if you will it, seize hold of this incalculable treasure Christ offers. Conversely, if you reject it, the treasure will be lost.

Through the ages huge intellects have fought to gain

some perspective on man's interaction with God, both before and after the new covenant of Christ. Desiderius Erasmus and Martin Luther tilted mightily around this subject. Erasmus, derided by Luther as a mere "humanist," somewhat reluctantly held out that even fallen man's will allows for a bit of input regarding his eternal destiny. Bombastic Luther responded with his "thunderbolt" that man's will with respect to moral matters is bound and effectively impotent. Ergo his eternal future is indeed destined, or perhaps more aptly, predestined.[3]

Interesting table talk (and type A paradox), but how does a believer or potential believer resolve this question? Too often, I fear, they punt and move on to the next paradox. But the soul still aches. Can man affect his own spiritual destiny? If yes, to what extent and how does he do it? If not, are we merely play actors parading about mumbling scripted lines? Has the play's writer already decided the actors' fates within the play?

Again, the easy conclusions may be dangerous to spiritual health. The complete-control-of-my-own-fate group concludes by replacing God with man's will. That is beyond dangerous; it's prideful. Opposite this group are the no-control people, those one could classify as true fatalists. Interestingly, most of the world's great belief systems are aligned with the latter group's thinking. Like it or not our eternal fate is sealed, they lament. Buck up and quit complaining. I would argue that neither is what Christ had in mind nor what He taught.

Paradox (3) HELL: God is all-loving, and part of his creation will spend eternity in hell. It seems contradictory that a beneficent Creator could allow His creation to experience the reality of hell.

Eternal punishment, the second death, weeping and gnashing of teeth, the lake of fire, etc. are all repulsive images of a place or condition that came to be known in the Greek as "hell." These images assault the natural human sense of justice and proportionality. Reactions to the possibility of such a reality range from *ipso facto* rejection to guilt induced paralysis. Hell and its perceived overstatement of punishment is probably today's single greatest stumbling block on the non-believers path to faith. To many it is incomprehensible that an all-loving Creator could generate beings capable of bringing such unrelenting horror upon themselves. It is a true type A paradox.

More repugnant still is the notion that the same Creator would predetermine that certain beings—prior to the beginning of time and prior to their creation—would be relegated to unspeakable, unending misery. Ostensibly such individuals must be created simply for the sake of torture or, even more perverse, for the sake of helping those who are not doomed to recognize their own good fortune.

Is it any wonder that non-believers are confused or reject such an "all loving" God out of hand? Better to reject such a tyrant and hope for reincarnation. Or maybe just drop the whole issue and cram as many pleasures as possible into the short time on earth. Believers cannot just fall back on the old saw that God has every right to do whatever he chooses to do, and everything He chooses to do is just. It is too easy—and too dangerous—to attempt to wrap God inside little aphorisms. They help us feel more comfortable about our own brand of theology. But unfortunately, aphorisms and pat answers almost never strike a chord with someone in need of repentance and salvation. Hell is a tough issue, one that needs to be addressed honestly and thoroughly.

Paradox (4) ATONEMENT: Jesus, who is God, became man to redeem man from the wrathful judgment of God. It seems contradictory that God would have to punish

Himself for the bad behavior of His creation.

Reconciling oneself to an historic figure, even one as unique and bold as Jesus, seems a bit odd. People do not normally talk about "reconciling" to a Julius Caesar, or a William Shakespeare, or an Abraham Lincoln. Myriad historical figures nudge our consciences into a sort of reckoning or re-evaluation or perhaps even renewal. None but Jesus, however, insists on *reconciliation*, a side-by-side and point-by-point personal acceptance or rejection of what He says and demonstrates. That is the magnitude of His power. He can be rejected and despised; He can be embraced and adored. But unlike any other historical figure, once you have heard about Him you must answer to Him.

Ironically, reconciliation between God incarnate (Jesus) and His creation is made possible and facilitated through the incarnate life and death of the Creator, not the creation. Delving into the mystery of atonement is often the point along the spiritual journey where skeptical seekers tend to throw up their hands in frustration. Often the incredulity gets voiced as follows: "God created man, right? And man screwed up big time and lost favor with God, right? Then why didn't God just let it go and forget this whole atonement thing and suffering and death on a cross? Why did Jesus have to atone to Himself (He's God, right?) for the lousy behavior of man?" Needless to say, it's another prickly type A paradox.

Paradox (5) THE SECOND COMING: Jesus said He will return to earth "soon" and almost two thousand years have passed since He departed. It seems contradictory that Jesus hasn't returned as He said He would.

Having mentioned four of the five facets of *Pentaparadox*, a mega-question looms. When is Jesus coming back? Being focused on timing, however, misses the crucial point of Jesus' warning: "Therefore keep watch, because you do not know on what day your Lord will come (Mt 24:42)." Strangely, in this instance the paradox (a type B one) is generated totally by man.

Jesus has put us on guard to continually watch for Him. Man, skeptical about the historicity of Jesus to begin with, has grown comfortable that He is way "past due." He seems so past due that for many the whole Jesus story falls apart. The opinion and expressed belief that Jesus will certainly return becomes increasingly unpopular and paradoxical as man increasingly disregards the charge to keep watch.

This situation is somewhat reminiscent of the 9/11/01 attack on the New York World Trade Center. Civil authorities had been warned for years that terrorists could use jetliners as huge incendiary bombs to massacre their enemies. A paradox developed that terrorists could and would attack in this manner. It was paradoxical in that popular opinion—despite real evidence to the contrary—held that modern man just would not do that sort of thing. Lack of resolve to deal with the paradox cost thousands of lives. The utter shock and dismay were complete.

For most of the world the probability of Jesus returning is very small, smaller than the likelihood of an attack on the WTC prior to 9/11/01. Jesus said He will return. Much of mankind, emboldened by the passage of time and self-interest, rationalizes that He will not. Try to imagine the cost of not heeding His warning.

Onward to the Land of Pentaparadox

Given all these paradoxes, it may seem like God is not making it any too easy for us to relate to Him, or at least to understand to some degree how the relationship works. That may seem to be the case, but I think it more likely that He wants us to know Him to the full extent of our capabilities. Though mankind fully comprehending the Creator is impossible, more clearly grasping seemingly paradoxical revelations about Him is not.

Glimpsing the meaning of several *interrelated* paradoxes, such as the ones mentioned above, is also within reach. Christian doctrine regarding Christ's second coming, for example, becomes a bit less opaque with a better grasp of His divinity. And both of these seem to make a bit more sense when the exercise of human will is understood as a means of relating to Him. Likewise, the hellish consequences of ignoring Christ's atoning act seem more just with a better understanding of why human will opposes divine will.

The single, most relevant document for delving into Biblical paradoxes is, of course, the Bible itself. Within that rather massive text I found it most enlightening to concentrate on Jesus' own words and teachings as recorded in the four Gospels. *The Book of Acts* is also critical as it completes Jesus' physical contact with humankind and elucidates the thinking and teachings of His early church. And John's *Revelation* stands alone as a lamp into the murky realm of the last days and Christ's return to earth. Together they serve as a trusty guide.

Since too-intense focus on any selection of Biblical canon may be misleading, other parts of Scripture are also quoted liberally. Outside sources are referenced fairly frequently, but my primary interest is to allow the scriptural text to speak for itself as much as possible. Hopefully, the outside sources and commentary (including my own) used to interpret and draw out the meaning of Scripture will prove to be helpful.

Chronologies of historical events as given in Strong's *Exhaustive Concordance of the Bible*[4] and *The NIV Study Bible*[5] serve as the basic organizational scheme for discussing Jesus' divinity. "Background" information and "asides" are provided along the way to stimulate thought and provide a little more depth regarding my own perspective on various issues. In keeping with the basic chronological scheme, the narrative flow moves through the four Gospels followed by events in *The Book of Acts* and *Revelation*.

Geographical references use the Roman designations in effect during Jesus' lifetime. The use of capitalized titles for the five paradoxes throughout the book (DIVINITY, WILL, HELL, ATONEMENT, and SECOND COMING) is intended to emphasize the inter-connections and interactions between them.

Paradox One

The Divinity of

Jesus

Jesus

Introduction

Attempts to relate mankind to some force or person—usually referred to as "God" or the "Divine"—have been going on for a very long time. The fact that such efforts have continued unabated is really not so mysterious as is often suggested. At its core the motivation behind this long-term pursuit is simple. Given that man exists (an easy proposition to satisfy by observation) and is sufficiently intelligent to reflect on himself and his surroundings, he attempts to explain or rationalize himself in relation to everything outside himself. The mere existence of intelligent consciousness capable of inner/outer reflection is sufficient impetus to initiate God-type questions.

Where did I come from? Are there others out there somewhere in space like me? Unlike me? How long will I have consciousness? What happens when I no longer have it? Asking these kinds of questions is inherent to mankind. They are the natural product of people operating in their natural environment. They flow from people because of their inborn qualities and capabilities.

People provide all sorts of answers to themselves and others based upon their life experiences. The phrase "life experiences," incidentally, is used here to mean any experience that humans are capable of having, including sensate, emotional, symbolic, metaphysical, etc. Four questions that raised my personal interest in what God might be like and how people might relate to Him developed over time in the following sequence:

(1) *Did I create myself*? As satisfying as it might be to answer this one yes, it became ever more apparent that I could not make that claim. There was the problem of

being born to parents who had some prior claim. And, of course, there was the problem of not being able to remember anything prior to the age of two or three.

(2) *Was I created by accident?* Surrendering the possibility of self-creation, there occurred the enticing possibility that I, along with the rest of the universe, might have just happened. The attractiveness of this option was the same as suggested in the first question. Being self-generated or randomly generated there is only one authority to be satisfied, namely me. Over time this notion became less and less tenable, and the possibility of it representing reality slipped to zero.

Truly random development (see chapter eight for a discussion of this concept) of a single human brain cell, let alone the co-ordination of the hundred-billion-plus brain cells as one organ in the human body, simply cannot happen. It cannot happen even given the billions of years of earth's existence and the additional billions since the origin of the universe. The probability of such an occurrence has been somewhat humorously described as attempting to produce the U.S. space shuttle by sequentially setting off a series of explosions in an extremely long string of junkyards. Voila! With enough time and explosion attempts the shuttle is bound to emerge, right? Wrong.

Truly random activity can be hypothesized, and hypothetically such activity could continue forever; but its continuance would not *necessarily* lead to anything of interest. There is simply no basis to assume that it could or would result in the hyper-complex living organisms and relationships that we observe on a daily basis. The mere existence of such organisms is no reason for concluding that the absolute random activity hypothesis has been substantiated in any way.

I use the qualifier "hypothetically" when referring to the notion of true randomness because it assumes that a result (and ultimately all results) can come to exist without a precipitating cause (or causes). But the notion of absolute or true randomness should not be confused with Charles Darwin's attempts to explain the biologic order of nature. *On The Origin of Species*[6] deserves a full reading for a good understanding of where his thoughts were leading him. And for an interesting discussion of "irreducibly complex" features of living organisms that pose current challenges to Darwinian theory I would recommend Michael Behe's *Darwin's Black Box.*[7]

(3) *How else could I have been created?* Folks with a scientific bent talk a lot about the "Big Bang," but grow uncomfortable with some of its implications. Big Bang theory posits that the stuff of the universe has not always been around, i.e. it was not pre-existent. And if the universe had a beginning, who or what made it begin? The spontaneous start of a universe from an immeasurably small speck of pure energy and its subsequent, unguided expansion is even more difficult to imagine than a universe that just happened to always be. Whence the speck of pure energy? How and why was the great explosion triggered? Was the Big Bang a controlled explosion, and, if so, how was it controlled?

Does it make sense to allow the legitimacy of such questions while simultaneously denying the possibility of a Creator God? Does it make sense that the "laws" of the expanding universe set off by Big Bang came about in a truly random fashion and yet are so exquisitely tuned as to provide the physical context for highly complex life forms? What is the real evidence for infinite universes that would allow for the possibility of ours being produced randomly? If we stretch the imagination to allow for this possibility, we have merely come full circle to the original question: how did *infinite* universes (rather than *the* universe) come into existence? How can one argue that the imagined infinite universes did not have their own

Bigger Bang?

The total absence of a God became less and less tenable to me as more detailed data about the universe and the life it sustains have poured forth. Personally, my belief in God was facilitated by the conclusion that the mounting body of scientific evidence is increasingly harmonizing with, rather than opposing other sources positing God. Slowly, mankind is reconciling his observations about his limited reality with ancient truths revealed by Holy Scripture—a source not limited to his observations. Truth is truth, but scriptural truth goes *beyond* scientific truth. If they reconcile within the physical reality of which they speak in common, what is the logic in *not* accepting the "beyond" of which Scripture speaks?

(4) *How do I reconcile the various sources of information concerning creation?* Having answered the big, initial God questions, people who begin to accept belief in a Creator still face a formidable task: making sense of all the so-called "revealed" information about God. All sorts of revelations, interpretations of those revelations, and codifications of the interpretations have been developed and passed down through history. If one were to apportion credibility solely on the basis of longevity, it seems the nod would have to go to one of the ancient Eastern belief systems such as Confucianism, near Eastern polytheism, or the Judeo-Christian tradition. Islam would not make the cut since it is a mere youngster originating some six hundred years later than Christianity (when defined as starting with Jesus Christ) and thousands of years later if the Judeo-Christian tradition is considered a unified whole.

As influential and helpful as it is, however, history is totally cerebral and insufficient for leading one to conviction regarding the metaphysical, supernatural...yes, the spiritual. That kind of conviction draws upon the complete range of a person's capabilities, including the cognitive, emotional and spiritual. To object that spirituality is merely some kind of projection of the physical does not obviate God, but it does close the door on the fullest possible appreciation of Him. Unwilling to do that, or to put it more positively, being willing to embrace the Creator and seek new insight into the God-type questions, it became necessary to trod religious grounds.

The decision to accept faith was the inflection point of my journey. Unfortunately, for many of us in Western culture, the process leading up to such a decision mimics a trip to the mall to buy new clothes, furniture, or, perhaps, a car. Based on a little homework and competing sales pitches, we make a decision and conclude the transaction. *Caveat emptor!* God is not part of a transaction, and salesmen are notoriously deficient at really knowing their products. The "spiritual journey," as it has been called, is a reasonably apt metaphor. But it is a continuous process of discovery, not the simple acquisition of someone's prepackaged God-in-a-box. And, incidentally, the first "step" along the spiritual journey need not be a fearsome "leap of faith" if one employs all of his or her God-given powers (including reason and emotion) in making it.

For me, the single most important aid in trying to find God and relate to Him was...well, God...or at least the putative God who makes such bold claims in the latter part of Judeo-Christian Scripture, the New Testament of the Bible. The God of the Israelites (Yahweh) and the Hebrew descendant (Jesus of Nazareth) who made direct claims of identity with God is truly unique. That's not to say that others were too timid to claim divinity. They did.

What others fell short of was the all-encompassing claim of *actually being* the singular Creator God of the universe. Jesus made that claim—a claim so far-reaching that believers of all persuasions must deal with it. If and when His claim can be sufficiently substantiated, i.e. made acceptable to the inquirer, all alternative paths to God effectively become dead ends.[8] It is for this critical reason that the first Biblical paradox, which must be addressed head-on, is the DIVINITY of the man named Jesus.

CHAPTER ONE

JESUS' EARLY YEARS

Greek portrait of Jesus and Mary at the Basilica of the Annunciation, Nazareth

Bethlehem in Judea, c. 5 B.C.

Matthew, sometimes called Levi and one of Jesus' chosen twelve apostles, targeted his Gospel primarily at Greek speaking Jews. He was especially concerned with proving to them that Jesus was the Messiah of their ancestors. He also wanted to transition his people to the proposition that the new Messiah was more than a super-king anointed in the manner of Saul or David. Accordingly, his Gospel has great relevance to the DIVINITY paradox. Only John's Gospel makes a more direct claim that Jesus is the Messiah, and that the Messiah is God.

From very early in his account of Jesus, Matthew establishes that Jesus was not Joseph's son. "This is how the birth of Jesus Christ came about: His mother Mary was pledged to be married to Joseph, but before they came together, she was found to be with child through the Holy Spirit" (Mt 1:18).[9] Two verses later an angel assures Joseph in a dream not to be afraid, "because what is conceived in her is from the Holy Spirit." Matthew follows up by quoting the prophet Isaiah who had stated seven centuries earlier: "The virgin will be with child and will give birth to a son and will call him Immanuel" (Is 7:14).

Leaving no room for speculation, Matthew explains that the word "Immanuel" means God with us. This use of "with us" is not in the sense of providing prophetic guidance, but in the sense of actual presence. It is the same presence that Moses and his generation experienced at the tabernacle. Matthew applies the term to Mary's son as the fulfillment of what Isaiah had spoken. He is emphasizing to his readers that the baby born to the virgin Jewish girl was of the Holy Spirit—God Himself. His name was to be "the Lord saves" (Jesus), but he was to be "called" (or spoken of) as "God with us."

Luke's recounting of Jesus' birth differs in detail from Matthew's. An angel communicates with Joseph in Matthew's account, whereas Gabriel appears directly to Mary in Luke's. Both events could easily have happened. As is often the case with apparent discrepancies between personal testimonies, they tend to highlight the genuineness of individual observations rather than potential disparities. Emphasis on Jesus' DIVINITY is the same in both accounts.

> In the sixth month, God sent the angel Gabriel to Nazareth, a town in Galilee, to a virgin pledged to be married to a man named Joseph, a descendent of David...You will be with child and give birth to a son, and you are to give him the name Jesus. He will be great and will be called Son of the Most High. The Lord God will give him the throne of his father David, and he will reign over the house of Jacob forever; his kingdom will never end (Lk 1:26-33).

"Most High" is a deferential name for God used fairly frequently throughout the Bible. One might argue that all people are "sons" of God in the sense that they are all part of His creation. Context, however, provides a much more specific meaning. This Son is described as a king who will reign "forever." Earthly kings cannot fit that description.

Luke, thought to be a trained physician and extremely skilled in the use of Greek, gives the most complete rendering of Jesus' actual birth. He tells of "shepherds living out in the fields nearby, keeping watch over their flocks at night" (Lk 2:8). An angel appeared to these uncomplicated, unpretentious men and announced the incomprehensible: "Today in the town of David a Savior has been born to you; he is Christ the Lord" (Lk 2:11).

In a single, declarative sentence the angelic messenger from God witnessed that the child born in Bethlehem was the one who would save them ("Savior"), the anointed one ("Christ" or Messiah) whom they had been waiting for, and the One who is supreme ("Lord" or God). Luke adds that the shepherds actually visited the infant Jesus and, "spread the word concerning what had been told them about this child" (Lk 2:17). Why would God use lowly shepherds to bear witness to such an earth-changing event? Certainly they were humble, perhaps suggesting the posture the new Messiah would assume.

Or, perhaps, it was because they were vulnerable to the truth.

A Brief Aside: The New Calendar

Sign celebrating the 40th anniversary of the reunification of Jerusalem under Israeli control; taken outside the western side of the Old City

Curiously, the historic timeline of Jesus' birth and thirty-plus years on earth is out of sync with the Gregorian calendar in use throughout most of the world today. Around A.D. 525 a Russian monk by the name of Dionysius Exiguus was asked by Pope John I to determine future dates for the celebration of Easter. Dionysius began the task by attempting to establish the date of Christ's birth relative to the founding of Rome, a common reference point for numbering years. He concluded that Christ was born 753 years after the founding.[10]

Under Roman Emperor Justinian I (A.D. 483-565) years began being numbered relative to Christ's birth date as established by Dionysius Exiguus. Year A.D. 1 in the new B.C./A.D. system was considered the 754th year of Rome as a city. After the institution of the B.C./A.D. nomenclature, however, it was discovered that the monk had made a mistake. He had placed Jesus' birth several years later on the old Roman system than it should have been. Year A.D. 1 (Jesus' birth year) in the new system, it turned out, actually occurred about four (or as many as six) years earlier than the A.D. year count indicated. Thus, the recorded A.D. numbers we currently use plus four would be a more accurate measure of the years that have passed since Jesus' birth.

Aside from the monk's miscalculation, it is interesting to note that a political leader felt the need to change the key reference point for measuring time. Most likely, Justinian I was politically motivated in making this historic change. The very obvious fact that it did occur is convincing evidence of the profound and pervasive influence of Christianity on Western society at that time.

Journey to Jerusalem, c. 5 B.C.

Forty days following Jesus' birth, Mary and her young family traveled the five miles from Bethlehem into Jerusalem. The time of purification according to the Law of Moses having been completed, Mary and Joseph presented their firstborn for dedication to the Lord. On this occasion two devout Israelites, Simeon and Anna, gave testimony to the Messiahship of infant Jesus. Praising God, Simeon exclaimed: "For my eyes have seen your salvation, which you have prepared in the sight of all people, a light for revelation to the Gentiles and for glory to your people Israel" (Lk 2:30-32).

It is fascinating to consider exactly what Simeon saw. He speaks of Jesus as God's "salvation" for all people, including non-Jews. Without question, Simeon and Anna had both patiently awaited the anointed one who would redeem their people. They were among the first to bear witness to the fulfillment of that long-standing expectation. But did they make the connection between the Messiah and

DIVINITY? In retrospect it is easy to infer that they must have. Within the context of Jewish ambivalence about the exact nature of the Messiah, it is much less certain. The text itself does not settle the point, but does strongly reinforce the notion that Jesus was indeed the Jewish Messiah. Further, it confirms that the Messiah involves all mankind, both Israel and the Gentile nations.

Northeast corner of Old City Jerusalem wall

Jerusalem in Judea, c. 4 B.C.

Sometime after his presentation at the temple and before the age of two another stunning witness about Jesus as Messiah occurred. This one involved a well known, ruthless Roman king named Herod the Great and a number of "wise" men, who were probably astrologers, and possibly highly placed counselors to royalty. Matthew indicates that these wise men "disturbed" Herod and the whole city of Jerusalem in their search for the one born king of the Jews. With seeming impertinence, Gentile foreigners tramped about the capital city of Judea asking about a Jewish king.

Herod, ever protective of his power, was also knowledgeable about Jewish tradition concerning a Messiah. There was widespread and long-standing expectation that a ruler of the Jews would emerge from Bethlehem in the land of Judah (see, for example Mic 5:2). His fear of possible competition from such a ruler led Herod to call meetings with the Sadducees and other leading Jewish scholars of the day. He also met with the wise men from the East to find out what they knew about the new king. What he learned confirmed his suspicions. And the fact that dignitaries had traveled from a distant land to pay homage was further validation that the Jewish king had actually arrived. Herod's response was typical of the line of Herodian kings: eliminate the competition.

The story of the wise men is a telling bit of Roman-dominated, Near Eastern history. It is laden with Jewish yearning for a resurgence of power, Roman political intrigue, and mysterious visitors traveling from a foreign country. But what elevates the story beyond historical interest is an unusual detail concerning the foreign visitors. They did not come to merely pay homage to a new king but to "worship him" (Mt 2:2). "Worship" is a word usually used in reference to deity. Of course, it is true that Roman emperors demanded homage as deities, but Jewish kings did not go that far.

Likewise, the method the visitors used to find the new king was, to say the least, unconventional. "After they had heard the king [Herod] they went on their way, and the star they had seen in the east went ahead of them until it stopped over the place where the child was" (Mt 2:9). Was the star actually a conjunction of Jupiter and Saturn, a supernova, a comet, or some other natural phenomenon? Matthew's description of the star-guide concurs with several naturalistic explanations. The critique that the whole story of the wise men is simply a fabrication of Matthew is a common one. But there is no real evidence that any of the Gospel writers attempted anything other than the recording of actual events.

The Nile Delta, Egypt c. 4 B.C.

Following the visit by the wise men, Matthew indicates that Jesus and His family fled to somewhere in Egypt to escape Herod the Great. Although the exact length of their stay is not known, they remained in Egypt until after Herod's death in 4 B.C. The family then set out for the "land of Israel" (Mt 2:20), most likely Bethlehem in Judea, until Joseph realized that the equally brutal Archelaus had replaced his father (Herod) in Judea. Joseph changed course to Nazareth, his and Mary's hometown, located in the southern portion of Galilee. Nazareth was outside of Archelaus's control. During this series of events Joseph was guided by instructions from an angel as he dreamed.

Almost everyone loves angels. Often we see them as fluffy, bright-faced creatures with huge, beautiful wings that go around helping hapless humans. Biblical accounts, however, more often describe them as enormously powerful messengers and executors of God's will. Their mention in the Bethlehem-Egypt-Nazareth scenario is not a direct allusion to Jesus' divinity, but it does speak of the great protective care given to "the anointed one."

Jerusalem in Judea, c. A.D. 7

The four Gospels included in the Biblical canon give scant coverage of the time between Jesus' return from Egypt and the beginning of his active ministry—a span of about twenty-nine years. Luke does give a glimpse of Jesus at age twelve as He observed the Feast of the Passover with His family. A precocious adolescent, Jesus got involved in serious discussion with several rabbis in the temple courts. "Everyone who heard him was amazed at his understanding and his answers" (Lk 2:47). Apparently, He was totally engrossed with the teachers, and He became separated from His family for three days.

Upon returning to Jerusalem and finding Him, Mary mildly scolded Jesus. " 'Son, why have you treated us like this? Your father and I have been anxiously searching for you'" (Lk 2:48). Jesus' response shows an early awareness of His unique relationship to God. " 'Why were you searching for me?'" he asked. " 'Didn't you know I had to be in my Father's house?'" (Lk 2:49). A more literal interpretation is: " 'Didn't you know I had to be in the things of my Father?'" Jesus distinguished between "my Father" and His mother's usage of "your father," Joseph.

This little vignette displays an interesting facet of the DIVINITY paradox. Jesus as a man went through the same learning and maturation processes as any other man. He shared Old Testament teachings with the rabbis and "grew in wisdom and stature, and in favor with God and men" (Lk 2:52). Yet, simultaneously, He was intimately aware of His own non-human Father.

Nothing conclusive can be inferred from the brief treatment given by the Gospel writers to Jesus' early years. Most likely the authors wanted to remain focused on recounting their particular perspectives of His teachings—Matthew's emphasis on the fulfillment of Messianic promise, Luke's special outreach to Gentiles, etc. In the context of their evangelistic missions, Jesus' actions and words subsequent to His baptism were of far greater importance than biographical detail of the preceding years.

CHAPTER TWO

CIRCA A.D. 26

Jordan River a few miles north of its entrance into the Sea of Galilee (Lake Kinneret)

Lower Jordan River, East of Jericho in Judea, c. Summer A.D. 26

Matthew writes that John the Baptist attracted crowds from the whole region of Judea and the city of Jerusalem. Baptism, a ritual used by John to signify cleansing and purification, was meaningful to his Jewish followers. He spoke to the crowds as a messenger of someone much greater than himself. "I baptize you with water for repentance. But after me will come one who is more powerful than I, whose sandals I am not fit to carry. He will baptize you with the Holy Spirit and with fire" (Mt 3:11). Among the crowds were Pharisees and Sadducees, members of two influential parties within Orthodox Judaism who came to examine John's message and ritual. John admonished them severely for depending on their lineage to Abraham as a grant of righteousness.

All three of the "synoptic" Gospel writers (Matthew, Mark and Luke)[11] relate the story of how Jesus came to John to be baptized. Jesus' baptism was a public event that marked the beginning of His public ministry. It redefined the baptism ritual, setting the stage for one of the most dramatic depictions of Jesus' DIVINITY in the entire Bible. Luke gives the following account:

> When all the people were being baptized, Jesus was baptized too. And as he was praying, heaven was opened and the Holy Spirit descended on him in bodily form like a dove. And a voice came from heaven: "You are my Son, whom I love; with you I am well pleased" (Lk 3:21-22).

This description of a heavenly Father speaking audibly to His Son and the Holy Spirit manifesting visually in the form of a dove is so perceptually bold that it raises reams of questions. Who actually witnessed the event? Since none of the Gospel writers were present, how were the details transmitted to them? Are the Gospel writers describing what Jesus alone experienced, or did all of those present share the experience? Are the Gospel accounts of Jesus' baptism merely collusion among four of His fanatical followers to convince gullible Jews and Gentiles that their man was the Messiah—and even God?

It is clear that the veracity of this powerful story hinges on the testimony of a limited number of witnesses. First and foremost is Jesus; He may have recounted the story at a later date to one of His apostles or disciples. Acting as one's own witness, however, has never been considered convincing testimony. Secondly, there are those who were baptized with Jesus, or were at least present during His baptism. Context of the synoptic accounts suggests that persons from among this group provided the detail. Finally, and perhaps most convincingly, there are the recollections of an individual with a very intimate perspective on what transpired—John the Baptist.

It is another John—John "the beloved" apostle of Jesus and author of the fourth Gospel—who gives insight into what the Baptist experienced. The apostle John quotes John the Baptist directly:

> Then John [the Baptist] gave this testimony: "I saw the Spirit come down from heaven as a dove and remain on him. I would not have known him, except that the one who sent me to baptize with water told me, 'The man on whom you see the Spirit come down and remain is he who will baptize with the Holy Spirit.' I have seen and I testify that this is the Son of God" (Jn 1: 32-34).

Thus, the person who performed Jesus' baptism reported a sensory experience very similar to those described in the synoptic Gospels. The same Spirit that came down and remained on Jesus was the Spirit that had sent the Baptist on his own mission of preparation. It was the same Spirit Jesus would impart in the new baptism.

Based on the four Gospel accounts, the one obvious conclusion that may be drawn is that Jesus' encounter with the Father and Holy Spirit at His baptism was *not* a private one. It, like the remainder of Jesus' ministry, was intentionally as public as the media of the time would allow. John the Baptist's witness about the one who would baptize with the Holy Spirit was demonstrably public; and Jesus publicly submitted to John's baptism. It would be inconsistent for the witness of God about His Son to have been private; i.e. it is reasonable to conclude that those present at Jesus' baptism shared in His experience. Curiously, the Pharisees and Sadducees could not bring themselves to accept John's baptism. And anything *beyond* John's baptism, such as baptism "with the Holy Spirit" (baptism with and into God Himself), was deemed blasphemous.

As regards the question of collusion among the Gospel writers, perhaps the more pertinent question is whether *any* piece of history (and particularly ancient history) can be objectively validated to satisfy the curious and skeptical mind of man. Opinions and conclusions are always based on incomplete information. They develop into hypotheses and theories that help stimulate new thought and new opinions. The cycle continues along with

From Belvoir Castle looking east across the Jordon valley

the search for truth. Ultimately, however, we have to trust and rely on others, past and present, to make any progress.

West of Jericho in Judea, c. Summer A.D. 26

Matthew's fourth chapter brings together several of the five paradoxes. The Spirit of God led Jesus into the Judean desert to be tested or "tempted." A somewhat puzzling exchange then took place between Jesus and Satan that begs DIVINITY related questions. Why would God put His Son in the position of being tempted? If Jesus was truly God, why did He have to prove it to Satan?

Satan was fully aware of whom he was tempting: " 'If you are the Son of God, tell these stones to become bread...If you are the Son of God, throw yourself down'" (Mt 4: 3-6). What appears to be the conditional "if" here has the meaning of "since." Satan knew the nature of his target and inadvertently gave testimony about Him. Jesus, as evinced by the Father's testimony at His recent baptism, was also aware of His DIVINITY and purpose. He rebuffed the tempter to focus on His primary mission—ATONEMENT.

Jesus was under no obligation to prove anything to Satan. He did, however, use their interaction to reveal key characteristics about Himself to mankind. The following were made apparent: Jesus was man and had the experiences of man; as acknowledged by Satan, Jesus had the power of God; Jesus used His power at His discretion, not as Satan suggested or man expected; and He was totally focused on achieving His purpose. Seen through the prism of multiple paradoxes, the encounter with Satan highlights the union between DIVINITY and ATONEMENT. The reconciliation between man and God was to be achieved by God-in-man. It would require DIVINE power and WILL to ATONE for mankind's willful submission to the power of Satan.

Cana in Southwest Galilee, c. Fall A.D. 26

John's Gospel omits any account of Jesus' temptation in the desert. He moves from the baptism to a short recollection of Jesus choosing his first five disciples (one of whom is John) and then immediately on to Cana in Galilee. During a wedding feast in that small town near Jesus' hometown of Nazareth, the first "miraculous sign" of the new Messiah took place. John, newly converted from John the Baptist, personally witnessed something that he considered physical proof of Jesus' DIVINITY. At his mother's request, Jesus saved a newly married couple's family from deep embarrassment. He did it by creating a rather large quantity of vintage wine on the spot.

Jesus shared in celebration with the wedding guests, and He did it in spectacular fashion. Amid all the hoopla John captures the real significance: "This, the first of his miraculous signs, Jesus performed in Cana of Galilee. He thus revealed his glory, and his disciples put their faith in him" (Jn 2:11). It suddenly became obvious to John: the new rabbi he was following *was God*! John used this experience later on as he described the purpose of his own written testimony: "The Word became flesh and made his dwelling among us. We have seen his glory, the glory of the One and Only, who came from the Father, full of grace and truth" (Jn 1:14).

The wedding feast at Cana was a joyous occasion, but Jesus didn't want to be involved in the wine problem because, as He put it, " 'My time has not yet come'" (Jn 2:4). He knew He could solve the problem, but His driving concern was His mission of ATONEMENT. Producing wine for a wedding party was somewhat premature and irrelevant to His real mission. Perhaps out of deference to his mother's wishes and compassion for the celebrants, Jesus did something that ordinary men cannot. Certainly

He understood that His action would be a faith-builder for His new disciples.

Time Out: A Word About Miracles

Modern and ancient societies have always been attracted to extraordinary events that go beyond human or natural power and are attributed to supernatural causes. The word "miracle" as used by John in describing Jesus' act of changing water into wine is a translation of the Greek word *saymion.* Besides the notion of something supernatural, *saymion* also conveys the idea of a token or indicator of divine authority or power.

Mosaic tile floor at the Church of the Multiplication of the Loaves and Fishes. Located at Tabgha, about eight miles north of Tiberias on the Sea of Galilee

John's repeated use of this shade of meaning is illustrative of Jesus' manner of teaching and John's mode of response. By suggesting that the miracle at Cana and the later miracles are tokens, John is pointing to the necessary involvement of those persons witnessing the miracles. Tokens are offered by one person and accepted by another. Miracles are indicators, not stand-alone proofs positive that Jesus is divine. It remains the choice of the witness of any supernatural event to characterize its actual meaning. John interpreted the changing of water into wine at Cana as a clear indication that Jesus was divine. Others did not make this connection.

One of the most noteworthy aspects of Jesus' miracles is that they never completely overwhelm the witness. They always allow for acceptance or rejection by the reader of the Gospels. Some come close to being totally compelling, most notably those instances where individuals are brought back to life from death. But even in those cases the reader can find "plausible deniability" if he or she chooses. Why is this allowed to happen? Why didn't Jesus just close the door and make His miracles so patently clear, so scientifically verifiable that they cannot be denied by mankind—ancient or modern?

Admittedly, this would be an extremely difficult thing to do. Mankind, after all, is intelligent, very curious, and skeptical. Nevertheless, if a divine being chose to do so, it would not be beyond His power to make the evidence of some particular act totally irrefutable. The answer to why Jesus does not "close the door" on the question of his divinity is quite simple and quite beautiful. He interacts with mankind in a truly relational manner. Jesus does not force Himself or His love on His creation, and He always allows created man to accept or reject Him.

Viewed from this perspective, Jesus' restrained use of divine, miraculous power is actually a vivid display of His love and respect for His creation. If His miracles were fully compelling demonstrations of His divinity, the nature of mankind would be changed in a manner opposing the Creator's original intent. Mankind, like the rest of creation, would become automatically responsive and obedient to the laws of the Creator. There would exist no freedom to engage in a truly meaningful relationship with the Creator. Amazingly, God allows His creation to reject Him and the signs of His divine power in order to preserve real relationship.

CHAPTER THREE

CIRCA A.D. 27

Jezreel valley looking north near Megiddo

Jerusalem in Judea, c. Spring A.D. 27

Only John records Jesus' activities during the eight-month period between the wedding at Cana and the beginning of His preaching in Galilee. Exactly why the Synoptics ignore this time frame is open to speculation. Most likely John felt confident about covering it since he was with Jesus and witnessed actual events. Mark and Luke had no direct witness of Jesus' life, and Matthew was a relative latecomer as a disciple and apostle. John's account fills out the early months of Jesus' public ministry.

Leaving Cana, John says that Jesus "went down" to Capernaum with His family and disciples (Jn 2:12).[12] They stayed at Capernaum a few days until it was almost time for Passover. John then describes Jesus' rampage through the Jerusalem temple. "So he made a whip out of cords, and drove all from the temple area, both sheep and cattle; he scattered the coins of the money changers and overturned their tables" (Jn 2:15).

Jewish leaders on the scene were shocked, as many still are today, that Jesus could be so angered and aggressive. Startled, they demanded a miraculous sign that would " 'prove your authority to do all this'" (Jn 2:18). In this instance Jesus responded by saying, " 'Destroy this temple and I will raise it again in three days'" (Jn 2:19). They had no clue what he was telling them, which is not surprising. These were the same leaders who allowed the total commercialization and degradation of orthodox ritual. Their blindness was nearly complete. Jesus' authority for cleansing the temple *of* God was simple: He *was* God. Destroy me, as I know you will, Jesus said, and within three days I will raise myself up. Watch for it. It can overcome even your blindness.

Incidentally, this first cleansing of the temple scene is not mentioned in the synoptic Gospels. Matthew and Mark both report a similar incident near the end of Jesus' public ministry; John does not. Are the Gospel writers taking liberties with history—one placing the scene more than three years prior to the others? Poetic license of this sort was common in Jesus time, as it is today, because authors did not necessarily feel constrained by chronological sequence. Sequencing of events could be arranged to emphasize certain points without the loss of any real content. Perhaps a more convincing possibility is that the events happened as the record states. Jesus may have shown anger at desecration of the temple on two separate occasions. Both are eyewitness accounts, but the details are dissimilar. Matthew's account of the chief priests' reaction to Jesus' actions, for example, is completely different from John's.

While at the Passover Feast many people listened to the teachings of Jesus and His disciples. Many "saw the miraculous signs he was doing" and came to believe in Him (Jn 2:23). Nicodemus, a Pharisee, was sufficiently impressed that he considered Jesus to be a teacher who came from God. In a secret meeting at night, Jesus explained a great deal to Nicodemus, leaving him somewhat befuddled. Unlike the instance at Cana where John had the breakthrough realization that Jesus was God, Nicodemus was stymied. His Pharisaic background as "Israel's teacher" appears to have been a roadblock rather than an aid in understanding Jesus (Jn 3:10).

But Jesus was unequivocal: "No one has ever gone into heaven except the one who came from heaven—the Son of Man" (Jn 3:13). He used his favorite self-description as the "Son of Man" to inform Nicodemus that His origin was actually DIVINE, i.e. "the one who came from heaven." Instead of making the connection at this time, Nicodemus's mind locked up. He was anticipating a powerful, political leader in the Pharisaic mold who would lead the Jewish people out of Roman oppression into the glories of the past. He was not looking for God in the flesh. He was not open to how God might operate in the future.

Jesus pressed on and laid out the future quite explicitly. He forged unbreakable links between DIVINITY, ATONEMENT, and salvation. Salvation is the result of atonement, which is the result of divine action. Jesus expressed it this way:

> "Just as Moses lifted up the snake in the desert so the Son of Man must be lifted up, that everyone who believes in him may have eternal life...For God did not send his Son into the world to condemn the world, but to save the world through him" (Jn 3:14-17).

Eternal life, Jesus said, is made possible only by the divine Son of Man being "lifted up" (crucified). Acts of man, even sacrificial acts of man as required of the Israelites in the past, do not provide the power to completely atone for (i.e. rectify or cover over) the mistakes of humankind, thereby providing eternal life. The atoning power is supplied directly by God; and the application of that power results from man submitting to the will of God.

Judean Countryside, c. Spring A.D. 27

Following the encounter with Nicodemus, Jesus and His disciples moved to the Judean countryside. The disciples performed baptisms there, but it was the work of John the Baptist that Gospel writer John found most noteworthy. The Baptist had moved about 40 miles north of Jerusalem to a small town on the Jordon River outside of Judea called Aenon. It was here that he reconfirmed his earlier testimony of Jesus' divinity. The manner in which he did it attests to the Baptist's true character—his honesty, humility, and obedience.

Disciples of the Baptist were concerned that he was losing followers to Jesus. John responded that it was his great joy that they were leaving him! This makes no sense in the normal human context. Having followers, and particularly a rapidly growing number of followers, was usually taken as evidence of the validity and forcefulness of one's teaching. Recognition and material rewards were often jealously pursued as they are today. John the Baptist, however, understood and completely accepted his subordinate position to Jesus.

" 'He must become greater; I must become less. The one who comes from above is above all; the one who is from the earth belongs to the earth and speaks as one from the earth. The one who comes from heaven is above all'" (Jn 3: 30-31). In this quote, the Baptist makes a simple and meaningful dichotomy: one from heaven and one from

Yarn spinning demonstration, Nazareth Village, Nazareth

earth, the Creator and the creation, God and man, Jesus and John. His heartfelt recognition of this relationship produced the true humility and joy of releasing his followers to the new Messiah. Jesus was to be followed not only because He was the long-awaited Jewish Messiah, but also because He was God Himself.

Sychar, Near Shechem in Central Samaria, c. Spring A.D. 27

The success that Jesus' disciples had in baptizing new believers gained the attention and opposition of the Pharisees. "When the Lord learned of this, he left Judea and went back once more to Galilee" (Jn 4:3). Instead of using the more direct route along the Jordon valley Jesus traveled west and north through Samaria. Sometime around midday He and His disciples stopped at Jacob's well at Sychar, near Mount Gerizim. This particular site was well known to both Jews and Samaritans. Jacob bought land in this area from the sons of Hamor (the father of Shechem), and it was this land that he gave to Joseph. Mount Gerizim had become the worship center of the Samaritans—roughly equivalent to Mount Zion in Jerusalem for the Jews.

As a Samaritan woman approached Jacob's well to draw water, Jesus unexpectedly initiated a conversation. It was a conversation that occurred on two levels. For the woman it was an exchange with a somewhat mysterious Jewish man who needed a drink of water. For Jesus it was an opportunity to reveal His true identity to non-Jews. He declared Himself to be the Messiah, one of the few occasions in the Gospels where the claim is so direct.

The context of the revelation is all the more interesting. Samaritans were somewhat fuzzy on what to expect in a new Messiah, accepting only the first five books of the bible, the Pentateuch, as valid Scripture.

Jesus noted: " 'You Samaritans worship what you do not know; we worship what we do know, for salvation is from the Jews' " (Jn 4:22). Samaritan understanding of the nature of God and the Messiah was limited. To help overcome this, Jesus explained His divine power as Messiah by promising, " 'whoever drinks the water I give him will never thirst. Indeed, the water I give him will become in him a spring of water welling up to eternal life' " (Jn 4:14).

Jesus went on to explain that the true nature of God is spirit, " 'and his worshipers must worship in spirit and in truth' " (Jn 4:24). The simultaneous joy and apparent confusion of the Samaritan woman is understandable. She encountered a man who claimed to be the Messiah, but not one in the Samaritan tradition. He intimated that he had divine power and that God is actually spirit, yet he was obviously flesh and blood. " 'Could this be the Christ?' " she wondered aloud (Jn 4:29).

Impressed by Jesus' knowledge of her past, the Samaritan woman blurted out to the people of Sychar: " '[He] told me everything I ever did' " (Jn 4:29). Jesus remained in the area a few days teaching the Samaritan people. The result was nothing short of astonishing. John records that the townspeople proclaimed, " 'we have heard for ourselves, and we know that this man really is the Savior of the world' " (Jn 4:42). In a few short days Jesus was accepted not only as the Messiah, but also as the "Savior of the world" by a people estranged from the Jews.

Return to Cana, Southwest Galilee, c. Spring A.D. 27

Following His warm reception by the Samaritans in Sychar, Jesus continued His journey northeast toward Galilee. His fame as a miracle worker was already established, and He was welcomed by the Galileans. At Cana Jesus acceded to the pleadings of one of Herod's officials and performed the second "miraculous sign" recorded by John. He healed the official's son who was located in Capernaum, about sixteen miles northeast of Cana. This is the second of eight signs in John's Gospel, but it is clear that Jesus had performed more than two miracles by this time.

John used the healing at Cana to reinforce his primary message of Jesus' DIVINITY. Jesus' power was shown to be unaffected by physical distance. A precise connection was also made between the timing of Jesus' declaration that " 'Your son will live'" and the son's actual recovery (Jn 4:50). The official's servants informed him that: " 'The fever left him yesterday at the seventh hour.' Then the father realized that this was the exact time at which Jesus had said to him, 'Your son will live' " (Jn: 4: 52, 53).

Though John's witness about the healing at Cana is dramatic and forceful, it can easily be denied if one so chooses. The precise timing mentioned above could have been coincidental. And the sixteen-mile distance between Jesus at Cana and the official's son at Capernaum does not necessarily prove Jesus' omnipotent power as deity. Recovery of the son may have been spontaneous. But John is building a case—almost in the manner one would present evidence before a court.

First there was the incident of turning water into wine. That, along with other miracles they had witnessed in Jerusalem, made an impression on many Galileans. Then another remarkable sign occurred in Cana; it was powerful enough to cause a Roman official and his entire household to become disciples of Jesus. John accumulates the evidence and presents it to the reader as his Gospel unfolds. As suggested earlier, however, the evidence brought by all of the Gospel writers maintains a "token" quality. It is intended to be increasingly persuasive, but it leaves the verdict of authenticity to the reader.

Reproduction of Nazareth synagogue in Christ's time, Nazareth Village, Nazareth

Nazareth in Galilee, c. Spring A.D. 27

Luke picks up the narrative at this point in Jesus' Galilean ministry. The time frame is the same as that of the second visit to Cana recorded by John. Apparently, while in the region, Jesus stopped at his hometown of Nazareth and taught there.

The text used by Jesus prophesies about the Messiah (Is 61:1-2). He concluded: " 'Today this scripture is fulfilled in your hearing'" (Lk 4:21). Though not a direct declaration of His deity, Jesus did affirm that He was the Jewish Messiah. Reaction of His audience to this monumental claim was a sort of subdued acceptance. Luke mentions that, "All spoke well of him and were amazed at the gracious words that came from his lips" (Lk 4:22). Nobody seemed unduly alarmed or opposed to the claim of Messiah, most likely because rumors of Jesus' miraculous signs were widespread. But there was a lingering sense of disbelief voiced as some questioned,

“ ‘Isn’t this Joseph’s son?’” (Lk 4:22).

Unyielding to the Nazarenes’ desire for their own special sign, Jesus used references to Elijah and Elisha to warn them of the consequences of unbelief. Indirectly, Jesus was teaching them that they needed to reconsider their view of the Messiah and their privileged position as Israelites. Ignore the Messiah from your own hometown, He suggested, and you will be bypassed in favor of the Gentiles. Curiously, it was this warning, and not who or what He claimed to be, that angered the crowd to the point of wanting to kill Him.

Why such furor at a warning? The answer probably lies in the strong sense of separateness and covenant endemic among the Israelites. Redemption, it was felt, had to do with hereditary ties to Jacob. The requirement that they shift their faith to a self-proclaimed Messiah—the local carpenter’s son—was simply too much to ask. Jesus had become a threat to a long-cherished and misunderstood promise.

Capernaum in Galilee, c. Early Summer A.D. 27

According to Matthew, when Jesus heard that John the Baptist had been arrested and put in prison, He withdrew from Nazareth and went to dwell in Capernaum, by the northern tip of the Sea of Galilee (Mt 5:12-13). Though all three synoptic Gospels record the “calling” of the first apostles at or near Capernaum, Luke’s version is a bit more detailed. He mentions that Jesus instructed Peter to put out into deep water to do some fishing. Disappointed at having caught no fish the prior evening, Peter reluctantly obeyed. The catch was enormous, and recognizing the miraculous nature of what had happened, Simon Peter “fell at Jesus’ knees, and said ‘Go away from me, Lord; I am a sinful man!’” (Lk 5:8).

Peter’s reaction to the huge catch was much the same

as John's reaction to the changing of water into wine at Cana. He immediately recognized that he was a sinful man in the presence of God. Peter, his brother Andrew, and their fishing partners James and John, the sons of Zebedee, were filled with bewildering amazement, almost to the point of terror.

It is interesting to note how such drama can become plausibly deniable when narrated by the Gospel writers. Though inspired by God, their recounting of what happened can be fairly readily dismissed. Peter caught a great number of fish, it might be explained, simply because he moved into the deeper waters where the fish had migrated. Possibly, but as usual such explanations of miracles raise other questions. Isn't it likely that experienced fishermen such as Peter and Andrew would have known the best times and places for catching fish? Could the depth of the water have made much of a difference, given the type of surface nets used in Peter's day? Again, the story is compelling, particularly to those actually present. But, by design, it does not and cannot force acceptance by the reader.

It should be added that at least three of the disciples chosen at Capernaum (Peter, Andrew and John) had already been greatly impressed by Jesus. From John's Gospel (1:37-49) it is apparent that they had already decided to follow Jesus almost a year earlier. The second calling at Capernaum was powerful enough so that they "left everything and followed him" (Lk 5:11). They gave up their livelihood as fishermen, dropped everything, and became Jesus' devoted companions.

Capernaum in Galilee, c. Summer A.D. 27

Mark and Luke now turn to an eventful Sabbath at the Capernaum synagogue. There a demon-possessed man directly addressed Jesus. This is the first mention in the

Gospels of "demons," a term which is synonymous with devils and unclean spirits. For many, demons are the flip-side caricature of angels; instead of being plump-faced, winged do-gooders they are often viewed as pointy-eared, pointy-tailed mischief makers in red tights. Along with the cute, cartoon characterization usually goes a wink and smile of disbelief. But the Bible is clear that they are real and that they are evil—not to be trifled with one might say.

Capernaum synagogue. The late fourth century A.D. white limestone synagogue was constructed upon the black basalt remains of the structure in which Jesus taught.

The word "demon" derives from the Greek *daheemown* and denotes a supernatural spirit of a bad nature. This bad nature was revealed in Jesus' earlier encounter in the desert with a very specific demon named Satan. Jesus finally dismissed him from His presence by name, a name that derives from the Greek *satanas* meaning adversary. Satan is no less than the adversary or opponent of Jesus, the followers of Jesus, and God Himself. Willful opposition to God and His Son is a pretty good definition of sin. Thus, the connection between demons/Satan and sin is obvious.

Jesus sternly ordered the demon to come out of the possessed man and it obeyed. "All the people were amazed and said to each other, 'What is this teaching? With authority and power he gives orders to evil spirits and they come out!'" (Lk 4:36). Those present were shocked that a demonic spirit would yield to the commands of a rabbi. They failed to understand that they had witnessed something more than a contest between a man and a demon. They had witnessed a contest of spirits. This truth was openly acknowledged by the demon: " 'I know who you are—the Holy One of God!'" (Lk 4:34). As Jesus had made clear to the Samaritan woman from Sychar, the true nature of God is spirit. The demon yielded to something more powerful than the commands of a rabbi. It yielded to a spirit much more powerful than itself—God in the form of man.

Jesus continued his display of divine power as He adjourned from the synagogue to Simon Peter's home. As it happened, Simon's mother-in-law was suffering from what Luke the physician called a high fever. "So he [Jesus] bent over her and rebuked the fever, and it left her" (Lk 4:39). As an indication of how immediate and extraordinary the effects of this healing were, Luke notes, "She [Simon's mother-in-law] got up at once and began to wait on them" (Lk 4:39).

At sundown on the same Sabbath, with travel and transport no longer restricted, what had been an eventful day developed into an almost hectic display of divine power.

When the sun was setting, the people brought to

> Jesus all who had various kinds of sickness, and laying his hands on each one, he healed them. Moreover, demons came out of many people, shouting "You are the Son of God!" (Lk 4:40-41).

Consistent with His action earlier in the day, Jesus rebuked the demons to be silent. Most likely He was dissociating Himself from them, desirous that His miraculous good works give testimony to His true identity.

The Region of Galilee, c. Late Summer A.D. 27

At this point begins what might be termed Jesus' first "preaching tour" of Galilee. His popularity and fame increased as He moved from town to town in the region. "Large crowds from Galilee, the Decapolis, [a group of ten Hellenized towns located south of Galilee and mostly east of the Jordon] Jerusalem, Judea and the region across the Jordon followed him" (Mt 4:25). Throughout the tour Jesus taught and preached the good news of His kingdom. And as He went the generous display of His divine healing continued unabated—undoubtedly a major contributor to His enormous attractiveness.

All three synoptic writers record an early and dramatic healing. Jesus came down from a mountain, the exact location of which is unknown, and was approached by a man with a serious case of leprosy. In all likelihood the man's malady was actual leprosy (Hansen's disease) not one of the several other skin diseases to which the Biblical term applies. The man knew of Jesus' healing powers but asked whether He was "willing" to heal him. In surveying biblical word usage one finds that "will" and its derivatives are near the top of the list. It is extremely important in denoting one of the functions of consciousness as well as verb tense.

Jesus told the leper: " 'I am willing…Be clean!'" (Mt

8:3). His response is a good example of a conjunction of paradoxes. Here, the DIVINITY (God-man) paradox and the operation of free WILL (divine vs. human) paradox come together. Jesus, the divine being, exercised his will to make an event happen, the healing of the leper. His will is what actually empowered or caused the healing. But note that the exercise of human will is also involved. The leper had already shown a strong desire to be healed. He was in agreement with the will of God; absent such agreement Jesus would most likely not have acted.

Following the healing, Jesus instructed the man to not tell anyone. Given Jesus' increasing fame throughout Galilee and beyond, this seems a bit curious. The effect of the healing may have been so immediate and dramatic that Jesus was concerned He would be overwhelmed by cure seekers. Apparently that did happen. "As a result, Jesus could no longer enter a town openly but stayed outside in lonely places. Yet the people still came to him from everywhere" (Mk 1:45).

Capernaum in Galilee, c. Early Fall A.D. 27

All of the synoptic writers record Jesus' return to Capernaum where he continued teaching and preaching. Heavy throngs of curious Gentiles and Jews followed his every movement. It was probably at Peter's home in Capernaum where onlookers pressed so closely that stretcher bearers were forced to dig a hole through the roof. They did this in order to lower a paralytic directly into Jesus' presence. "When Jesus saw their faith, he said, 'Friend, your sins are forgiven'" (Lk 5:20). As is often the case, Jesus reaction to excited, desperate human activity seems restrained and perhaps even a bit off-key. But it is always helpful to remember that Jesus' perspective was divine as well as human. His immediate comment to the paralytic was actually a prelude to an enormously powerful act designed to influence Gentile and Jew alike.

Pharisees and their scribes in the crowd, already sensitized to Jesus' seemingly rebellious teachings, quickly took affront. They thought to themselves " 'Who is this fellow who speaks blasphemy? Who can forgive sins but God alone?'" (Lk 5:21). Their theology was sound. No one but God can truly forgive sin because it is God that sin most deeply offends. The one offended must do the forgiving. Their presumption that Jesus was not God was the fallacious part, and Jesus used the occasion to completely refute their presumption.

He first demonstrated an omniscient knowledge of their thoughts, asking: " 'Why are you thinking these things in your hearts?'" (Lk 5:22). He then posited, through an interrogative, that it is "easier" to forgive sin than physically cure disease because the power to forgive cannot be directly verified. " 'Which is easier: to say, "Your sins are forgiven," or to say, "Get up and walk?"'" (Lk 5:23). The Pharisees' apparent silence indicates that they accepted the premise.

Jesus then flatly asserted that he would do something that would attest to his DIVINITY. He would do something more difficult than forgiving sin—something that could be directly verified. Jesus put it this way: " 'But that you [Pharisees and teachers of the law] may know that the Son of Man has authority on earth to forgive sins…I tell you [the paralyzed man], get up, take your mat and go home'" (Lk 5:24). He then brought about an immediate cure to the paralytic. Logically, the Pharisees and scribes should have accepted Jesus' DIVINITY since he accomplished something that they considered to be more difficult than forgiving sin, one of their own measures for defining God.

The *Amplified Bible*[13] captures the forcefulness of Jesus' action. "And overwhelming astonishment and ecstasy seized them all…We have seen wonderful and strange and incredible and unthinkable things today!" (Lk 5:26). What easily could have been a turning point in Pharisaic thinking did not happen. The display of power was palpable, and yet the Pharisees and their scribes chose to retreat back into denial—denial of the Messiah, His DIVINITY, and His offer of a new covenant.

Perhaps one of those unable to deny such power was Levi, a low-level, despised Jewish tax collector. His self-described conversion and his renaming as Matthew occurred shortly after the healing of the paralytic. "As Jesus went on from there, he saw a man named Matthew sitting at the tax collector's booth. 'Follow me,' he told him, and Matthew got up and followed him" (Mt 9:9).

CHAPTER FOUR

CIRCA A.D. 28

Entrance to the pools of Bethesda, Old City Jerusalem

Jerusalem in Judea, c. Early Spring A.D. 28

Only John records the healing at the pool of Bethesda in Jerusalem. It is the third of John's signs pointing to Jesus' DIVINITY. Along with the subsequent discourse, it is one of the clearest, most revealing descriptions of the nature of Christ (Christology) in all of Scripture. John does not name the specific feast on which the miracle occurred. Most likely it was Passover or Purim; the latter would indicate winter rather than springtime.

Essentially, Jesus used this visit to Jerusalem as an object lesson to the Pharisees about who He was. It was no accident that He performed the miracle in the most populous and orthodox city in the entire region. Nor was the Sabbath timing coincidental. These circumstances suggest a deliberate confrontation with the Jewish leaders. Even the choice of whom to heal seems deliberate—an invalid who had been seeking assistance for almost four decades.

Jesus began by asking the long-term invalid whether he wanted to get well. Though in search of a cure and quite willing to be healed, he displayed no apparent faith in Jesus. Uttering the words " 'Get up! Pick up your mat and walk,' " Jesus effected an immediate cure (Jn 5:8). But as in the recent case of the healing of the paralytic at Capernaum, the Jewish leaders became defensive. This time they fell back on non-Mosaic, tradition-generated law that prohibited any kind of transport on the Sabbath!

Once again Jesus did not relent. He entered into a detailed explanation of His total human dependency on the Father *and* His simultaneous spiritual equality. First, notice the references to His unique position as the one who had surrendered divine prerogative to take on human form: " 'I tell you the truth, the Son can do nothing by himself...By myself I can do nothing...If I testify about myself, my testimony is not valid'" (Jn 5: 19,30,31).

Along with these declarations of human limitation Jesus revealed His divine character. He spoke of Himself, along with the Father, as the source of all life.

> For just as the Father raises the dead and gives them life, even so the Son gives life to whom he is pleased to give it...I tell you the truth, whoever hears my word and believes him who sent me has eternal life and will not be condemned...I tell you the truth, a time is coming and has now come when the dead will hear the voice of the Son of God and those who hear will live. For as the Father has life in himself, so he has granted the Son to have life in himself... (Jn 5: 21,24,25-26).

As the originator or, if you prefer, co-originator of life, Jesus also lay claim as its rightful judge. " 'Moreover, the Father judges no one, but has entrusted all judgment to the Son, that all may honor the Son just as they honor the Father...And he has given him authority to judge because he is the Son of Man'" (Jn 5: 22,27).

In addition to his claims of being the originator and judge of life, Jesus made several other unmistakable claims of His DIVINITY and equality with the Father.

> My Father is always at his work to this very day, and I, too, am working...For the Father loves the Son and shows him all he does...He who does not honor the Son does not honor the Father, who sent him...I have testimony weightier than that of John. For the very work that the Father has given me to finish, and which I am doing, testifies that

> the Father has sent me. And the Father who sent me has himself testified concerning me (Jn 5: 17,20,23,36-37).

The special relationship Jesus claimed with the Father, like the warning to the Nazarenes about ignoring him as the Messiah, infuriated his listeners. "For this reason the Jews tried all the harder to kill him; not only was he breaking the Sabbath, but he was even calling God his own Father, making himself equal with God" (Jn 5: 18).

Besides the obvious references to Jesus' divinity, John's recording of the miracle at the pool of Bethesda illustrates the interaction of the will of Jesus and the will of individual people. Jesus and the paralytic both willed physical healing. Jesus, who is the source of all life, wills *eternal* life to all of those who exercise their individual will to believe in Him.

Traveling Through Galilee, c. Early Spring A.D. 28

North of Capernaum near the Jordan River

Roads in Jesus' time were limited to a few main arteries, and side roads were more like wide footpaths that often bordered directly on arable private land. Moving through Galilee, Jesus and his disciples passed by grain fields on the Sabbath. They picked heads of grain, rolled them in their hands to remove the chaff, and chewed the grain to relieve their hunger. Pharisees in the entourage incorrectly charged that this activity violated Sabbath law. In fact, Mosaic Law did not prohibit minor labor on the Sabbath in order to satisfy one's own hunger. Deuteronomy states: "If you enter your neighbor's grainfield, you may pick kernels with your hands, but you must not put a sickle to his standing grain" (Deut 23:25). The Pharisees had misapplied another part of the law, which prohibited the harvesting of grain for profit on the Sabbath.

Rabbinic traditions accumulated over the years and were treated by the Pharisees as the equivalent of Mosaic Law. Such traditions were often legalistic, and they easily became more of a hindrance to normal human needs rather than the meaningful expression of devotion. In responding to the Pharisees' charge of violating the Sabbath, Jesus asked if they had read about David eating the bread of the presence, or the priests working on the Sabbath. As devotees of the law they should have been able to understand the difference between technical violations and willful disregard of its intent. Attempts to be pious in the eyes of their followers resulted in the Pharisees trivializing the real purpose of the law. In effect, they were using the law for their own purposes.

Jesus then completed His point regarding the God-inspired holiness of the Sabbath by making a direct assertion of His own DIVINITY. " 'I tell you that one greater than the temple is here…For the Son of Man is Lord of the Sabbath'" (Mt 12:6-8). To paraphrase, Jesus was saying: I, God in the flesh, am greater than the temple building which was only visited by the true God; I, God in the flesh, have complete dominion over the day set aside to honor me and provide rest to my creation.

Jesus next appeared in a Galilean synagogue. The Pharisees still wanted to use charges related to the Sabbath to bring Him before the Sanhedrin. Directly confronting their ignorance of the law, Jesus instructed a man with a withered right hand to stand before them. He then asked: " 'Which is lawful on the Sabbath: to do good or to do evil, to save life or to kill?' " (Mk 3:4). Their misinterpretation of the law about healing on the Sabbath exposed—doing good not being prohibited—the Pharisees remained silent. Knowing their thoughts about misusing the law to bring charges against Him, Jesus "looked around at them in anger and, [was] deeply distressed at their stubborn hearts…" (Mk 3:5). Then, with miraculous, divine power He immediately restored the man's withered right hand in full view of all present.

Once again the reaction of the Pharisees is almost unexplainable. "Then the Pharisees went out and began to plot with the Herodians how they might kill Jesus" (Mk 3:6). Involvement of the Jewish Herodian party suggests political motivation, but the Pharisees' nearly reflexive animosity was probably more basal, more human. They were deeply humiliated by their inability to defend their legalistic interpretations and expansions on Mosaic orthodoxy. That, along with their particular expectations about the Messiah, seems to have been enough for the Pharisees to deny the obvious, miraculous healing and embrace hatred.

Why, some ask, didn't Jesus attempt to avoid confrontation with the Pharisees and the adverse reaction it could bring? In short, He was driven by the truth of the Father. Jesus knew their hearts and their thoughts. His divine will would not yield to the willful ignorance, vanity and stubbornness of His creation.

Aware of the Pharisees' desire to kill Him, Jesus withdrew to the Sea of Galilee. By this time in His ministry miraculous healings had become frequent and widespread. Mark indicates that when people heard all that He was doing they came to the lake from as far as, "Judea, Jerusalem, Idumea, and the regions across the Jordon and around Tyre and Sidon" (Mk 3:8). Crowds pressed in to hear Him and to be healed of their diseases. "Those troubled by evil spirits were cured, and the people all tried to touch him, because power was coming from him and healing them all" (Lk 6:18-19).

Jesus' display of divine power had reached such scale that it became difficult for the Gospel writers to capture. His miraculous work among the crowds usually receives only brief mention. Nevertheless, His nearly unrestrained healing and driving out of demons points directly to His DIVINITY. He was not merely an agent who occasionally exercised divine power. Rather, He was the actual source of divine power, and it flowed from Him almost continuously.

Around this same time, Jesus, after a full night of prayer, selected twelve men from among His disciples and appointed them as apostles.

> These are the twelve he appointed: Simon (to whom he gave the name Peter); James son of Zebedee and his brother John (to them he gave the name Boanerges, which means Sons of Thunder); Andrew, Philip, Bartholomew, Matthew, Thomas, James son of Alphaeus, Thaddaeus, Simon the Zealot and Judas Iscariot, who betrayed him" (Mk 3:16-19).

They were given special power to heal and drive out evil spirits, and they were instructed to go first, not to the Gentiles, but to "the lost sheep of Israel" (Mt 10:6).

The word "apostle," from the Greek *apostolos,* translates literally as "one sent forth," with the connotation of being sent forth as a special messenger, delegate, or ambassador. Jesus speaks of Himself as an apostle in describing His relation to the Father (see Jn 17:3); its usage in naming the twelve is intended to draw a parallel to His own mission.

The twelve were personally chosen by Jesus to carry forth His good news message that redemption and salvation had arrived. They had arrived in the person of Jesus. He was indeed a man—or the "Son of Man" as He called himself—but His spirit was God, the source of all power. Like Jesus, the apostles were men, but their created spirits were not God. They did not inherently possess divine power as Jesus did. Therefore, Jesus vested them with power to help convey and validate His message.

This transference of power from Jesus to His apostles is a reminder that the flow of *all* power is from God. Throughout history mankind has tended to lose sight of this fact. Today's culture has pretty well convinced itself that power flows from man and his accomplishments. This thinking leads to a self-serving conclusion: power is vested in man, not by God, but by an extremely long, fortuitous, and completely random series of naturally occurring events. *Fortuitous randomness*, it could be termed, has emerged as a philosophy which strives to rationalize mankind as self-centered and, ultimately, uncreated.

On A Mountainside Near Capernaum In Galilee, c. Spring A.D. 28

Following the selection of the twelve apostles, Matthew and Luke record what is widely recognized as one of the most cogent, elegant and complete summaries of Jesus' basic teachings, the Sermon on the Mount. Whether the two versions actually relate to the same specific event is uncertain. Jesus preached almost continuously during this period in his ministry. Matthew's fuller rendering of the sermon may have been repeated in briefer form at other locations.

Thematically, the Sermon on the Mount is a natural sequel to the two previous encounters with the Pharisees regarding Sabbath day activities. As in those instances, Jesus corrected misinterpretations of Old Testament law. He challenged the shallow, hypocritical interpretations and applications of Scripture such as those dealing with charitable giving, prayer, and fasting.

Jesus then moved beyond correction. He explained his teachings as integral with the Old Testament—at one with, and in fulfillment of it. In reading what He said, one experiences a definite excitement and sense of newness. The profound teachings that pour forth radiate a sense of the extraordinary. Many people point to the sermon as an example of how revolutionary His teachings were, and remain. Loving your enemies and treating others as you wish to be treated, for example, still seem radical. "Revolutionary" does describe the principles brought forth when compared to the then-current moral code, one epitomized by Pharisaic rules. But nothing that Jesus said changed or opposed the long-standing teachings of the Old Testament.

Perhaps more revolutionary is the absolute clarity with which Jesus expounded his teachings, particularly the moral imperative to salvation: " 'Be perfect, therefore, as your heavenly Father is perfect'" (Mt 5:48). Salvation requires *perfection*! This quote speaks of true perfection, as the Father is perfect, not the precise observance of rules and ritual preached by the Pharisees. Individuals, by themselves, cannot attain that kind of perfection. Jesus' sermon highlights mankind's unwillingness and inability to truly obey the revealed law of the Old Testament.

Most revolutionary about the Sermon on the Mount is Jesus' portrayal of his own DIVINE role in achieving perfection. He alluded directly to this as he finished:

> Not everyone who says to me, "Lord, Lord," will enter the kingdom of heaven, but only he who does the will of my Father who is in heaven…Therefore everyone who hears these words of mine and puts them into practice is like a wise man who built his house on the rock (Mt 7:21,24).

Perfection requires doing the will of the Father, which, in turn, requires obeying the Son. As the simile suggests, hearing and putting Jesus' words into practice—putting faith in Him—is the only means of withstanding the rain of judgment.

At Capernaum, c. Spring A.D. 28

Upon leaving the mountain Jesus returned to Capernaum. Elders of the Capernaum synagogue approached Him acting on behalf of a Roman centurion, an officer in command of up to one hundred soldiers. Apparently there was mutual respect between the centurion and the Jewish population of Capernaum as is evinced by the elders' plea: "This man deserves to have you do this, because he loves our nation and has built our synagogue" (Lk 7:4-5). The centurion had heard about Jesus, but was deferential about approaching Him directly. He was sensitive to Jewish rules regarding ceremonial cleanliness.

It is noteworthy that the centurion related to and commented upon authority, a synonym for power. He understood power, and he saw power in Jesus.

> "But say the word, and my servant will be healed. For I myself am a man under authority, with soldiers under me. I tell this one, 'Go,' and he goes; and that one, 'Come,' and he comes. I say to my servant, 'Do this,' and he does it" (Lk 7:7-8).

He was absolutely convinced, and believed in Jesus' power

to perform supernatural acts such as healing his dying servant. Given such power, it was a simple conclusion for the centurion that his servant would be healed if Jesus gave the order. Matthew records that Jesus did give the order, "And his servant was healed at that very hour" (Mt 8:13).

Luke indicates that Jesus marveled[14] (*thoumadzo* in the Greek) at the words of the centurion (Lk 7:9). "Marvel" indicates wonderment and implies admiration. It is a term very seldom used to characterize Jesus' reaction to anything. Why would such a powerful, even DIVINE figure such as Jesus marvel at the words of a Roman soldier? Possibly He was admiring the Father's inspirational work of faith in the centurion, and, perhaps, the centurion's submission to it.

Nain in Southern Galilee, c. Spring A.D. 28

Tombs in Jewish cemetery on the Mount of Olives, outside the eastern wall of Old City Jerusalem

Aside from His own resurrection, the New Testament records three specific instances of Jesus raising people from the dead. (Jesus' resurrection, incidentally, was a unique display of divine power. Its implications regarding the issue of DIVINITY are discussed following the account of His death.) The first took place as a funeral procession drew near the entrance gate at the small town of Nain. Moved by a deep sense of compassion for the dead man's mother, Jesus touched the open coffin. He spoke with power: " 'Young man, I say to you, get up!' " With those words, "The dead man sat up and began to talk, and Jesus gave him back to his mother" (Lk 7:14,15).

It is difficult to imagine a more convincing display of power than restoring life through a spoken command. Miraculous physical healings—usually the reversal of degenerative physical processes—are certainly inspiring. But reinstating life after it has completely ceased is so powerful, unusual and beyond the reach of man as to demand a special category. So-called miraculous procedures of modern medicine do not even come close. They may help extend life, but are never capable of reversing death. Perhaps the only phenomenon that exceeds the sheer power of resurrection at a spoken command is the divine creation of life *de novo*.

As suggested earlier, however, Jesus' exercise of power, even resurrection power, is not irrefutable evidence of his DIVINITY. If one searches hard and long enough, the miracle at Nain can be rationalized. For example, the case can be made that the widow's son may not have been medically dead, even though he was in a funeral procession on the way to burial.

Opponents of Jesus' divinity might even allow that He exercised supernatural power to raise dead people. But they would likely conclude that He was acting as God's agent, and that the exercise of such power does not necessarily confer divinity. The basic logic of this conclusion is correct. Indeed, the prophets of old exercised supernatural power, and Jesus himself instructed his twelve apostles to raise the dead: " 'Heal the sick, raise the dead, cleanse those who have leprosy, drive out demons' " (Mt

10:8).

Ambivalence regarding whether Jesus was actually God incarnate is sometimes drawn from the comments of those present at Nain. "They were all filled with awe and praised God. 'A great prophet has appeared among us,' they said. 'God has come to help his people'" (Lk 7:16). Jesus is called a "prophet" and there is recognition that God was at work. The text can be read that God was working through a prophet as in the past or, more literally, that God in the person of Jesus had come to help his people.

Passages in Luke and Matthew follow the miracle at Nain with the question raised by John the Baptist about Jesus' true identity. " 'Are you the one who was to come, or should we expect someone else?'" (Lk 7:20). Jesus replied by simply restating what He was doing. " 'Go back and report to John what you have seen and heard: The blind receive sight, the lame walk, those who have leprosy are cured, the deaf hear, the dead are raised, and the good news is preached to the poor'" (Lk 7:22).

Jesus was showing great compassion and exercising miraculous power. But most importantly, and most powerfully, he was preaching the good news to the poor—the news that eternal salvation exists and that his DIVINE person makes it possible. Jesus comforted the Baptist to not be discouraged because of the way he was going about His mission. " 'Blessed is the man who does not fall away on account of me'" (Lk 7:23).

In effect, Jesus' response to John the Baptist was commentary on how His miracle-working activity related to His true purpose and identity. Yes, the miracles were powerful signs that focused listeners' attention and helped validate His claims. But they did not define Jesus' purpose or identity as God. Those were established by what He taught and the ATONEMENT He accomplished.

Jesus was aware of peoples' varied reactions to the

persuasive power of miracles, and He cautioned against being overly skeptical about them.

> Woe to you, Korazin! Woe to you, Bethsaida! If the miracles that were performed in you had been performed in Tyre and Sidon, they would have repented long ago in sackcloth and ashes…And you, Capernaum, will you be lifted up to the skies? No, you will go down to the depths. If the miracles that were performed in you had been performed in Sodom, it would have remained to this day (Mt 11:21-23).

Korazin, Bethsaida, and Capernaum are all towns located in the northern Galilee region where Jesus taught extensively. He was warning the inhabitants of those towns, and mankind in general, that the willful disregard of miraculous signs has negative consequences. " 'But I tell you that it will be more bearable for Sodom on the day of judgment than for you'" (Mt 11:24).

Along with His statement about the unrepentant, Jesus boldly reiterated His DIVINITY and sovereignty along with the Father. "All things have been committed to me by my Father. No one knows the Son except the Father, and no one knows the Father except the Son and those to whom the Son chooses to reveal him" (Mt 11:27).

Return to Capernaum, c. Spring A.D. 28

Upon returning to His headquarters at Capernaum, a Pharisee by the name of Simon invited Jesus to dinner. At the dinner table an unnamed woman, known by many of those present to be a prostitute, approached Jesus. (Incidentally, there is no reason to assume that this woman was Mary Magdalene, who is mentioned later in Luke's text.) She showed great humility and devotion toward Jesus by cleansing His feet with her tears, wiping them with her hair, and perfuming them with costly ointment.

Simon and Jesus had opposite reactions to the woman's uninhibited expression of guilt. Simon assumed that a true prophet would be defiled by the woman's actions. Jesus, understanding her deep need for forgiveness, did what only God could: He forgave her sins. Rather than grasping Jesus' lesson that great sin requires great forgiveness, and that forgiveness engenders love, "those who were at table with Him began to say among themselves, Who is this Who even forgives sins?" (Lk 7:49).[15] The Pharisees completely doubted Jesus' DIVINITY.

Luke mentions that following the event at Simon the Pharisee's home, Jesus "traveled about from one town and village to another, proclaiming the good news of the kingdom of God" (Lk 8:1). This was his second "preaching tour" in the Galilean countryside; it occurred outside Capernaum where much of His ministry was focused. All twelve apostles traveled with him, along with a group of women. Mary Magdalene, Joanna the wife of one of Herod's officials, and Susanna are specifically mentioned. Luke adds: "These women were helping to support them out of their own means" (Lk 8:3). Though financial and material support were often provided to teachers, it was unusual for women to do so. Jesus' message and personal appeal apparently cut across all segments of society.

Capernaum, c. Summer A.D. 28

> Then Jesus entered a house, and again a crowd gathered, so that he and his disciples were not even able to eat…And the teachers of the law who came down from Jerusalem said, "He is possessed by Beelzebub. By the prince of demons he is driving out demons"

(Mk 3:20-22).

Mark doesn't mention the healing of the blind mute that gave rise to the Pharisees' comments in the above quote. But knowing their thoughts Jesus used the occasion to teach about the stark contrast between the Godly and Satanic. Satan is internally consistent and unified. " 'If Satan drives out Satan, he is divided against himself. How then can his kingdom stand?'" (Mt 12:26). Jesus and the Holy Spirit of God are also unified and internally consistent. " 'But if I drive out demons by the Spirit of God, then the kingdom of God has come upon you'" (Mt 12:28).

The two, however, are diametrically opposed, and completely antithetical in what they represent. True miracles, such as the healing of the blind mute, are the work of a pure, holy and beneficent Creator. To consciously and willfully attribute such work to God's opposite for one's own purposes constitutes unforgivable blasphemy. " 'Anyone who speaks a word against the Son of Man will be forgiven, but anyone who speaks against the Holy Spirit will not be forgiven, either in this age or in the age to come'" (Mt 12:32). Jesus' self-description as the Son of Man places emphasis on his human characteristics. Speaking against the man can be forgiven. Willfully assaulting the true God—the context here is equating Satan with the true God—cannot be forgiven.

Jesus' teaching on the "unforgivable sin" was prompted by a miracle. It completes His earlier teachings on the use of divine power to persuade belief (note, for example, the healing of the paralytic at Lk 5:17-26). Miracles, which are observable and recordable, are the most potent physical evidence of divine power available to the human senses, logic, and emotion. People weigh what they personally observe along with the recorded accounts of others in attempts to determine their credibility and meaning. The credibility threshold varies widely among individuals, but eventually most people accept or reject miracles as factual occurrences.

There are three principal arguments used to challenge the veracity of Jesus' miracles and thereby refute His DIVINITY. The simplest and most frequent argument denies the possibility of supernatural occurrences. As mentioned earlier, rationalizations can always be found that even the most dramatic displays of power never happened, or did not happen as recorded. Notably, this kind of disclaimer was almost never used by the scribes and Pharisees, the most likely reason being that they were too close to many of the recorded miracles. They could not protest and deny what their own human senses were telling them.

The second means of challenging miracles and their relationship to divinity was frequently used by the scribes and Pharisees. They recognized that Jesus exercised supernatural power, but they attempted to separate the miracles from his person. He was construed as an agent of God (such as a prophet), but not the actual source of divine, sovereign power. Jesus' actions and words consistently contradicted this interpretation on numerous occasions. He clearly demonstrated that it was the immediate exercise of His own will (or His will in union with the Father and Holy Spirit), and not that of some other authority, that brought about miraculous results (see, for example, Lk 5:18-25; Mk 5:25-30; Lk 7:1-10; Jn 5:1-9; Mt 8:23-27; Jn 11:1-44).

It was precisely this connection—the unity between Jesus and DIVINITY—that most confused and threatened non-believers, including the Pharisees. And it was precisely this connection that Jesus so adamantly exhorted his followers to believe. In effect, Jesus had proclaimed His divinity so boldly that the Pharisees felt the need to oppose him more aggressively. They abandoned their position that he was an *agent of God* and put forth a third explanation of his miracles—one that could reconcile the miracles they had observed and simultaneously nullify his claims to divinity. They accused him of being the agent of another authority, a dark power—Beelzebub.

The perversity of that accusation (and the argument from which it flowed) was so extreme that Jesus expressed His unwillingness to forgive those who accepted it. The scribes and Pharisees may have bought into it because Jesus did not meet their expectations of the Messiah as a forcefully dominant king. They understood the pivotal role of divinity with respect to the rest of Jesus' teachings. Once His divinity is accepted, the truth of all His teachings, including His unique ability to ATONE for mankind's imperfections, takes on a consistent and coherent logic. Once His divinity is accepted, His teachings make sense as fulfillment and continuation of the Judaic belief system instead of oppositional heresy.

Jesus' solemn rebuke of the Pharisees' distorted logic and selfish motives would seem sufficient to silence them, at least for a time. But they immediately challenged him: "Teacher, we want to see a miraculous sign from you" (Mt 12:38). Many such signs had already been given—acts of mercy and healing, rather than the show-stopping, grand displays of physical power the Pharisees wanted. They were demanding proof on their terms that Jesus was the Messiah.

Jesus again roundly chastised the Pharisees' stubborn narrow-mindedness and disregard of divine power that had been repeatedly shown to them. They would be condemned, Jesus said, by the men of Nineveh—apostate Gentiles—and the Queen of the South (Sheba)—yet another Gentile—for their obstinate spiritual blindness. The Ninevites had been warned by the prophet Jonah and repented, and the Queen of the South cherished the great king Solomon's wisdom.

But the Pharisees, snug in their promise of

inheritance, totally discounted powerful signs and totally overlooked the fact that, " 'now one greater than Jonah is here...and one greater than Solomon is here' " (Mt 12:41,42). Jesus' self-proclaimed status as one greater than a prophet and greater than the wisest and wealthiest of Judah's kings is a not-so-veiled allusion to His DIVINITY.

Capernaum by the Sea of Galilee, c. Summer A.D. 28

According to the writers of the synoptic Gospels, Jesus began teaching in parables at about this time (see Mt 13:1-52; Mk 4:1-34; Lk 8:4-18). Though John's Gospel employs other figures of speech to describe Jesus' method of teaching, the Synoptics use parables almost exclusively from this point forward. The word "parable" stems from

Ruins of Capernaum looking toward the Sea of Galilee (Lake Kinneret)

the Greek *parabolay* meaning to throw or lay beside. Implicit with that action is the purpose of drawing a comparison and bringing forth a lesson—in Jesus' case, spiritual lessons. One may think of a parable as an extended analogy containing a message. Jesus made liberal use of them, most often to draw spiritual meaning from natural phenomena.

One of the interesting qualities of parables and other figures of speech as teaching devices is how they run counter to exacting literal interpretation. By design, they are intended to expand understanding beyond the literal. They use the familiar and literal to help explain the unfamiliar and non-literal. Jesus commented that he used them as a means of reaching out to the spiritually dull. This is not to suggest that the Gospels, and Scripture in general, does not have its more literal moments, but it does point out that the full range of language is widely used to convey the truths of the Bible.

With respect to Jesus' DIVINITY, this instance of teaching in parables by the Sea of Galilee is not particularly significant. What might be called the "kingdom of heaven" parables that Jesus used at this time explain most directly what that kingdom will be like. Obvious inferences about the king (Jesus) can be drawn from them by simply replacing "kingdom" with "king." For example, people receive the message of the king differently (farmer sowing his seed parable); or the king will start small but become great (mustard seed parable); or the king will not allow all to enter his kingdom (nets and seeds parables); or the incalculable value of the king (hidden treasure and pearl of great price parables).

Sailing on the Sea of Galilee, c. Fall A.D. 28

Mark records: "That day when evening came, he said to his disciples, 'Let us go over to the other side'" (Mk 4:35). Context suggests that Mark may be speaking of the same day on which Jesus first taught the kingdom of heaven parables. Jesus and His disciples set out from Capernaum and: "A furious squall came up, and the waves broke over the boat, so that it was nearly swamped" (Mk 4:37). Jesus, exhausted from the day's activities, lay asleep in the stern of one of the boats. Near panic, His disciples awoke him asking, " 'Teacher, don't you care if we drown?'" (Mk 4:38). Jesus, the frail human in need of rest, rose from His slumber and performed a mighty act of DIVINE power. "He got up, rebuked the wind and said to the waves, 'Quiet! Be still!' Then the wind died down and it was completely calm" (Mk 4:39).

It seems ironic that Jesus, at sea with just a few of his disciples, commanded nature to obey in the fashion that the scribes and Pharisees eagerly sought as proof of His claims. Those few disciples, already committed to Jesus but still weak in faith, were permitted the spectacle of the Creator's control over nature. They asked rhetorically, " 'Who is this? Even the wind and the waves obey him!'" (Mk 4:41). Exactly who it was riding beside them was confirmed: man and God.

For those not inclined to believe in miracles, perhaps the only rational way around this one is total denial. The Gospel writers, it might be claimed, are either fabricating an interesting story, or the squall and its subsidence were only natural occurrences. But assuming that the Synoptics are not deliberately lying, one should consider the circumstances surrounding this event.

The men accompanying Jesus, most of whom were experienced fishermen, were familiar with the violent storms generated on the Sea of Galilee. That body of water's position below sea level makes it easily capable of producing such storms. Men who earned their living there were not likely to be panicked by even serious storms. This one must have been gigantic. It may have diminished naturally just as it arose, but apparently it was still in full rage when the disciples approached Jesus. That the timing of the sea's calming would fortuitously coincide with Jesus' command, rather than in response to it, is possible but not really tenable. Furthermore, sailors have a strong sense of when storms are building and unwinding. Had this one been diminishing naturally, they would not have turned to Jesus for protection.

Having survived the storm, the small flotilla continued on to the other side of the Sea of Galilee. Exactly where they made landfall is debatable because there are three place names identified with the "region of the Gadarenes" mentioned by Matthew (Mt 8:28) and the "region of the Gerasenes" mentioned by Mark and Luke (Mk 5:1; Lk 8:26). Gadara, one of the free cities of the Decapolis, was situated south, directly opposite Capernaum, about six miles inland. Gerasa, capital city of the Decapolis, was about 30 miles further south of Gadara. Both of these towns probably had political and commercial influence over the smaller town of Gersa (now called Khersa or Kerza), located about midway on the eastern coast of the Sea of Galilee. Gersa closely matches the physical description in the synoptic texts of an area with steep banks, near the sea, and with tombs nearby.

It was probably near Gersa that Jesus met two violent, possessed men, one of whom spoke to Him. When Jesus asked the man's name the controlling demons within him responded, " 'legion'" (Lk 8:30). Today's most terrifying horror shows cannot match this scene. Imagine being possessed by a multitude of militant demons. Roman "legions" were made up of about six thousand tough, disciplined soldiers. As in other cases where Jesus confronted demons, they gave immediate recognition to Him as Son of "the Most High God," a Gentile name for the Supreme Being.

The demons were also obedient to Jesus' DIVINE spirit. "He said to them, 'Go!' So they came out and went into the pigs, and the whole herd rushed down the steep bank into the lake and died in the water" (Mt 8:32). Having completed the exorcism, and at the request of the townspeople, Jesus and His followers prepared to leave. Those wishing Jesus to leave knew little or nothing about Him. They had never been taught by Him, likely they resented the loss of their animals, and they did not know what to make of His obvious spiritual power. The healed man, on the other hand, begged to go with Jesus; he had experienced His mercy and power first hand.

Northwest shore of the Sea of Galilee

Sailing Back to Capernaum, c. Fall A.D. 28

Crossing back over the Sea of Galilee to "the other side," almost certainly back to Capernaum, Jesus was welcomed by a large crowd (Mk 5:21). The crushing throngs of people attest to His popularity at this time, and to the building expectation that great, even miraculous things could happen. Jesus did not disappoint. Before He was even able to move away from the shore, a man named

Jairus fell at His feet. Jairus was a ruler (administrative official) at the local synagogue who was apparently influenced by Jesus and came to have faith in Him. He begged Jesus to save the life of his young daughter who was near death. Jesus responded by agreeing to go with Jairus to see the daughter.

Along the way the excited crowd pressed around Jesus. Among the crowd was a woman who had been seriously ill with internal bleeding for many years. Mark writes that she had "suffered" under many doctors and became poor seeking relief. She secretly touched the hem of Jesus' cloak believing that, " 'If I just touch his clothes, I will be healed'" (Mk 5:28). Her faith was rewarded and, "Immediately her bleeding stopped and she felt in her body that she was freed from her suffering" (Mk 5:29).

Of note here is that healing power flowed directly from the person of Jesus to the faithful woman. The manner in which this power was applied is made clear by Jesus' own description of what had taken place. He halted the crowd and demanded to know who had touched Him. " 'Someone touched me; I know that power has gone out from me'" (Lk 8:46). Jesus the God-man was not acting as an agent of divine authority; the DIVINE spirit within Him was the power from which healing flowed.

While Jesus was still comforting the healed woman, Jairus was informed that his daughter had died. Her death was confirmed by the presence of people wailing and mourning as Jesus arrived at Jairus's house. Speaking euphemistically Jesus said the child is " 'not dead but asleep'" (Lk 8:52). The crowd "laughed at him, knowing that she was dead" (Lk 8:53). It may have been the crowd's skepticism about His power to resurrect the girl that led Jesus to "put them all out" of His presence (Mk 5:40). Only the child's mother, Jairus, and the disciples who were with Jesus were allowed to witness the miraculous resurrection. Jesus took the girl by the hand

and said to her, " 'Talitha cumi'—which translated is 'Little girl, I say to you, arise!' And instantly the girl got up and started walking around—for she was twelve years old. And they were utterly astonished" (Mk 5:41-42).[16]

As mentioned earlier, the sheer power of resurrection makes these events in Jesus' ministry stand apart. Note that he used the first person "I" along with the direct imperative "arise." This is the language of one person speaking directly to another. Jesus the DIVINE took personal action and exercised the power within Him to bring the young girl back to life.

Another miraculous event, recorded only by Matthew, probably occurred soon after the resurrection of Jairus's daughter. Two blind men following Jesus called out for mercy and healing. Jesus asked them about their faith in a very telling way: " 'Do you believe that I am able to do this?'" (Mt 9:28). He was asking whether they believed that He, as an individual person, had the power to heal them. Once again it is the language of one person speaking directly to another. The men replied "Yes Lord" giving recognition to his divinity, and their sight was restored (Mt 9:28).

Return to Nazareth and the Final Tour of Galilee, c. Fall A.D. 28

Mark and Matthew mention that around this time Jesus and His disciples returned to Nazareth. As usual, Jesus taught in the synagogue and He was again met with skeptical disbelief. It was from this episode that the famous lines, " 'Only in his hometown, among his relatives and in his own house is a prophet without honor'" were recorded (Mk 6:4). Jesus' male siblings (James, Joseph, Judas, and Simon) are also named, and mention is made of his "sisters" (Mk 6:3). Context suggests that these sisters were not female disciples but also siblings.

Moving out from Nazareth, Jesus parted company with His chosen twelve. He began a third teaching tour in the Galilean countryside where He, "went around teaching from village to village" (Mk 6:6). It was a new stage in His ministry in which He traveled alone, and the apostles actively imitated their master's teaching, preaching, and healing.

Before sending out his twelve "ambassadors" Jesus gave them explicit and rather detailed how-to instructions. Matthew's rendering is the most complete. They were told not to go among the Gentiles, not to take along provisions because they would be provided, and not to expect a warm reception to the message: "The kingdom of heaven is near" (Mt 10:7). Toward the end of his talk, Jesus explained His relationship with those whom the apostles would be teaching. "Whosoever therefore shall confess me before men, him will I confess also before my Father which is in heaven" (Mt 10:32).[17]

"Confess," sometimes translated "acknowledge," is from the Greek *homologeho* meaning literally to speak the same thing, and by extension to agree or assent. The construction of the verb here conveys the thought of acknowledging allegiance to Jesus as Lord and Master. Those who so acknowledge Him publicly before their peers (men), Jesus will acknowledge before His peer (the Father) as loyal followers and servants. The interaction between Creator and creation is clear. Jesus acts as the intermediary between God and man; those who *consciously acknowledge* Him—an act of human WILL—He will consciously acknowledge before the Father. Because He has special standing with the Father as an equal, Jesus' acknowledgement has the enormous consequence of bestowing eternal life.

To add clarity and emphasis to the teaching on confessing Him, Jesus spells out the opposite set of conditions. " 'But whosoever shall deny me before men, him will I also deny before my Father which is in heaven'" (Mt 10:33).[18] "Deny" in this context has the sense of actively disowning a person, and is used to counterpoint confessing allegiance. It is critical to understand that confessing Jesus as Lord precedes being accepted by Jesus and the Father. However, and this is a big "however," confession, of itself, does not satisfy the divine demands on the relationship. In order to relate to the DIVINE, who is perfect, people must somehow also be made perfect. Jesus' mission on earth was to enable that perfection.

Jesus concluded his instructions by graphically describing the profound effect that individual choices regarding His Lordship would have. They would cause severe conflict as both confessions and denials are made.

> "For I have come to turn 'a man against his father, a daughter against her mother, a daughter-in-law against her mother-in-law—a man's enemies will be the members of his own household'" (Mt 10:35-36).

It is a conflict that must occur—choices that must be made—before Jesus' final objective of peace on earth can be achieved.

One might wonder whether choosing to make Jesus Lord of their life is worth the struggle. Anticipating this, Jesus used intimate human relationships in an attempt to give some scale to the enormous value of a relationship with Him.

> "Anyone who loves his father or mother more than me is not worthy of me; anyone who loves his son or daughter more than me is not worthy of me; and anyone who does not take his cross and follow me is not worthy of me" (Mt 10:37-38).

An Aside: Machaerus in South Perea, c. Winter A.D. 28

An interesting historical note is placed in the text between the time the apostles leave and return from their first missionary trip. All the synoptic writers ascribe the murder of John the Baptist directly to the Roman ruler (or, as Mark calls him, the "king") of the Galilee and Perea regions. Technically, Herod Antipas was a tetrarch or ruler of about one quarter of the kingdom of his father, Herod the Great. Undoubtedly the relationship between John the Baptist and Herod Antipas was a rocky one. Antipas was both drawn to John and fearful of him. "When Herod heard John, he was greatly puzzled; yet he liked to listen to him" (Mk 6:20). So Herod placed John in a sort of protective custody by imprisoning him in the fortress at Machaerus, on the eastern side of the Dead Sea. The protection was necessary, it seems, since Herodias, the wife of Antipas, wanted to kill John. Her violent indignation was fueled by John's repeated and public denunciations of her incestuous marriage to Antipas.[19]

Herodias used her daughter's lascivious dancing to extract a promise from Antipas; and Antipas being honor bound, though in fact notoriously duplicitous, yielded up the head of John on a platter. It is not known exactly when John's murder took place, and may be sequenced in the writings as the authors (specifically Matthew) became aware of it. The location at Machaerus is attributed to Josephus, the Jewish historian.

All kinds of questions fall out from this piece of history. Wasn't John just asking for it in using Levitical law (Lev 18:16) to criticize a secular Roman ruler? Wasn't John just meddling in the personal affairs of a government official? Shouldn't John have been much more considerate of the separation of church and state? Who did this John the Baptist think he was anyway?

There is an interesting side note that goes along with the story of John's murder. It confirms that Jesus' fame had reached all echelons of society, and that there was general confusion concerning who He was and what He represented.

> Some were saying "John the Baptist has been raised from the dead, and that is why miraculous powers are at work in him [Jesus]." Others said "He is Elijah." And still others claimed, "He is a prophet, like one of the prophets of long ago" (Mk 6:14-15).

The guilt-laden reaction of Herod Antipas was that Jesus must be, " 'John, the man I beheaded...raised from the dead!'" (Mk 6:16). One can imagine Herod squirming at the thought of being haunted by John the Baptist. But apparently Herod came to his better senses. Luke notes that, "Herod said, 'I beheaded John. Who, then, is this I hear such things about?'" (Lk 9:9). His interest in Jesus was sufficiently strong that he expressed a desire to see Him. That meeting did occur, but probably not under the circumstances that Herod Antipas expected.

CHAPTER FIVE

CIRCA A.D. 29

Looking east across the Sea of Galilee from the shore at Tiberias

Near Bethsaida, East of Capernaum, c. Spring A.D. 29

When the apostles returned, they reported to Jesus what they had done" (Lk 9:10). They then set out together on the Sea of Galilee in search of a private place for some rest. Landing at or near the town of Bethsaida, they were discovered and a large crowd formed. Given the relatively sparse population of the region, the number of those who gathered on this particular occasion was astounding. Capernaum and Bethsaida, for example, are estimated to have had a combined population of about five thousand. All four Gospel writers report that five thousand *men* were present;

the total number could easily have been more than ten thousand, including the women and children with the men.

As evening approached, the apostles began to worry about feeding the massive number of followers. "Taking the five loaves and the two fish and looking up to heaven, he [Jesus] gave thanks and broke the loaves. Then he gave them to the disciples, and the disciples gave them to the people. They all ate and were satisfied…" (Mt 14:19, 20). Perhaps the most intriguing part of this story is the physical multiplication of the fish and loaves of bread. What are the mechanics involved? How was it possible to produce the huge quantity of food required to satisfy an enormous crowd? The short answer, it seems, is creation; food was materialized from nothing.

Creation, of course, is the hallmark of DIVINITY. Examining the writers' language sheds some light on the manner in which the food was produced. When the Synoptics say that Jesus "gave" the loaves and fishes to the disciples, the prolonged form of that verb (in the Greek, *didomee*) is used. In other words, Jesus kept on giving the food to the disciples, and the disciples kept on giving it to the people. This description suggests that the creation or materialization of the loaves and fish occurred simultaneously in Jesus' and the disciples' hands as they distributed them.

Could it be that the Gospel writers are talking about some kind of tremendous acceleration of the natural food production cycle instead of creation? Collapsing the fish spawning and growth cycle into a few milliseconds, for example, might get the job done. Likewise, the growth and production of barley loaves could be hyper-compressed. Interesting, but that kind of control of natural processes would also seem to qualify as supernatural.

Or, somewhat more simply, could it be that the crowd shared food that was brought along for the occasion? Some may have had food, but all the writers allude to the need to acquire food that very evening. Jesus himself asked, " 'Where shall we buy bread for these people to eat?' " (Jn 6:5). Furthermore, if the crowd had brought its own food, why would all the Gospel writers have recorded the story of Jesus distributing food? Perhaps the simplest and most obvious conclusion of all is that spontaneous crowds do not plan or prepare for anything. Thus, the people either had to disperse and locate their own food, or someone had to provide it for them.

Having fed the crowd, Jesus instructed His disciples to get into the boat and go to the other side, probably meaning that they should sail back toward Capernaum. He then dismissed the crowd and went off by Himself to pray. And then the spectacular happened, the kind of sign that the Pharisees demanded. Jesus took a long walk (the Greek indicates "many stadia," possibly more than a mile) across choppy waters to rejoin His disciples. His majesty, power and control of the elements shone forth. The Gospel writers are not talking about a ghost skimming across the top of the Sea of Galilee as the disciples, seeing Jesus approach, first feared. This was an awesome display of DIVINE power controlling the natural, allowing the physical body of Jesus to tread on water as though it were dry land. Was Jesus being capricious? What was the point of this showy display of power?

All of Jesus' actions, including miracles, were focused on His earthly mission. Feeding the five thousand at Bethsaida and walking on the Sea of Galilee are no different. He was always demonstrating and explaining whom He was and why He had come. Without question it was difficult for the people of His time to connect all the dots. For the Jews it was made more difficult because their expectations were out of sync with His teachings. As with all Jesus' miracles, these two point directly to His DIVINITY. They were initiated, directed, empowered and executed by the spirit within Him. Jesus was giving His apostles insight into His unique position as the embodiment of the divine—insight that would help build faith in Him as the true Messiah and Savior.

One can easily conclude that powerful signs such as walking on water would eventually have their intended effect. But we should also remember that Jesus was dealing with humans, a proud, headstrong, often chameleon-like group. Those in the boat proclaimed, " 'Truly You are the Son of God!' " as Jesus rejoined them (Mt 14:33). Certainly they were impressed, and what they meant is clear. The word "Son" is from the Greek *hweeos*; it stresses the quality and essence of one so resembling another that distinctions between the two cannot be made. *Hweeos* is combined repeatedly with man (*anthropos*) and God (*thehos*) throughout the New Testament in reference to Jesus. Those around Him frequently acknowledged Him as "Son of God," a characterization He never denied. His self-description as "Son of Man" had two purposes. He was assuming the Messianic title first used by Daniel (Da 7:13) while acknowledging His physical human condition.

But the apostles' understanding of Jesus and His mission still seems spotty at the time of these two momentous signs. Mark notes that when Jesus climbed into the boat: "They were completely amazed, for they had not understood about the loaves; their hearts were hardened" (Mk 6:51, 52). Though they had been privy to astounding miracles, they, like unbelievers, were not yet completely receptive to Jesus' message. And the masses lagged behind the apostles; they still cherished the old Messianic tradition. John says that just after being fed by Jesus, "they [the crowd] began to say, 'Surely this is the Prophet who is to come into the world.' Jesus, knowing that they intended to come and make him king by force, withdrew again to a mountain by himself" (Jn 6:14, 15).

Gennesaret and Capernaum, c. Spring 29 A.D.

According to John, when the crowd "realized that neither Jesus nor his disciples were there, they got into the boats and went to Capernaum in search of Jesus" and "…they found him on the other side of the lake" (Jn 6: 24, 25). Both Capernaum and Gennesaret, a plain south and west of Capernaum, are on the other side of the lake, opposite Bethsaida. Matthew and Mark indicate that Jesus and His disciples landed at Gennesaret, and the mass healings continued there.

> And wherever he went—into villages, towns or countryside—they placed the sick in the marketplaces. They begged him to let them touch even the edge of his cloak, and all who touched him were healed (Mk 6:56).

John does not mention the activity in Gennesaret; the "bread of life" discourse, which he next relates, probably occurred in Capernaum. It was in this exchange with the crowd that Jesus crystallized the purpose of His earthly mission. He explained the interaction of three of the great paradoxes of His teachings—His DIVINITY, His offering as ATONEMENT for the sin of mankind, and the operation of His WILL in relation to that of man. The teachings within this discourse lay out the foundations of Christianity; they are Christianity in a nutshell.

But the teachings were not simple, nor were they familiar to the crowd. Their newness, and the language Jesus used to convey the profound truths about Himself, resulted in consternation and rejection by many. Many considered his teachings "hard," not incomprehensible, but hard to accept. Jesus' popularity began to fade subsequent to the bread of life discourse as He focused on His real message.

John's account of the discourse is relatively brief, but it is packed with meaning. Within twenty-six verses, Jesus referred to having "come down from heaven" six times (Jn 6:33-58). This obvious, heavy emphasis on his DIVINITY took on personal meaning for those in the crowd when he declared, " 'I am the bread of life'" (Jn 6:35). In saying this, Jesus identified Himself as the source and sustainer of eternal life—for individuals and all mankind.

Jesus continued, " 'If anyone eats of this bread, he will live forever'" (Jn 6:51). How does one eat of this bread? The crowd was in wide-eyed suspense, and Jesus' answer was shocking: "This bread is my flesh, which I will give for the life of the world" (Jn: 6:51). His incarnate body, He said, is the source of life. Somehow that special bread or "flesh" must be eaten to gain eternal life. He connected the eternal life (salvation) He provides with the ATONEMENT which makes it possible, telling of His intention to surrender His body for the "life of the world."

The Bread of Life Discourse: God Relates to Man

Giving up his life at the cross—when He allowed His DIVINE spirit to be separated from His earthly body—is the critical conjunction between DIVINITY, WILL, and ATONEMENT. The operation of the divine will to permit the separation of Jesus' earthly body and divine spirit (His physical death) is the atoning act that eliminates sin.

In contemplating this relationship, it is important to keep in mind what Jesus meant by "my flesh." It denotes the physical body and blood of the person of Jesus, and it also refers to the teachings delivered through His physical person while on earth. Jesus confirmed the importance of this second meaning toward the end of the discourse. " 'The Spirit gives life; the flesh counts for nothing. The words I have spoken to you are spirit and they are life'" (Jn: 6:63). In other words, the life-giving part of Jesus' flesh is not the flesh itself. It is the words spoken through the spirit while in the flesh, and the willingness of the divine spirit to be separated from the flesh that give eternal life.

At this juncture the literalist attitude and thinking of some of those following Jesus got them into trouble. They were attracted largely by His ability to control the material world; for example, by His ability to provide food for their human bodies at will. But in talking about eating His flesh and drinking His blood, Jesus was talking about the non-literal, second meaning mentioned above. His followers are to totally consume, to swallow whole, to completely absorb His teachings to the point that they become completely internalized. Jesus' teachings are to become the standard for human behavior, the moral yardstick that will lead to eternal life. Consuming or "eating" His message, and adhering to it, is the responsibility of those who choose to follow Him.

Jesus' actual *corpus* or physical body also had to be consumed by man—but not in the sense of being taken into the bodies of humans. The meaning in this context is that Jesus' body would be consumed by death at the hands of man. It was through the surrendering of his earthly life unto death that Jesus effected or *empowered* eternal life for mankind. He made that life *accessible* through his teachings. Jesus' suffering and death is remembered in a physical way with the consumption of bread and wine at the Lord's table. The symbolism of the physical remembrance, however, should not be confused with Jesus' physical person.

Briefly stated, Jesus' physical death as a human being, which is the essence of ATONEMENT, was an act of DIVINE forgiveness. By surrendering to horrendous suffering and death Jesus declared the forgiveness of the sin of humankind. The "debt" of sin, if you choose to think of it in accounting terms, was forgiven—declared null and void by Jesus' death on the cross. Mankind's "account" or relationship with God was "reconciled" or set right by the DIVINE spirit in Jesus. Reconciliation with the divine was only possible through willful action of the divine. The separation of Jesus' divine spirit from his human body is the ultimate sign of forgiveness. Why that beautiful statement of forgiveness is linked to such brutal treatment at the hands of man is central to the ATONEMENT paradox.

The Bread of Life Discourse: Man Relates to God

Street vendor, Old City Jerusalem

Human WILL interacts with and relates to the DIVINE WILL. This relationship is explained in almost syllogistic form within the bread of life discourse. Someone in the crowd asked Jesus point blank " 'What must we do to do the works God requires?'" (Jn 6:28). Jesus had already given the answer that eternal life is a gift that He, the Son of Man, was going to give them. It is not something that individuals can earn, regardless of what they do. Your indispensable part in this relationship, Jesus explained is, " 'to believe in the one he has sent'" (Jn 6:29). The "work" God requires is to believe in His Son, Jesus. Equating work with believing may seem a bit unusual. Work always requires effort and, sometimes, initiative on the part of the individual. Believing may require mental effort, but does it take *initiative* on the part of the individual to believe in Jesus?

How belief and relationship are initiated is not really a surprise. The initiator of the universe and everything of which it is capable is the Creator.

> "All that the Father gives me will come to me, and whoever comes to me I will never drive away…And this is the will of him who sent me, that I shall lose none of all that he has given me, but raise them up at the last day" (Jn 6:37,39).

Here we see the very intimate relationship and unity of purpose between Father and Son. Creator God offers to His Son, as a gift, those who believe in His Son. Exactly who these individuals given by the Father are, and how they become included in this group, were the obvious next questions on everyone's mind. But by this point in the discourse the crowd was grumbling, and again raising doubts that Jesus was just, " 'the son of Joseph'" (Jn 6:42). The path he was going down seemed demanding and unfamiliar.

" 'Stop grumbling among yourselves,'" Jesus answered. " 'No one can come to me unless the Father who sent me draws him, and I will raise him up at the last day'" (Jn 6:43, 44). Those who come to Jesus—the same ones given to him by the Father—are also "drawn" by the Father. The action of the Father in drawing individuals to the Son—his action of initiating the relationship with them—is pivotal in understanding the overall relationship. The Father exercises His DIVINE WILL to draw or attract His created human beings, i.e. to appeal to their created HUMAN WILL.

Exactly what the Father does is highlighted in the Greek. The action verb to "draw" is differentiated between *helko*, meaning to draw or drag with some force, and *suro*, meaning to draw or drag with violent force. *Helko,* which is used by John to describe how the Father draws individuals, indicates that His attraction is forceful but not violently overwhelming. He does not neutralize or overpower the will of His created subjects. *Suro* almost certainly would have been used to indicate a more violent, irresistible dragging or drawing. In other words, when the Father initiates relationship with His creation He exerts a strong draw or pull upon them, but He does not override their ability to ignore or resist Him.

Interestingly, Jesus does not comment directly on whom it is that the Father will "draw" to Him within the bread of life discourse. After His triumphal entry into Jerusalem on Palm Sunday, He does make it clear. " 'But I, when I am lifted up from the earth, will draw all men to myself' " (Jn 12:32). The word "all" has its usual meaning here. Also, notice that Jesus' statement that He will draw individuals to Himself is exactly equivalent to the Father drawing individuals to Him. Their mutual design, intent and purpose in Jesus' crucifixion and resurrection are in perfect unison; indeed, their very DIVINE being is in perfect unison. Jesus' death on the cross, and His resurrection from that death, draw all individuals to Him in union with the will of the Father. Their spiritual relationship is so intricately and intimately close that they cannot be separated.

The Bread of Life Discourse: Relating and Believing

If God initiates the relationship, what is left for mankind to do in pursuing it? Individuals must " 'believe in the one he has sent,' " a requirement that Jesus emphasizes and repeats: " 'I tell you the truth, he who believes has everlasting life' " (Jn 6:29, 47). The Gospels make it clear that the path to belief is not the same for everyone. Some readily became faithful followers while others grew resistant and hostile. Given people's varied backgrounds, life experiences, and temperaments, how can they come to believe?

Jesus answers this question by referring to the prophets, Isaiah in particular: " 'It is written in the Prophets: "They will all be taught by God." Everyone who listens to the Father and learns from him comes to me' " (Jn 6:45). People cannot be passive; they must listen to the Father and learn from Him. His teachings, of course, include the teachings of His Son. And people must do something with what they learn. They must exercise their human WILL to accept or reject the drawing of the Father. Rejection, unlike acceptance, can take a more passive form; individuals can effectively reject belief by simply ignoring the evidence placed before them.

Through His crucifixion, Jesus is, in one sense, throwing a life preserver to man as he wallows in a sea of death and despair. Man has the choice of grabbing hold of the life preserver—the *eternal* life preserver—or drowning. And yes, mankind, bobbing around out there in that black sea, is not yet fully dead. He cannot save himself and swim to some shore that does not exist. But he still has the ability to heed the words of the Father and grasp hold of the life preserver, the hand of his Son, as he mercifully extends it. Were man a mere corpse floating about, the Father would not call to it, and Jesus would not reach out.

Pharisees and teachers of the law traveling from Jerusalem again approached Jesus sometime after the bread of life discourse. Possibly, they had heard of His declining popularity and sought to capitalize on it. They continued to challenge and oppose Him, and they raised the question of why His disciples disregarded the tradition of ceremonially washing their hands before meals. Jesus' answer was a strong refutation of their man-made rules, rules that had the effect of nullifying the word of God. It also reinforced His earlier point in the bread of life discourse regarding the relative importance of the material (flesh) and non-material (spirit).

> "What comes out of a man is what makes him 'unclean.' For from within, out of men's hearts, come evil thoughts, sexual immorality, theft, murder, adultery, greed, malice, deceit, lewdness, envy, slander, arrogance and folly" (Mk 7:20-22).

Food goes into a person from the outside and gives physical nourishment as it passes through. It is material and necessary for physical life, but by its nature it is morally neutral, neither good nor evil. What originates from within people, from within their hearts (the immaterial thoughts and desires), is what makes them unclean. That kind of defilement is sin, which has eternal consequences. Sin does not occur naturally as material things do; it requires human participation. It is the product of man's "heart," the center of his being—his mind, emotions and spirit.

Tyre and Sidon in Phoenicia, c. Spring A.D. 29

Matthew and Mark report that Jesus and His disciples again attempted a retreat, this time at a greater distance from their home base at Capernaum. They were likely trying to escape the press of the crowds and the mounting opposition of the Pharisees. Jesus was also seeking time and privacy to instruct His disciples. Even in the Tyre-Sidon region on the Mediterranean coast, a heavily Hellenized, commercially devoted, Gentile region escape was impossible. One memorable event is Jesus' response to the persistent requests of a local woman, a Gentile. He rewarded her persistence and "great faith" by ridding her daughter of demon possession (Mt 15:28).

Decapolis, c. Spring A.D. 29

Having traveled the twenty or so miles from Tyre to Sidon, Jesus and his disciples turned eastward. They crossed the Jordon River, moved south along the eastern shore of the Sea of Galilee and into the region of the Decapolis. The crowd picked up again and followed after Jesus day and night. Given that the Decapolis was primarily Gentile, it is likely that the crowd was also largely Gentile. Matthew writes of the continuing abundance of healing miracles: "Great crowds came to him, bringing the lame, the blind, the crippled, the mute and many others and laid them at his feet; and he healed them." In response, the people "praised the God of Israel" (Mt 15:30, 31).

Mark is the only one to record a particular, rather peculiar sounding healing that occurred during this period.

> After he took him aside, away from the crowd, Jesus put his fingers into the man's ears. Then he spit and touched the man's tongue. He looked up to heaven and with a deep sigh said to him, "Ephphatha!" (which means, "Be opened!") At this, the man's ears were opened, his tongue was loosened and he began to speak plainly (Mk 7:33-35).

Some have suggested that Jesus' gestures were sign language to the man that He was about to heal his maladies.

After traveling with Jesus for three days, the crowd grew weary and hungry. Just a few short weeks prior, and probably near the place they gathered, a very similar scene had played out. The crowd was not quite as large this time—four thousand men and their families instead of five thousand. And they were probably even more needy, having followed Jesus for several days instead of spontaneously assembling on the same day. The disciples once again betrayed their lack of faith by asking, " 'where in this remote place can anyone get enough bread to feed them?' " (Mk 8:4). Jesus again established for the record that only a minute amount of food was at hand—this time seven loaves of bread and a few small fish. With great human compassion, Jesus the DIVINE again created food to satisfy the earthly needs of His fellow man.

Dalmanutha, c. Spring A.D 29

From the eastern side of the Sea of Galilee Jesus and His disciples crossed over to an area called Dalmanutha (or Magadan) on the western side, just south of the plain of Gennesaret. The Pharisees and Sadducees met them there and tested Jesus by asking for a sign from heaven—some ultra-convincing, large-scale display in the skies—that might convince them of His divine authority. Jesus again refused to overwhelm their stubborn unbelief in this manner. Miraculous signs, though perhaps not the type the Pharisees were demanding, were happening on a daily basis. They were witnessed by thousands of people in Galilee and the bordering regions, but the Pharisees chose to ignore them. Jesus left, crossing back to the eastern shore at Bethsaida.

Yeast is the metaphor Jesus used to describe the pervasive, damaging effects of the Pharisees' false doctrine and teachings to His disciples. It turned men's hearts away from the true teachings of the Father. " 'Be careful,' Jesus said to them. 'Be on your guard against the yeast of the Pharisees and Sadducees' " (Mt 16:6). Interpreting the word "yeast" literally, the disciples confused Jesus' warning with a shortage of bread. " 'Why are you talking about having no bread? Do you still not see or understand? Are your hearts hardened?' " (Mk 8:17). The disciples' spiritual obtuseness, it seems, was not so different from that of the Pharisees—perhaps just a matter of degree.

Lack of faith resulted in stubborn rejection on the part of the Sadducees and Pharisees. Little faith on the part of the disciples prevented them from seeing beyond the most basic, literal meaning of language to its fuller content.

Upon reaching Bethsaida, Mark records a second miracle not mentioned in the other Gospels. A blind man was brought to Jesus and, "his eyes were opened, his sight was restored, and he saw everything clearly" (Mk 8:25). Curiously, in this instance Jesus laid His hands on the man's eyes twice before his sight was fully restored. No explanation is given for the second laying-on of hands. Physical restoration of sight was an awesome display of Jesus' DIVINE control of the natural combined with His deep sense of human compassion. It can also be taken as an allegory of the restoration of spiritual sight to a creation blinded by sin. Laying His hands on the eyes of the blind man a second time may speak of the persistence of Jesus' faith, and the persistence His followers must have in overcoming spiritual blindness.

Caesarea Philippi, c. Spring A.D. 29

"Jesus and His disciples went on to the villages around Caesarea Philippi," a region north and east of Bethsaida and about 27 miles northeast of Capernaum (Mk 8:27). There Jesus exposed the widespread misunderstanding of His identity and purpose when He asked His disciples the question: " 'Who do the people say the Son of Man is?'" There seemed to be a general consensus that Jesus was different, perhaps extraordinary, but the possibility that He may have been the long-awaited Messiah had not yet taken hold among the populace. "They replied, 'Some say [you are] John the Baptist; others say Elijah; and still others, Jeremiah or one of the prophets'" (Mt 16:13,14). The apostles themselves, however, had become convinced by this time that Jesus was indeed the Messiah, and that He even surpassed the Jewish world's expectations about the Messiah. Peter, speaking for the group, proclaimed: " 'You are the Christ, the Son of the living God'" (Mt 16:16).

Peter equated the Christ (or Messiah) with the ancient God of the Israelites, and Jesus confirmed his bold statement. " 'Blessed are you, Simon son of Jonah, for this was not revealed to you by man, but by my Father in heaven'" (Mt 16:17). Heretofore the link between the Jewish concept of Messiah and DIVINITY had always been indirect or undefined. *Mawsheeakh* (Messiah in the Hebrew) refers to a special rubbing or anointing with oil. It implies an anointing for a special office or function such as the anointing of Saul as the first king of Israel. It was usually expressive of divine purpose but not divinity *per se*.

Over time, expectations about the anointed one who would deliver Israel from captivity undoubtedly increased. Still, there was no general presumption in Jesus' day that the Messiah would be God incarnate. Jesus elevated the contemporaneous meaning of Messiah. His chosen twelve grasped this new, fuller meaning when Peter made his confession. Most others continued mulling over the possibility that Jesus was some kind of prophet, not the Messiah, let alone a God-in-the-flesh Messiah.

Later, but while still in the region of Caesarea Philippi, there was a decided, somber change in the focus of Jesus' ministry. He turned his attention from public healing and teaching to preparing His disciples for His death.

> From that time on Jesus began to explain to his disciples that he must go to Jerusalem and suffer many things at the hands of the elders, chief priests and teachers of the law, and that he must be killed and on the third day be raised to life (Mt 16:21).

The Messiah—the Son of the living God—to be struck down at the direction of the Jewish court? How could this be? Why should this be? Peter's understanding of the Messiah did not allow for such defeatism. He rebuked Jesus, and was in turn rebuked for his own misunderstanding. Jesus would first achieve reconciliation with mankind through the forgiveness of sin. This would involve His trial and shameful execution on a Roman cross. The kind of Messianic power that Peter and the apostles expected would follow later. Jesus did allude to the future demonstration of such power at Caesarea Philippi: " 'For the Son of Man is going to come in his Father's glory with his angels, and then he will reward each person according to what he has done' " (Mt 16:27).

Mount Hermon, Northeast of Caesarea Philippi, c. Summer A.D 29

Jesus then took Peter, James and John with Him to a high mountain to pray. Exactly which mountain they climbed is not recorded. Given that it was a "high" mountain (Mk 9:2) and that they had recently been traveling about Caesarea Philippi, Mount Hermon fits the circumstances well.

> As he was praying, the appearance of his face changed, and his clothes became as bright as a flash of lightning. Two men, Moses and Elijah, appeared in glorious splendor, talking with Jesus. They spoke about his departure, which he was about to bring to fulfillment at Jerusalem (Lk 9:29-31).

Luke is careful in his choice of words, choosing not to use the term "transfigured" as do Matthew and Mark. "Transfigured" (*metamorfoo* in the Greek) means to change into another form. Luke was probably concerned that his Gentile readers might confuse such a physical changeover with the metamorphoses often attributed to heathen gods.

What happened on the mount of transfiguration was, at the very least, difficult to describe. Jesus' face "shone like the sun" (Mt 17:2), and apparently His clothes emitted bright flashes of light. Peter, bold and impetuous, was so shaken and disoriented that he started babbling about erecting tents. "While he [Peter] was still speaking, a bright cloud enveloped them, and a voice from the cloud said, 'This is my Son, whom I love; with him I am well pleased. Listen to him!' " (Mt 17:5). The words are the same as those spoken by the Creator Father at Jesus' baptism. As on that occasion, the Father openly and directly confirmed His DIVINE relationship with the Son.

Obviously, there can be no greater, more credible witness of Jesus' divinity than that of the Creator. The written record of supernatural events such as the transfiguration on the mount can be questioned, doubted, challenged, denied, and rewritten. If the original record is accurate, however, all the mental manipulation in the world cannot diminish the credibility of the personal witness of the Creator God that Jesus was His Son.

As suggested earlier, the accuracy of the record remains for individual people to decide. By design, written testimony—including the testimony of the Creator of the universe—does not *force* acceptance of the Son as DIVINE. What was the purpose of this relatively isolated event, if not to bring complete closure on the divinity question? Interestingly, John did not write about it though he was present, and he was deeply concerned with conveying the divinity of Jesus to mankind. He left it to the other Gospel writers to describe the Father's second direct testimony.

If one is to garner additional purpose from this episode, it may be best to imagine what Peter, James and

John were experiencing. Not yet ironclad in their faith, they needed help and reassurance. They needed a more complete grasp of just whom it was they were following—and would ultimately follow to their deaths. They received that help on the mount of transfiguration, and became emboldened to give the doubting world a truer picture of the long-awaited Messiah. They would not overwhelm the world, just as Jesus would not overwhelm the world. Theirs was a position of great privilege, responsibility and power—but not unrestrained power.

Apparently Jesus and the three apostles spent the evening on the mount of transfiguration (see Lk 9:37). When they descended a large crowd met them. The other apostles were there, arguing with the "teachers of the law" (Mk 9:14). A man in the crowd whose son was possessed by a "spirit that has robbed him of speech" explained the argument (Mk 9:17). The man had asked the disciples who had remained at the base of the mountain to drive out the evil spirit, but they failed. Their failure probably encouraged the skeptical teachers of the law. The questions no one seemed quite able to answer were simple and direct. Why were the disciples of the great miracle worker unable to do what He had been doing with great regularity for many months? Had not the disciples been reported to have healed the sick and driven out demons on their own? Had the power left Jesus and His disciples?

Jesus responded with questions of His own to all those present: " 'O unbelieving and perverse generation...how long shall I stay with you? How long shall I put up with you?'" (Mt 17:17). In private, Jesus responded more directly to His disciples. You failed, " 'Because you have so little faith'" (Mt 17:20). Faith in the power of God, a power shared directly by God with Jesus, had slipped away. Power was still present, but it was not inherent in the disciples. For these men who had experienced the power of God and administered that power, it was an easy mistake to make.

It is so human to presume that power originates and wells up from within. But power does not just happen, does not self-generate within people. God is the power supply, and He requires faith in Him as the source of power. Jesus was able to immediately drive the demon from the boy because His DIVINE spirit—like the DIVINE spirit of the Father—is the source of power. Lack of faith, both on the part of the boy's father and the disciples, disconnected them from healing power.

Jesus concluded with an emphatic "I tell you the truth" statement about the key role of faith in the relationship between God and man. " 'I tell you the truth, if you have faith as small as a mustard seed, you can say to this mountain, "Move from here to there" and it will move. Nothing will be impossible for you' " (Mt 17:20).

Late fourth century A.D. Capernaum synagogue

Through Galilee and Back to Capernaum, c. Summer/Fall A.D. 29

Leaving the area of Caesarea Philippi, Jesus and the disciples passed through Galilee. "Jesus did not want anyone to know where they were, because He was teaching His disciples" (Mk 9:30). For a second time He informed the twelve that He was going to be betrayed and killed. The seeming incongruity of such talk with their improved understanding of Jesus as the true Messiah was confusing. It made no sense and it was frightening: "But they did not understand what he meant and were afraid to ask him about it" (Mk 9:32).

Upon their return to Capernaum, Matthew, the former tax collector, relates a rather amusing story, which speaks of Jesus' divine status and power. Collectors of the two-drachma (two days' wages) temple tax questioned Peter whether Jesus paid the tax. Peter returned home and, before uttering a word, was asked by Jesus what he thought about the tax. " 'From whom do the kings of the earth collect duty and taxes—from their own sons or from others?'" (Mt 17:25). Peter agreed that the taxes should be collected from others. It followed then, Jesus implied, that His disciples were sons of the heavenly King and should be exempt from the temple tax. To avoid controversy Jesus set aside the "exemption." He instructed Peter to go fishing, retrieve a four-drachma coin from the mouth of the first fish he caught and pay the temple tax for the two of them. Jesus did have a sense of humor! And, assuming that Peter followed up on his instructions, even Jesus' humor is laced with fabulous power.

At Capernaum, c. Fall A.D. 29

On their way back to Capernaum an argument erupted among the twelve about "who was the greatest" (Mk 9:33). Position and status—in this case the relative position among Jesus' followers—were valued and coveted as they are today. Humans tend to gauge their innate worth on the basis of their relative position to other people. The relative scale can be almost anything, physical appearance or size, wealth, knowledge, etc. Jesus' power was impressive and the kingdom of which He spoke excited the imagination. It was natural for the apostles to seek to advance their own positions and attempt to establish a pecking order within their teacher's new kingdom.

But they were also probably embarrassed about their ambitions. Mark indicates that they "kept quiet" (Mk 9:34) about the matter around Jesus, and Luke suggests that "knowing their thoughts" (Lk 9:47) Jesus took the initiative to correct them. Matthew's rendering of the incident is the most complete. It begins his famous fourth discourse. Incidentally, Matthew indicates that the disciples came to Jesus and asked, " 'Who is the greatest in the kingdom of heaven?' " (Mt 18:1). He phrases the question as though it were asked in a more rhetorical, personally removed manner. But Jesus knew that status weighed heavily on the twelve and responded as such.

"When he was in the house" (probably the one owned by Peter and Andrew), Jesus brought a young child into their midst (Mk 9:33). Using simile, He taught that to enter the kingdom of heaven and to be the greatest there His disciples must, " 'become like little children' " (Mt 18:3). This was another shocker for the disciples since they were certainly not attracted to the lowly status of small children. But the likeness of which Jesus spoke was not the youth or physical characteristics of children; it was their unpretentious trust in and dependence upon their parents. Whoever humbles himself like a young child—whoever believes in and depends on and is obedient to the Father—is the one most valued and "greatest" in the kingdom of heaven. The old markers used by humankind to measure success and status are meaningless in the realm

Boys at play in the Jewish Quarter of Old City Jerusalem

of Jesus and the Father.

Childlike belief is valued for the correct relationship it acknowledges with the Creator, and because, " 'whoever welcomes a little child like this in my name welcomes me'" (Mt 18:5). In other words, those who have child-like faith in Jesus act as representatives of Him and His teachings. Being His representative is the most meaningful status anyone can achieve. It has profound implications for the believers themselves, and for those to whom they represent Jesus.

Using hyperbole, Jesus warned that believers must move decisively to avoid sin. " 'If your hand or your foot causes you to sin, cut it off and throw it away. It is better for you to enter life maimed or crippled than to have two hands or two feet and be thrown into eternal fire'" (Mt 18:8). Individuals have the responsibility to exercise WILL and take action on their own behalf; and those with influence over others have additional responsibility. " 'But if anyone causes one of these little ones who believe in me to sin, it would be better for him to have a large millstone hung around his neck and to be drowned in the depths of the sea'" (Mt 18:6). Being the agent of sin—the opposite of being Jesus' representative—is spiritually deadly. " 'Woe to the world because of the things that cause people to sin! Such things must come, but woe to the man through whom they come!'" (Mt 18:7).

Switching to another figure of speech (metaphor), Jesus explained His purpose in coming to earth as, " 'to save that which was lost'" (Mt 18:11). (Note that Mt 18:11 is absent from some manuscripts; it is quoted here from the King James Version.) He told the story of a man who owned a hundred sheep and one of them wandered away. What was the man to do about the lost sheep? Forget about it and protect the remaining ninety-nine? Jesus, as the good shepherd, would go in search of the one lost sheep. And upon finding it, " 'I tell you the truth, he [the good shepherd] is happier about that one sheep than about the ninety-nine that did not wander off'" (Mt 18:13). As always, Jesus' thoughts and teaching were in complete sync with the Father. " 'In the same way your Father in heaven is not willing that any of these little ones should be lost'" (Mt 18:14). "Little ones" in this story parallel the little ones with childlike faith. God's will is to save them all, whether they have faithfully remained in the fold or wandered off. He refuses to exercise His will to abandon any of His little ones.

Jesus knew that sins or wrongs, violations of the moral code he was teaching, would occur among his followers. He laid out a series of practical steps for the faithful to use in maintaining harmony among themselves. At the extreme, an offender should be removed from the body of the faithful until he or she could be won back as a " 'pagan or a tax collector'" might be (Mt 18:17). Another practical step, mentioned only by Mark and Luke, concerned the activities of a man driving out demons in Jesus' name, but who was not one of His followers. " 'Do not stop him,'" Jesus said, " 'for whoever is not against you is for you'" (Lk 9:50). It was a clear message to John the apostle that his understanding of discipleship was too narrow, and it remains as a rebuke of modern day sectarianism.

Peter picked up on the underlying message that Jesus was trying to get across. There are practical steps that should be taken when wrongs are committed, but, more importantly, Jesus' instructions implied that the wrongs must be forgiven. The desire for retribution must be dropped. "Then Peter came to Jesus and asked, 'Lord, how many times shall I forgive my brother when he sins against me? Up to seven times?'" (Mt 18:21). Seven times undoubtedly seemed extremely generous to Peter. When Jesus responded, " 'not seven times, but seventy times seven,'" the critical importance of forgiving became apparent (Mt 18:22).

Seventy times seven is figurative speech for without limit. Forgiving without limit is one of those teachings that can only be characterized as truly *revolutionary*. To explain this kind of thinking Jesus used a parable. A servant owed a king ten thousand talents, was unable to pay, and begged for mercy. Showing great pity, the king canceled or forgave this almost immeasurably large debt. But the servant was unwilling to imitate the king's generosity. He had a fellow servant thrown into prison for failing to repay him a relatively trifling amount, a hundred denarii. Hearing of this, the king had the servant whose debt he had forgiven severely punished. " 'This is how my heavenly Father will treat each of you unless you forgive your brother from your heart,'" Jesus concluded (Mt 18:35).

As it relates to DIVINITY and the other paradoxes, the parable of the ten thousand talents brims over with meaning. A key characteristic of the divine Father and Son is their willingness to forgive. They have it in their hearts to forgive almost any offense of their human servants. Ten thousand talents is symbolic of the magnitude of debt they will dismiss. As discussed earlier, there is such a thing as "unforgivable" sin against God. It is limited and specific; and there is no offense of one man against another that is equally grave and perverse. Thus, Jesus established a key rule of relationship between the Creator and His human creation: to be forgiven you must be WILLing to forgive as God is WILLing to forgive. Unlike God, there are no unforgivable offenses against man.

For humans, unlimited forgiveness may seem like an enormous expectation and demand on God's part. In contemplating this last part of Matthew's fourth discourse, however, it may be helpful to remember the following. First, God's willingness to forgive is perfect and flawlessly executed; He knows that ours is not. This is not a hedge against the requirement to forgive. It is merely the recognition of our unequal natures. Secondly, one's perspective on forgiveness is improved by recalling Jesus' attitude as He departed Capernaum. Luke indicates that, "Jesus resolutely set out for Jerusalem" (Lk 9:51). In doing so He was resolutely exercising His WILL to travel to the place where He knew He would be brutally murdered. He was focused on the purpose of ATONEMENT, and He was willing to do anything that He called upon His creation to do. He knew that the crucifixion and death that awaited Him would *be* the ATONEMENT. They would be the final act and sign of forgiveness that would re-establish harmony with mankind.

It is not coincidental that Jesus placed such great emphasis on forgiveness as the basis of harmony among His followers.

On the Road to Jerusalem, c. Fall A.D. 29

Jesus' five-month "journey" to Jerusalem (the period between the fall Feast of Tabernacles and the spring Feast of the Passover) is most completely chronicled by Luke and John. It was not a journey in the sense of traveling directly from one place to another, but more the resolute

Inside the northern wall of the Temple Mount, Old City Jerusalem

progression toward atonement as mentioned above. His actual travels began with a sojourn to Jerusalem to observe the Feast of Tabernacles. From there He moved to other parts of Judea, on to Perea, Galilee, Jericho and finally back to Jerusalem.

Jesus' familial half-brothers, the other sons of Mary and Joseph (James, Joseph, Judas and Simon), had suggested that He should make the trip to Jerusalem and Judea to gain publicity and to, " 'show yourself to the world'" (Jn 7:4). But knowing His own brothers' skepticism and unbelief, and operating on His own schedule, Jesus demurred. The right time for Him to achieve salvation had not yet come. A bit later He did choose to go in secret to the Feast of Tabernacles. Jesus and some of His disciples traveled from Galilee by way of Samaria. Like most pilgrims to Jerusalem, they were not welcomed by the Samaritans. James and John became indignant and asked Jesus if they should not call down fire and destroy the Samaritans. Jesus rebuked them severely. Those closest to Him, His apostles and brothers, still had much to learn about His true spirit.

Jerusalem, c. Fall A.D. 29

The Feast of Tabernacles lasted seven days with a closing assembly on the eighth day. It was the custom of rabbis to teach in the temple courts during the feast, and Jesus started teaching midway through it. His claims of being the Messiah and being DIVINE had mixed reception among the several groups described by John.

The group John labels "the Jews" were Jewish leaders (chief priests, Pharisees and Sadducees) who were hostile to Jesus and his teachings (Jn 7:11-52).[20] The plot to get rid of Jesus was originated and carried out by this group. "Crowd" or "crowds" in John's context refers primarily to Jewish pilgrims from Palestine and beyond who swelled the population of Jerusalem during the large feasts. They were largely unaware of the plot against Jesus and were generally interested in His message. Many among the crowd put their faith in Him. The "people of Jerusalem" were a subset of the crowd, and were comprised mainly of local Jews who were not involved in the plot against Jesus but may have known of it.

"The Jews," amazed at Jesus teachings, wanted to know how he understood the Scripture so well without having studied under a prominent rabbi. Though they rejected His interpretation of and claims upon Scripture, they were deeply impressed by His knowledge. " 'My teaching is not my own,'" Jesus told them. " 'It comes from him who sent me'" (Jn 7:16). There was no rabbinic teaching involved; the Father was the source of the teaching and He was one with the spirit of Jesus.

With piercing insight Jesus then challenged His questioners: " 'Why are you trying to kill me?'" (Jn 7:19). He knew their thoughts and reflected back upon them their misunderstanding of Scripture that gave rise to those murderous thoughts.

> " 'Now if a child can be circumcised on the Sabbath so that the law of Moses may not be broken, why are you angry with me for healing the whole man on the Sabbath? Stop judging by mere appearances, and make a right judgment.'" (Jn 7:23-4).

"The Jews" took pride in their knowledge of the Scripture. But it was faulty and inflamed their desire to kill him.

The "people of Jerusalem" then began some fairly serious discussion about whether Jesus might actually be the Messiah. In their minds, however, there was no strong scriptural argument that He was. Resorting to irony, Jesus attempted to draw out the truth. He cried out: " 'Yes, you know me, and you know where I am from'" (Jn 7:28). They did not really know either. Some knew He was the man that the Jewish authorities wanted to kill, but they did not know that He was the Messiah and the Son of God. They knew He had traveled from Galilee, but they did not know that He was born in Bethlehem, and that His spirit was from the Father. They, like the Pharisees, knew the incidentals but were ignorant of the big picture.

Jesus immediately followed with a statement of His actual identity and origin. " 'I am not here on my own, but he who sent me is true. You do not know him, but I know him because I am from him and he sent me' " (Jn 7:28-9). As on prior occasions, the peoples' response to assertions of special relationship and equality with the Father was intense. Some tried to seize Him, but others believed in Him.

As talk among the crowd about Jesus possibly being the Messiah increased, the Pharisees became alarmed and sent temple guards to arrest Him. The guards heard for themselves some of Jesus' prophecies, such as this one concerning his death: " 'I am with you for only a short time, and then I go to the one who sent me. You will look for me, but you will not find me; and where I am, you cannot come' " (Jn 7:33-4). Largely misunderstood by His listeners, it was actually quite revealing about His nature. The "I" Jesus talked about—his actual identity—was not simply the physical person His audience could observe. His essential identity was spirit, and it could not be found or followed back to its source. Nor would it be possible to find His physical body. At death His spirit would separate from His body; but the spirit would rejoin His transformed body at resurrection. Jesus' return to the Father would leave no trace of His temporary physical presence on earth.

On the last day of the feast Jesus used a water metaphor to depict His role as the true Messiah. It was a particularly apt figure of speech for the occasion, since drawing water from the pool of Siloam had become an accepted ritual for the final day of the feast.[21] Rising to his feet, Jesus said in a loud voice: " 'If anyone is thirsty, let him come to me and drink. Whoever believes in me, as the Scripture has said, streams of living water will flow from within him'" (Jn 7:37, 38).

John explains the living water metaphor. Jesus identified himself—his teachings and actions—as the source of eternal life. Water sustains physical life as the spirit of God sustains eternal life. Whoever seeks or is thirsty for real, everlasting life must believe in Jesus the Messiah, the source of that life-giving water. Again, Jesus shed light on his DIVINE nature. In being one with the Father, i.e. in being God himself, He is capable of providing access to the life-sustaining spirit of God. That spirit—the Holy Spirit—will accompany or be "within" whoever believes in Jesus. The personal interaction between Jesus and individual people was made clear. He provides access to the living water or spirit, and individuals must believe in Him as the divine provider. Some in the crowd were moved by this powerful metaphor to declare, " 'He is the Christ'" (Jn 7:41). But the people remained divided.

Unbelief among "the Jews," however, did not waiver. When the temple guards sent out to seize Jesus came back empty handed, the chief priests and Pharisees grew frustrated that their plot had failed. Their reaction to the guards highlights how distorted their sense of morality had become. They considered their knowledge of the law—actually a knowledge and observance of made-up additions to the law—as the sole basis of judging Jesus' authenticity. " 'Has any of the rulers or of the Pharisees believed in him? No! But this mob that knows nothing of the law—there is a curse on them'" (Jn 7:48-9). Their knowledge of the law, and less-than-perfect knowledge of Scripture, could not reveal the truth.

Context suggests that when Jesus next spoke to the people the Feast of Tabernacles was over. Jesus then made the second of His self-revealing "I am" statements. " 'I am the light of the world. Whoever follows me will never walk in darkness, but will have the light of life'" (Jn 8:12). "Light" has its usual meaning as an energy source that enables the discernment of many things about physical reality. Jesus, being one with the Creator, is the source of that light. It is also used metaphorically here, and indicates truth penetrating into the mind and heart of the viewer.

The Pharisees immediately challenged Jesus' claim of being the light of the world on the basis that He was being His own witness. Claims under Jewish law required a minimum of two witnesses to be valid. " '…I am not alone,'" Jesus answered. " 'I stand with the Father, who sent me…I am one who testifies for myself; my other witness is the Father, who sent me'" (Jn 8:16-18). It is from statements such as these that the doctrine of the Trinity—three persons in one God—derives. Jesus made a sharp distinction between his own spirit and that of the Father.

For us as humans, heavily influenced by the physical side of our nature, it is difficult thinking of three persons in one God. Might that be something like Siamese triplets? It may be easier to abstract a bit and think of three personalities rather than physical persons. Immediately after making the point about his being distinct from the Father, however, Jesus spoke of their unity. " 'You do not know me or my Father,'" Jesus replied. " 'If you knew me, you would know my Father also.'" (Jn 8:19)

On a later occasion the Jews asked point blank: " 'Who are you?'" (Jn 8: 25). " 'Just what I have been claiming all along,'" Jesus replied (Jn 8:25). He had been claiming that He was the Son of Man, the Messiah, and the great I AM, i.e. the uncreated, eternal God of the ancient Israelites. He again emphasized His spiritual unity with the Father saying: " 'The one who sent me is with me; he has not left me alone, for I always do what pleases him.'"

(Jn 8:29)

The conjunction "with" in the above quote is best understood as *inseparable from*, not merely alongside or accompanying. This distinction is important because God was also with Jesus the physical man, but in another sense. God resided in Him—much as He had been present in the temple's Holy of Holies. Physical death could separate the spirit of God from the physical person of Jesus, but it could not separate the DIVINE spirit indwelling Jesus from the Father. The spirit of God is truly singular, though made spiritually perceptible to mankind in three distinct persons or personalities.

Among the "Jews who had believed him" Jesus then made a startling statement (Jn 8:31). " 'I am telling you what I have seen in the Father's presence, and you do what you have heard from your father...You belong to your father, the devil, and you want to carry out your father's desire'" (Jn 8: 38, 44). Jesus knew these people not to be His disciples as they had apparently at one time professed to be. They still relied on their ancestral lineage to Abraham as their source of salvation. It was totally inadmissible to them that they could be children of the devil.

" 'If God were your Father,'" Jesus told them " 'you would love me, for I came from God and now am here. I have not come on my own; but he sent me...He who belongs to God hears what God says. The reason you do not hear is that you do not belong to God'" (Jn 8:42, 47). These are powerful words. God Himself spoke through the person of Jesus; and Jesus said that it is the sincere belief in His word that separates the children of God from the children of the devil. Relating to God as Jesus described it was something new—a new covenant between the God of Abraham and His people (See Jer 31:31-34). But it was only new in the sense that Jesus, the promised Messiah, had come to complete and fulfill its meaning.

Jesus' declaration of a new covenant completely repulsed some of the Jews. They answered with one of the worst epithets they could muster, "Samaritan" along with a charge of being "demon possessed" (Jn 8:48). Under such attack Jesus again spelled out his authority for all that He said and did. He was DIVINE and spoke with the authority of the divine spirit. " 'My Father, whom you claim as your God, is the one who glorifies me. Though you do not know him, I know him…I tell you the truth,'" Jesus answered, " 'before Abraham was born, I am!'" (Jn 8:54, 55, 58). He had claimed to be the bread of life and the light of the world, but the claim "I am" was an unmistakable assertion of being the Creator God.

Jerusalem, c. Fall A.D. 29 Continued

As He went along, possibly outside the temple grounds, Jesus and His disciples came upon a man blind from birth. The man's blindness was not the result of his own sin or that of his parents. It "happened so that the work of God might be displayed in his life" (Jn 9:3). His affliction was in accord with God's plan to present Jesus as the Messiah. In fulfillment of the plan Jesus put mud on the man's eyes and told him to wash in the Pool of Siloam. The man followed Jesus' instructions and became sighted.

Giving sight to the physically blind is a predicted Messianic activity (see Isa 29:18; 35:5; 42:7) that Jesus fulfilled several times. It is also a powerful metaphor for His greater mission of overcoming spiritual blindness. The Pharisees staunchly denied the specific healing mentioned above despite the convincing testimony of those involved. Basic facts surrounding the case were not really open to dispute: the man was congenitally blind, a condition verified by his parents; community members recognized him as a blind beggar; his sight was not merely restored (which would imply that he was sighted at one time), but

Western wall of Old City Jerusalem, near the Jaffa (Yaffo) Gate

effectively created on the spot.

But as convincing as these facts may seem, the Pharisees stubbornly clung to their opinion that Jesus' dramatic action in giving sight to someone born blind was not a sign from God. That was an odd conclusion, as the man who received sight pointed out, because the Pharisees' denial contradicted their own teaching. " 'We know that God does not listen to sinners,'" said the healed man to the Pharisees. " 'He listens to the godly man who does his will. Nobody has ever heard of opening the eyes of a man born blind. If this man [Jesus] were not from God, he could do nothing'" (Jn 9:31-33).

It was only through the conscious and persistent exercise of human WILL that the Pharisees could deny the facts laid before them. Jesus noted at the end of the story that such stubbornness can bring moral culpability. " 'If you were [spiritually] blind, you would not be guilty of sin; but now that you claim you can see, your guilt remains'" (Jn 9:41). The Pharisees would have remained blind to Jesus' message had they not been provided clear evidence.

They would have had insufficient basis for making a choice, and could not have been deemed guilty. But their guilt "remained" because they chose to oppose Jesus in the face of strong evidence that He was who He claimed to be.

Jesus transitioned at this point to a solemn but loving description of His role as caretaker of His people. He applied the double metaphor of sheep gate and good shepherd in explaining His relationship to His people and the cost of caring for them. " 'I am the gate; whoever enters through me will be saved…I am the good shepherd. The good shepherd lays down his life for the sheep' " (Jn 10:9, 11). Sheep herding was an ancient pursuit of near-eastern peoples that continued into New Testament times virtually unchanged. The symbolism associated with it had a long history among the Israelites, and Jesus likely used it as a familiar and relatively easy-to-understand portrayal of Himself.

Sheep pens were protective barriers, often constructed of stone, with a single opening. In identifying himself as the gate to the sheep pen the symbolism is clear. He is the one point of access to the safety (or salvation) of the sheep pen and to the pasture (life sustaining food) outside the pen. There is no other way to the eternal life and security of which He speaks except through Him.[22]

Besides being the gate, which seems rather inanimate and impersonal, Jesus is also the good shepherd. Here His tender, devoted and DIVINE character shines through.

> "I am the good shepherd…The reason my Father loves me is that I lay down my life—only to take it up again. No one takes it from me, but I lay it down of my own accord. I have authority to lay it down and authority to take it up again" (Jn 10:14, 17-18).

As protector of His sheep Jesus was willing to take the extraordinary step of dying for them to protect them and save their lives. Note the linkage between the two metaphors. Two things must happen to achieve salvation. The sheep must use the gate that has been provided for them, and the shepherd must be willing—even unto death—to fend off their enemies. In the absence of this total commitment, access to the safety of the pen and life sustaining pasture cannot be assured.

The Father loves the Son for His total commitment to their plan of salvation. Again, the distinctness and simultaneous unity between Father and Son is brought forth. Jesus operated in unison with the Father, something that required obedience and co-operation with the Father's wishes. But as DIVINE spirit, the Son Himself—the spirit of Jesus—had the authority to allow the physical death of Jesus the man. He also had the authority to raise Jesus' dead body back to life. Followers of Jesus will also experience resurrection back to life. As with Jesus, it will be a life no longer under the constraints of space and time.

Luke continues the account of Jesus' activity in the region of Judea. As He had done in Galilee, He sent out disciples "two by two ahead of him to every town and place where he was about to go" (Lk 10:1). This time seventy-two (some manuscripts indicate seventy) were given instructions about how to carry this message: " ' "The kingdom of God is near you' "" (Lk 10:9).

Interestingly, Jesus referred to some of His own prior activity in Galilee as "miracles" or "mighty works." His comments stand as confirmation by the person who actually performed the miracles that those actions were beyond the ordinary, beyond the natural. " 'Woe to you, Korazin! Woe to you, Bethsaida! For if the miracles that were performed in you had been performed in Tyre and Sidon, they would have repented long ago, sitting in sackcloth and ashes' " (Lk 10:13). He was repeating two basic principles to His disciples. First, some will experience more overt, direct evidence than others that the Messiah has arrived. Secondly, as in John's story of the healing of the congenitally blind man (see Jn 9), accountability and culpability are increased as the evidence provided to individuals is increased.

When the seventy-two returned with exciting stories of the power they had exercised, Jesus reminded them that He was the DIVINE source of that power. " 'I have given you authority to trample on snakes and scorpions and to overcome all the power of the enemy; nothing will harm you'" (Lk 10:19). Luke immediately follows up Jesus' statement about power with insights into the Father-Son-Spirit relationship. He indicates that Jesus was "full of joy through the Holy Spirit" and gave praise to His Father (Lk 10:21). He describes once again the special Father-Son unity and intimacy, and how they relate to mankind. " 'All things have been committed to me by my Father. No one knows who the Son is except the Father, and no one knows who the Father is except the Son and those to whom the Son chooses to reveal him'" (Lk 10:22).

Region of Judea, c. Fall A.D. 29

Jesus continued ministering, mostly in the region of Judea, up until the time of the Feast of Dedication in December. Shortly afterwards (according to Mt 19:1, Mk 10:1 and Jn 10:40) He traveled to the region of Perea, east of the Jordon river. Before embarking on His last Perean ministry, however, Luke records several important and oft-cited events on the Judean side. He tells the parable of the Good Samaritan (Lk 10:30-37), and notes Jesus' instructions to his disciples on how to pray (the "Lord's prayer," Lk 11:2-4).

But there is little in Luke's text prior to the departure for Perea (Lk 10:25-13:21) that deals directly with DIVINITY. Luke does describe a miracle that occurred at this time that is not recorded by the other Gospel writers. Jesus, teaching in one of the synagogues on the Sabbath, called forward a woman, "who had been crippled by a spirit for eighteen years. She was bent over and could not straighten up at all" (Lk 13:11). Jesus put His hands on the woman and she immediately straightened up and praised God.

As miracles go this one may not seem especially impressive or convincing—except, perhaps, to the crippled woman. It is another of those instances where Jesus used the Sabbath and His DIVINE power to reveal the hypocrisy of the Pharisees. Rather than sharing the woman's joy, they took umbrage at what they considered a violation of Mosaic Law, healing on the Sabbath. Jesus pointed out their twisted interpretation and, "When he said this, all his opponents were humiliated, but the people were delighted with all the wonderful things he was doing" (Lk 13:17).

Jerusalem, c. Winter A.D. 29

John's account picks back up at the Feast of Dedication (Hanukkah) in Jerusalem. "The Jews gathered around him [Jesus], saying, 'How long will you keep us in suspense? If you are the Christ, tell us plainly' " (Jn 10:24). Jesus replied that His actions, including miracles, were done in His Father's name and they spoke for Him. And He went on to confirm that He was the DIVINE Christ (Messiah) saying: "I and the Father are one" (Jn 10:30). To the Jewish leaders it was blasphemy—an indisputable assertion that He was God.

Jesus affirmed their conclusion somewhat indirectly by distinguishing between gods (with lower case "g") and the God of Abraham, Isaac and Jacob. In the past, Jewish judges and rulers were spoken of as "gods" because of their divine appointment to exercise authority, not because of their inherent nature. Jesus, on the other hand, can be validated as true deity on the basis of His exemplary teaching and actions. " 'Do not believe me unless I do what my Father does. But if I do it, even though you do not believe me, believe the miracles, that you may know and understand that the Father is in me, and I in the Father'" (Jn 10:37-38).

What lay behind the Jewish leaders' intransigent disbelief? Why did they so adamantly reject Him as the Messiah and the Son of God? The answer to this fundamentally important question combines elements of both the DIVINITY and WILL paradoxes. Jesus' simple response was that: " 'you do not believe because you are not my sheep'" (Jn 10:26). The determining factor for being one His "sheep" is contained in the following verse. " 'My sheep listen to my voice; I know them, and they follow me'" (Jn 10:27). These two key verses are not correctly interpreted as the Calvanistic doctrine of predestination would have it. They do not indicate that God has pre-selected His sheep and that they follow Jesus solely on the basis of God already having determined that they would do so.

The key operative word in these two verses is "listen" (or "hear" in the King James version). Listening requires active involvement by the sheep. As any good teacher knows, actual listening demands as much if not more conscious involvement than speaking. Relating requires the focused participation of both parties. Jesus' sheep are receptive and open to what he says and does. Listening is the precise opposite of the Pharisaic attitude of stubborn rejection. The ones Jesus "knows," the ones who "shall never perish," and the ones the Father has "given" to him are the ones who listen. They actively, consciously (i.e. WILLfully), and humbly choose to receive the word of God.

Jesus and the Father know, and have known since before the dawn of time, precisely who would have such a heart attitude—precisely who would be their sheep. But their knowledge does not obviate or mitigate the key role of the believer in choosing to listen to God. It is equally important to remember, however, that no choice or act on the believer's part effects, i.e. truly *causes* his or her own salvation. Salvation is uniquely the work of the Son in union with the Father and Holy Spirit. As mentioned elsewhere in this text, the believer's choice to listen merely allows God's miraculous saving power to have its impact. Human choice to listen to God turns on the switch that allows the miraculous power of salvation to flow to each individual.

In and Near the Region of Perea, c. Winter A.D. 29

Leaving Jerusalem, Jesus went through the towns and villages of Perea. Luke mentions that He was invited to the home of a prominent Pharisee where, "he was being carefully watched" (Lk 14:1). The careful watching was not in the sense of giving rapt attention; it connotes more a sense of the Pharisees carefully observing Him for their own purposes. Again, the issue of the lawfulness of healing on the Sabbath was raised. As in the instance of the man with the shriveled hand (see Lk 6:6-11), Jesus questioned the Pharisees before taking any action: " 'Is it lawful to heal on the Sabbath or not?'" (Lk 14:3).

Jesus likely kept returning to this issue as a didactic tool for contrasting the original intent of the Mosaic Law with the erroneous accumulation of rules that had built up around it. He was attempting to make the inconsistent logic of Pharisaic thinking as plain as possible. As had happened before, they remained silent when the question was put directly to them. There simply was no logical (or revealed) basis for prohibiting healing on the Sabbath. Jesus then proceeded to heal a man with dropsy, a condition that results in the accumulation of fluid and is indicative of disease in other parts of the body (Lk 14:4).

Miraculous healing in this context was not only a demonstration of Jesus' DIVINE authority over the physical realm. It also evinced His authority to set the record straight on DIVINE revelation—Mosaic Law in this case.

Bethany Near Jerusalem, c. Winter A.D. 29

While in Perea Jesus received word from Mary and Martha, who were in the town of Bethany, that their brother Lazarus was sick. Jesus decided to visit them despite the fact that He had enemies there who had recently tried to kill Him. During the visit a great miraculous sign occurred and was recorded by John. It was the seventh and final sign included in his Gospel—a dramatic climax to his case arguing for Jesus' DIVINITY. That sign, of course, was the resurrection of Lazarus from the dead.

It is fair to say that the Gospel writers were selective in choosing which events in Jesus earthly life they would emphasize. Given the then-current ability to record events, and given the frenetic pace of Jesus' ministry, the exhaustive kind of coverage we might expect today was impossible. John recognizes this fact at the very end of his Gospel: "Jesus did many other things as well. If every one of them were written down, I suppose that even the whole world would not have room for the books that would be written" (Jn 21:25). Each Gospel writer had a specific audience in mind as he wrote. Each had his own recollections, reminders, and personal experiences. And there was at least some awareness among the writers of what their fellow authors had written.

Resurrection, for example, was something of a hot topic in Jesus' day. All the Gospel writers recognized its importance. Then, as now, there was great appeal in the possibility of returning to the land of the living from *sheol* or *hades*. The three Synoptics all deal with Jesus' resurrection of Jairus's daughter. But only Luke describes the raising of the widow's son at Nain. That John gave such emphasis to the resurrection of Lazarus is understandable. There is reason to believe that he personally witnessed the event, an event that was central to his basic message. He used it to illustrate Jesus as he personally knew Him, the incarnation of God.

The absolute boldness and power of Jesus' words and actions at Bethany tug mightily on the human WILL to believe in Him. He was so convincing that it takes more effort to deny the miracle of Lazarus than accept it. In the final analysis, the only logical means of rejecting this monumental happening is to impugn the messenger. One can argue that human transmission of the story is somehow flawed. But if one accepts that what John says is accurate, Jesus' tug draws one to Him.

Think about the circumstances surrounding the account of Lazarus. Jesus announced ahead of time that He was going to raise him from the dead. " 'Our friend Lazarus has fallen asleep; but I am going there to wake him up...Lazarus is dead, and for your sake I am glad I was not there, so that you may believe. But let us go to him' " (Jn 11:11, 14). It is clear that Jesus intended to openly demonstrate a supernatural act.

Next, Jesus was careful to leave no room for doubt that Lazarus had in fact died. Having personal knowledge that Lazarus was already dead, He purposely stayed away from Bethany for another two days. During this period the body began to decompose. Martha, the sister of Lazarus, attested to this condition when Jesus directed that the gravestone be rolled back: " 'But Lord,' " she said " 'by this time there is a bad odor, for he has been there four days' " (Jn 11:39).

The verifiability of his death provides an extra measure of credibility to the Lazarus account. In the cases of Jairus's daughter and the widow of Nain's son, the decomposition process had not yet begun. Also, remember that there was a fairly large crowd present as Jesus approached the tomb of Lazarus, including a number of non-believing Jews. There were numerous eyewitnesses as, "The dead man came out, his hands and feet wrapped with strips of linen, and a cloth around his face" (Jn 11:44). John records that, "many of the Jews who had come to visit Mary, and had seen what Jesus did, put their faith in him" (Jn 11:45).

Jesus' obviously premeditated display of power harmonizes perfectly with the stated reasons for His actions. Before heading off to Bethany Jesus said, " 'This sickness will not end in death. No, it is for God's glory so that God's Son may be glorified through it'" (Jn 11:4). That was an extremely bold prediction and a clear disclosure of DIVINE purpose. The entire event was to simultaneously give glory to God and the Son of God. Since God and His Son are one in spirit, Jesus' actions brought glory to both at the same time.

Before raising her brother Jesus explained to Martha: " 'I am the resurrection and the life. He who believes in me will live, even though he dies; and whoever lives and believes in me will never die'" (Jn 11:25). This revelation went beyond Martha's somewhat vague understanding of resurrection. Jesus spoke of an identity with it; He is the essence of it; He personally defines resurrected, eternal life. Note that Jesus did not say that anyone who believes in Him will *become* Him or *be* God. But they will have eternal access to Him and the power of eternal life. Jesus promised life-giving sustenance forever; He will abide with believers beyond time.

Finally, as with all of Jesus' miraculous acts, raising Lazarus was to stand as testimony to the DIVINE plan. " 'Father, I thank you that you have heard me. I knew that you always hear me, but I said this [i.e. that if Martha believed she would see the glory of God] for the benefit of the people standing here, that they may believe that you sent me'" (Jn 11:41,42). Though Jesus knew that the act of raising Lazarus would be extremely persuasive, he did not WILL it to be totally compulsive. He desired that the people might believe, not that they must believe.

With the raising of Lazarus the resolve of the Pharisees and Sadducees to kill Jesus solidified. Their great fear was that, " 'If we let him go on like this, everyone will believe in him, and then the Romans will come and take away both our place and our nation'" (Jn 11:48). They feared the loss of status and power. Aware of their intent and in keeping with His own schedule, "Jesus no longer moved about publicly among the Jews" (Jn 11:54). He withdrew about fifteen miles north of Jerusalem to the village of Ephraim, outside their immediate grasp.

CHAPTER SIX

CIRCA A.D. 30

Excavations at the southeast corner of Old City Jerusalem wall. Picture taken outside the Dung Gate, looking east

The Final Journey to Jerusalem, c. Early A.D. 30

Luke and the other Synoptics chronicle the events between Jesus' retreat to Ephraim and His return to Bethany immediately prior to Passover. Traveling along the border between Samaria and Galilee, Jesus encountered a group of ten men suffering from "leprosy," a term which can indicate any of various skin diseases. As lepers they were unclean outcasts, so they shouted from a distance: " 'Jesus, Master, have pity on us!'" (Lk 17:13). Jesus did respond and healed them all. Only one of the ten—a Samaritan and "foreigner"—came back, threw himself at Jesus' feet and gave thanks. " 'Rise and go; your faith has made you well'" Jesus told the man (Lk 17:19). The demonstration of faith making the man "well" is often interpreted as more than the curing of his physical ailments. When rendered " 'your faith has saved you,'" it appears that Jesus was also rewarding the man with eternal salvation.

Perea, c. Early A.D. 30

As Jesus ministered in the region of Perea, east of the Jordon, a young man ran up to him and fell on his knees. " 'Good teacher,' he asked, 'what must I do to inherit eternal life?' " (Mk 10:17). Instead of giving direct instructions as He did to Martha at Bethany (see Jn 11:25), Jesus challenged the man's understanding of salvation. " 'Why do you call me good?'" (Mk 10:18). This question is sometimes taken as an implicit denial of Jesus' DIVINITY on the presumption that Jesus was questioning His own goodness. Context indicates the opposite.[23]

The young man was unaware that more than nominal adherence to the commandments was required to be saved. For him, salvation would require giving up all his wealth and then following Jesus. Though he had correctly referred to Jesus as being "good" (a descriptor of inherent character that can be correctly applied only to God), the young man was unaware that he had said something profound, and had not merely shown deference. In effect, when Jesus asked " 'Why do you call me good?'" He was prompting the young man to consider Jesus' true character relative to God. He had already spoken the truth and Jesus wanted him to understand what he had said.

While Jesus was in the region of Perea He made the third prediction of His death recorded by the Synoptics. This particular foretelling was more detailed than the prior ones and was linked directly to the Old Testament.

> "We are going up to Jerusalem, and everything that is written by the prophets about the Son of Man will be fulfilled. He will be handed over to the Gentiles. They will mock him, insult him, spit on him, flog him and kill him. On the third day he will rise again." The disciples did not understand any of this. Its meaning was hidden from them, and they did not know what he was talking about (Lk 18:31-34).

Though they were familiar with Old Testament prophecy, they could not understand why Jesus was consciously focused on an ignominious death. And though Jesus taught and demonstrated resurrection, His mention that He would rise again remained a mystery.

Old Testament prophets (see, for example, Ps 22; Is 53; Dan 9:26; and Zec 13:7) foreshadow, sometimes with uncanny detail and accuracy, an "anointed one" who would sacrifice his life and bear the burden of the iniquities of his people. The exact nature of this personage and the full implications of the salvation that he would bring, however, were left for Jesus to define. True salvation was something much grander than Jesus' contemporaries inferred from the prophets.

At this particular time the apostles were still unable to reconcile their Old Testament conceptions of the Messiah with the work of salvation that the living Messiah, Jesus, was intent on performing. That work was the *eternal* salvation of mankind, nothing less—not the physical deliverance of the Jewish nation, and not the immediate establishment of an earthly kingdom. Ironically, even though the apostles were convinced that Jesus was the true Messiah and that He was DIVINE, His primary goal and the realization of it remained obscure. The notion that salvation could be achieved only by God was not likely the source of the apostles' confusion. Rather, it was more likely the *manner* in which He would accomplish it—through suffering and death—that confounded them.

From the text of Matthew and Mark's Gospels it appears that John (the "beloved disciple") and his brother James had a typically human reaction to Jesus' pronouncement of His impending death: ambition mixed with pathos. The brothers approached Jesus with a special request for position and honor. " 'Let one of us sit at your right and the other at your left in your glory'" (Mk 10:37). Their immediate concern was not for their master but for their own standing in His future kingdom.

Some interpret Jesus' reply to this heartfelt but selfish entreaty as another disclaimer of His DIVINITY. " 'You will indeed drink from my cup, but to sit at my right or left is not for me to grant. These places belong to those for whom they have been prepared by my Father'" (Mt 20:23). Position within the eternal kingdom, so the argument goes, is controlled by the Father. Therefore, the Son is not equal to the Father and not divine. But note that the wording, "prepared by my Father" in no way excludes the full knowledge and participation of the Son and the Holy Spirit. To the contrary, Scripture indicates that there is complete sharing between the personages of God (see, for example, Jn 7:28-29 and 10:14-15). The sharing is so complete that it is correct to think of them as one.

Actually, the passages about the brothers' request are more of a commentary on the interaction between divine and human WILL than on divinity. When Jesus indicated that the places being sought by John and James, " 'belong to those for whom they have been prepared,'" He was notifying them in very kindly fashion that the eternal kingdom is established and ordered solely according to God's will. It is not subject to the will of man.

Mankind's impotency to affect the divine order may seem at odds with the eternal consequences of choosing to place one's faith in Jesus. In one sense the choices individuals make while on earth do have momentous, eternal impact: they are linked to eternal communion with or separation from the Creator. Their eternal significance, however, lies in their being divinely empowered and not in the human component of choosing. Absent the forbearance, grace and power of the Creator, human WILL has no consequence beyond the temporal realm.

Near Jericho, c. Early A.D. 30

Jesus attracted large crowds as He worked His way south through Perea. In part the renewed popularity may have reflected the dramatic and recent resurrection of Lazarus at Bethany. Near the ancient city of Jericho another incident took place that is instructive in the interaction of DIVINE WILL and human WILL. There the blind son of Timaeus (Bartimaeus) pleaded directly with the Son of David to have mercy on him as Jesus passed nearby (see Mk 10:47). "Son of David" is a Messianic title (see Isa 11:1-3; Jer 23:5-6; and Eze 34:23-24), and Bartimaeus's use of it indicates that he placed special trust in Jesus. Calling Bartimaeus forward Jesus confirmed that, "'your faith has healed you.' Immediately he received his sight and followed Jesus along the road" (Mk 10:52).

As on other occasions, supernatural healing power was directed by the DIVINE WILL to restore a blind man's sight. What distinguishes Bartimaeus is the persistence of his faith. "Many rebuked him and told him to be quiet, but he shouted all the more, 'Son of David, have mercy on me!'" (Mk 10:48). His will in exercising his faith was unshakeable; Bartimaeus knew what he wanted and believed Jesus could accomplish it.

Return to Bethany, c. Spring A.D. 30

Six days before the Passover, as John reports, Jesus arrived back in Bethany where Martha and Mary prepared a dinner in His honor. According to John, it was at this time and place that Mary poured expensive perfume on Jesus' feet and wiped them with her hair. Also mentioned is that Lazarus, "whom Jesus had raised from the dead" was present (Jn 12:1). The power of Lazarus's resurrection continued to reverberate throughout the region. When it became known that Jesus was visiting there again, a large crowd came, "not only because of him but also to see Lazarus" (Jn 12:9).

So threatened were the chief priests by the credibility of Lazarus's resurrection that they plotted to kill him along with Jesus. Due to that one event, "many of the Jews were going over to Jesus and putting their faith in him" (Jn 12:11). True conversions were being made. Jesus' own people were accepting Him as the Messiah and the Son of God. It seems ironic, almost contradictory, that the same DIVINE act of restoring life was leading some to choose salvation and steeling others in denial. Such is the operation of human WILL in the face of DIVINE purpose.

Bethany to Bethphage to Jerusalem, Palm Sunday c. A.D. 30

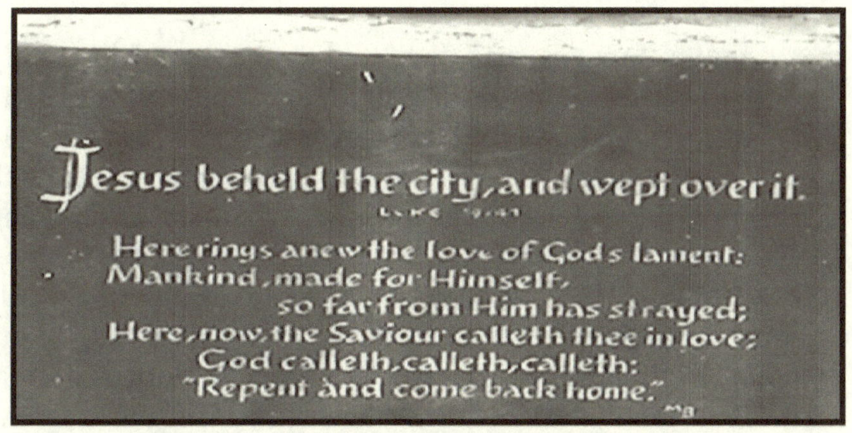

Plaque at Dominus Flevit Church on the Mount of Olives, east of Old City Jerusalem. It marks the spot where Jesus wept over the city the Sunday prior to His crucifixion.

What has come to be known traditionally as Palm Sunday or the Triumphal Entry of Jesus into Jerusalem is also charged with irony. One of the few events recorded in all four Gospels, it describes a time of excited celebration by disciples who lay garments and leafy branches in the path of their king. Indeed, the man who raised people from the dead was acclaimed as more than king. Jubilantly, the throngs received him as "Son of David," yes Messiah!

Human expectation and emotion were at a fever pitch. But the real triumph of Jesus' entry into Jerusalem has to be seen from the DIVINE perspective, disentangled from the hoopla and trappings of mercuric human emotion. Many of those who cheered as Jesus rode a donkey's foal into the great city would soon be clamoring for His death. The city itself would be reduced to rubble in a few short decades and the population all but annihilated. Nevertheless, in the larger sense, the celebration of Palm Sunday was not in vain. Though its fuller meaning remained obscured to virtually everyone present, the true Kingdom was officially and very publicly proclaimed.

True Salvation was declared.

Palm Sunday was the day that Jesus deliberately chose to confirm to the world in no uncertain terms that He was the anointed one for whom they had been waiting. He acted out in detail the well-known prophecy of Zechariah (9:9) to come to Jerusalem as a king, "righteous and having salvation, gentle and riding on a donkey, on a colt, the foal of a donkey" (see also 1 Ki 1:33,44). Pilgrim crowds jammed the holy city preparing for Passover, many anticipating an appearance by the miracle worker. Some had witnessed Jesus' power first-hand in the regions outside Jerusalem. His self-proclaimed enemies were also there, hoping to strike before all was lost.

Along the road from Bethany the crowds acknowledged Jesus' Messianic claims. "The crowds that went ahead of him and those that followed shouted, 'Hosanna to the Son of David!' 'Blessed is he who comes in the name of the Lord!' 'Hosanna in the highest!'" (Mt 21:9). These expressions are all clear Messianic references (see, for example, Ps 118:25-26). Mark adds that the crowd shouted, " 'Blessed is the coming Kingdom of our father David'" (Mk 11:10), an allusion to the Messianic kingdom promised David's progeny (see 2 Sa 7:11-14).

There was, without question, clear acceptance by the excited crowd of Jesus' claim of being the Messiah. One can imagine that Jesus was pleased by his apparently warm reception. But Luke suggests a much more somber, pensive mood. "As he approached Jerusalem and saw the city, he wept over it and said, 'If you, even you, had only known on this day what would bring you peace—but now it is hidden from your eyes' " (Lk 19:41-42). Their excitement at simply having the Messiah in their midst seems to have displaced a deeper understanding of what that truth implied—DIVINITY delivering eternal salvation.

As Jesus acted out Messianic prophecy He also

proclaimed His Godly nature. When He came near the place where the road descends from the Mount of Olives into the city, some Pharisees in the crowd told Jesus to rebuke His disciples for the praise they were giving Him. " 'I tell you,' he replied, 'if they keep quiet, the stones will cry out' " (Lk 19:40). Scripture has numerous references to inanimate creation reflecting and praising its Creator—references which the Pharisees knew well. Jesus was unambiguously identifying himself as the Creator God worthy of His creation's praise. Only minutes later the famous weeping scene mentioned above took place. Jesus lamented the judgment He knew would befall the city, " 'because you did not recognize the time of God's coming to you'" (Lk 19:44). He was commenting on His own "coming" to the Israelites and, in a more particular sense, His entry as the incarnate God into Jerusalem.

CHAPTER SEVEN

MONDAY-WEDNESDAY

OF PASSION WEEK

Jerusalem, Monday of Passion Week, c. A.D. 30

Jesus stayed in Bethany the evening following His triumphal entry and each evening through Wednesday of Passion Week. He had faithful friends there (e.g. Mary, Martha and Lazarus), was within walking distance of Jerusalem, and was not so readily accessible to His enemies. He continued to maintain control of the timing of His death.

Early Monday morning, as Jesus and His disciples were on their way back into the city, He grew hungry. Noticing a fig tree in leaf by the road, He went up to it to see if it had fruit. Finding no fruit Jesus "cursed" the tree: " 'May no one ever eat fruit from you again' " (Mk 11:21,14). Matthew, most likely compressing the chronology of the narrative somewhat, reports that, "Immediately the tree withered" (Mt 21:19). Mark's account indicates that the disciples noticed the tree had, "withered from the roots" the following day (Mk 11:20).

The cursing of the fig tree is widely interpreted as a parable of judgment against Israel (see Hos 9:10) for its failure to embrace the Messiah. Jesus, however, used this display of DIVINE power only to illustrate that enormous power is available through faithful prayer.

> "I tell you the truth, if anyone says to this mountain, 'Go, throw yourself into the sea,' and does not doubt in his heart but believes that what he says will happen, it will be done for him. Therefore I tell you, whatever you ask for in prayer, believe that you have received it, and it will be yours" (Mk 11:23-24).

Is this another instance of Jesus using hyperbole to emphasize a teaching point? Or is it possible, in the literal sense, for prayer with faith to move mountains? Context suggests the latter—that the natural world as human beings experience it is subject to the supernatural. Jesus had just shown this to be the case by making a tree "wither from the roots," (i.e. to be completely destroyed from the roots up) simply by speaking to it.

A Brief Aside: The Human Exercise of Free Will

Moving a physical mountain from one location to another would seem to entail the application of supernatural power on a large scale. The Jewish leaders unsuccessfully pressed Jesus for such displays of power on several occasions. What distinction might Jesus have been making between their requests and those of His followers faithfully seeking God's power "in prayer?" Human WILL is key to the answer because we use it to relate to God.

Metaphysical power brought to human consciousness in the manner requested by the Pharisees can effectively overcome or neutralize human WILL, thereby eliminating moral choice. Indeed, the desire (or will) to have one's own will "overcome" expresses a desire to escape the moral responsibility (and possible culpability) inherent in the notion of free will. If we truly have free will, we have the capacity to make morally correct and incorrect choices. Along with this great freedom of will goes the responsibility of abiding its results.

God, of course, has full knowledge of the moral dynamics taking place in His universe and the results they will produce. He fully understands what motivates human will. Human consciousness, on the other hand, is capable of convincing itself that its desire to escape responsibility is completely innocent and blameless. But humankind cannot have it both ways: it either has free will and responsibility or it does not. For free will to remain "free" and in the image of God it cannot call on God to overwhelm it for the purpose of being held blameless.

Man must remain free to express his innermost desires with the full freedom and power endowed by God. If God were to short-circuit this process by completely overwhelming man's will, He would vitiate man's special spirit nature, including free will. However, when God answers requests for power motivated by the desire to be in harmony with His own will, man's God-like spirit is enhanced not diminished. His spirit better understands God's spirit and becomes more capable of true moral discernment.

Monday of Passion Week, contd.

Upon entering the temple area on Monday, Jesus overturned the tables of the moneychangers and the benches of those selling doves. As mentioned previously, Jesus may have also shown his outrage at such activity a few years earlier (see Jn 2:12-16). Matthew notes that amidst the hubbub the blind and lame still came to Him, and He healed them (Mt 21:14). Seeing the, "wonderful things he did and the children shouting," the chief priests and teachers of the law again challenged Jesus. They were indignant that even children were shouting, " 'Hosanna to the Son of David'" (Mt 21:15). Jesus replied that He heard the children and He quoted directly from Psalm 8:2, which is about praising God: " 'From the lips of children and infants you have ordained praise'" (Mt 21:16). He again affirmed to the Jewish leaders that He had the right to be worshipped as God.

There are three occasions in the Gospels where audible communication between God the Father and Jesus takes place. Mark (1:11) and Luke (3:22) write about it at Jesus' baptism; and all three Synoptics describe it at the transfiguration (Mt 17:5; Mk 9:7; and Lk 9:35). John is the only one to write about the third such event, which happened early in Passion Week, probably on Monday.

Jesus became "troubled" and considered asking the Father to save Him from impending death. Instead, He called for the Father's name to be glorified. "Then a voice came from heaven, 'I have glorified it, and will glorify it again.' The crowd that was there and heard the voice said it had thundered; others said an angel had spoken to him" (Jn 12:28-29). Jesus explained that the voice was for the crowd's benefit—to show that: " 'Now is the time for judgment on this world; now the prince of this world will be driven out'" (Jn 12:31). Satan and sin were to be conquered by the ATONING sacrifice of the DIVINE Son.

Two other quotations directly referencing Jesus' DIVINITY follow the voice-from-heaven incident. Commenting on the Jews' continued rejection of Jesus, John quotes Isaiah. " 'He has blinded their eyes and deadened their hearts, so they can neither see with their eyes, nor understand with their hearts, nor turn—and I would heal them'" (Jn 12:40 quoting Is 6:10). Isaiah made this prophecy hundreds of years earlier, John says, "because he saw Jesus' glory and spoke about him" (Jn 12:41). The "He" who blinded the Israelites' eyes and deadened their hearts in Isaiah 6:10 was Yahweh, Creator God of the Old Testament. John makes no distinction between Him and Jesus. Jesus' glory, which was about to be revealed in the crucifixion, resurrection and exaltation, therefore, is at one with the glory of God spoken of by Isaiah (see, for example, Is 6:3).

John's equating Jesus with God also points to Christ as the one who would blind the Israelites eyes and deaden their hearts. This intimateness and oneness of Jesus and the Father are repeated in John's final quote from Jesus' public ministry: " 'For I did not speak of my own accord, but the Father who sent me commanded me what to say and how to say it. I know that his command leads to eternal life. So whatever I say is just what the Father has told me to say'" (Jn 12:49-50).

Jerusalem, Tuesday of Passion Week, c. A.D. 30

Though all of the synoptic authors cover the events of Passion Week Tuesday at some length, Matthew's account (including his fifth or Olivet discourse) provides the greatest detail. It was a lengthy and intense day of teaching, and as is typical, Matthew tells the story from the Jewish perspective. He uses Jesus' teachings to reveal an unfamiliar Messiah who fulfills prophecy in an unexpected manner. Matthew sequences Jesus' oratory in a manner that progressively enlarges the power and purpose of the Messiah, redefining the traditional Jewish view as the day unfolds. It is a fitting summary of Jesus' earthly ministry specifically crafted for the Jewish nation—one that the rest of the world would also come to treasure.

Beginning in chapter 21, Matthew establishes that Jesus was a person of authority. As He taught in the temple courts, the chief priests and elders asked: " 'By what authority are you doing these things? And who gave you this authority?'" (Mt 21:23). The "things" they spoke of were Jesus' teachings and actions, most likely including His recent expulsion of moneychangers and vendors from the temple.

Implicit in their questions was the recognition that Jesus did in fact have authority. What raised questions in the minds of the Sanhedrin members was the incongruity between their Messianic expectations and the teaching and actions of Jesus. Similar questions had been asked and answered numerous times. This time, instead of responding directly, Jesus put His questioners in exactly the position they were attempting to put Him, i.e. where any direct answer would be deemed unacceptable. " 'John's baptism—where did it come from? Was it from heaven, or from men?' " (Mt 21:25). If they replied "from heaven," they could be criticized for not believing John even though he spoke "heavenly" (Godly) truth. And if they answered "from men," they would face severe criticism from the populace, many of whom believed John was a true prophet.

Matthew next uses a series of parables to help fill out his portrayal of Jesus as Messiah. In the parable of the two sons he uses the familiar imagery of the vineyard (representing the nation of Israel) to make the point that what one does is more important than what one says (see Mt 21:28-32). One of the sons refused to work in the vineyard but changed his mind and then went to work. The other son did precisely the opposite. Jesus likened tax collectors and prostitutes to the first son. They were rebellious and despised by Jewish society, but some were willing to change. Those recognizing no need for change, including the Pharisees, were like the second son who did no work.

John the Baptist, Jesus said, came to show, " 'the way of righteousness, and you [Pharisees] did not believe him, but the tax collectors and the prostitutes did. And even after you saw this, you did not repent and believe him" (Mt 21:32). The "way of righteousness" to which Jesus referred is the path of repentance and faith in God, which John preached. In the more personal sense Jesus was referring to Himself. John's mission was to proclaim the coming of the Messiah, and his testimony was that Jesus is the Messiah.

In the next parable Matthew again uses vineyard imagery to explain the Messiah. A landowner planted a vineyard, rented it to some farmers and went away on a journey. As harvest time drew near he sent servants to collect his share of the fruit. The tenants mistreated the servants, and ultimately the owner resorted to sending his own son to do his bidding. Expecting to gain ownership of the vineyard by eliminating the heir to the property, the tenants, "took him and threw him out of the vineyard and killed him" (Mt 21:39). When asked by Jesus what the owner would do to the tenants when he came, the chief priests and Pharisees passed stern judgment. " 'He will bring those wretches to a wretched end,'" they replied, " 'and he will rent the vineyard to other tenants, who will give him his share of the crop at harvest time'" (Mt 21:41).

The words just out of their mouths, Jesus confirmed that they had judged themselves. He quoted from one of the most poignantly Messianic texts in Scripture, Psalm 118. " 'Have you never read in the Scriptures,'" Jesus asked, " ' "The stone the builders rejected has become the capstone; the Lord has done this, and it is marvelous in our eyes?"'" (Mt 21:42). He used Old Testament, Messianic imagery of the rejected stone to identify the slain son of the vineyard owner. The Messiah would be rejected and killed by the "tenant" authorities of the nation of Israel (the vineyard).

These scriptural connections were not lost upon His listeners. "When the chief priests and the Pharisees heard Jesus' parables they knew he was talking about them" (Mt 21:45). Jesus spelled out their self-imposed, "wretched end" at the end of the parable.

> "Therefore I tell you that the kingdom of God will be taken away from you and given to a people who will produce its fruit. He who falls on this stone will be broken to pieces, but he on whom it falls will be crushed" (Mt 21:43-44).

Flustered, but not yet totally humiliated, the Pharisees continued in their attempts to entrap Jesus. They searched about for questions that might elicit a response that could be construed as a serious offense of Jewish law—a capital offense such as blasphemy. To establish grounds for accusation, they solicited the help of their political opponents, the Herodians. Together, the Herodians and disciples of the Pharisees approached Jesus. Following a bit of flattery, they put out the bait: " 'Tell us then, what is your opinion? Is it right to pay taxes to Caesar or not?'" (Mt 22:17).

It was the old, all-answers-are-wrong trick, and Jesus handled it masterfully. "Then he said to them, 'Give to Caesar what is Caesar's, and to God what is God's' " (Mt 22:21). It made perfect common sense, and unfortunately for the Pharisees and Herodians, it was completely innocuous, both politically and theologically. Innocuous but brilliant. Embedded in that short answer was the inescapable implication of who God is *not*. God is not Caesar. God is not to be confused with a mere man, even a mighty king with the stature of Tiberius Caesar Augustus, whose image appeared on the common Roman coin, the denarius. Though Roman emperors claimed a sort of DIVINITY, Jesus sharpened the definition to exclude them. DIVINITY belongs to God and, as the teaching that day would continue to make clear, to the Messiah.

Jesus Himself then raised the issue of the nature of the Messiah. "While the Pharisees were gathered together,

Jesus asked them, 'what do you think about the Christ? Whose son is he?' " (Mt 22:42). Their reply was the most common Messianic reference of the time: " 'The son of David.'" An heir to the great king David, they believed, would be the anointed one who would deliver them out of bondage into the new order. Pursuing this line of thought, Jesus asked: " 'How is it then that David, speaking by the Spirit, calls him "Lord"? For he says, "The Lord said to my Lord: 'Sit at my right hand until I put your enemies under your feet.'""'" David's "Lord" or superior, and ultimately the Messiah (see Psalm 110), is addressed in this quotation by *The* Lord, i.e. by Yahweh God. " 'If then David calls him "Lord,"'" Jesus concluded, " 'how can he be his son?'" (Mt 22:45). Is it possible for the one who David recognized as his Lord and Messiah to be his own son?

Unlike the Pharisees' verbal thrusting, Jesus' questions were intended to elicit reflection and improved understanding. He was recognizing the Messiah as someone far greater than a human descendant of king David. Messiah is the Lord of David who sits at the right hand of the Lord God. This seems to have been a difficult relationship for the Pharisees to grasp. Not only is the Messiah the anticipated, physical "son of David," he is also David's "Lord" and in special relationship to Yahweh. He is, in other words, both man and God. Finally, and in this instance one could say regrettably, the Pharisees were silenced. "No one could say a word in reply, and from that day on no one dared to ask him any more questions" (Mt 22:45). Rather than pursuing the knowledge that Jesus was divulging about Himself, His questioners once again fell back into the defensive mode of denial.

Jesus then embarked on what is sometimes referred to as His "last sermon." Also referred to as "the seven woes," this public address painted the Messiah as judge—judge of those who feign righteousness and reject the

Messiah in their midst. Seven times Jesus intoned " 'Woe to you,'" teachers of the law and Pharisees (see Mt 23:13-32). The condemnation as symbolized by the sevenfold repetition was complete, an expression of the great grief and distress they would experience as a result of their hypocritical behavior. Their offenses were laid out in detail: shutting the kingdom of heaven in men's faces, making converts to become sons of hell, teaching others to swear falsely, focusing on minutiae and neglecting the important matters of the law, being obsessed with external appearances while ignoring the wickedness within, and shedding the blood of the prophets.

Rhetorically, Jesus asked: " 'How will you escape being condemned to hell?'" (Mt 23:33). Knowing they would not change even though He would send, " 'prophets and wise men and teachers'" to guide them, Jesus passed judgment. " 'And so upon you will come all the righteous blood that has been shed on earth, from the blood of righteous Abel to the blood of Zechariah son of Berekiah, whom you murdered between the temple and the altar'" (Mt 23:36). Most consider this judgment to have been fulfilled when Jerusalem was razed in 70 A.D.

Matthew further develops the theme of Messiah-as-judge as Jesus retreated with his disciples to the Mount of Olives for private instruction. The so-called "end of the age" (see Mt 24:3) and the accompanying judgment of mankind are the subjects of the Olivet discourse. At the end of the age the DIVINITY of the Messiah will become totally undeniable. The truth of the nature of the Son of Man will become so patently obvious that, " 'all the nations of the earth will mourn'" (Mt 24:30). They will mourn for having rejected the Messiah blazing in glory before them.

The critical aspects of the SECOND COMING of the Messiah as they relate to DIVINITY are laid out nicely by Matthew. Starting in chapter twenty-four, he records

Jesus' warning that others would falsely claim the mantle of Messiah at the end of the age. " 'Watch out that no one deceives you. For many will come in my name, claiming, 'I am the Christ,' and will deceive many'" (Mt 24:5). The end of the age will also experience enormous physical and mental affliction. " 'For then there will be great distress, unequaled from the beginning of the world until now—and never to be equaled again'" (Mt 24:21).

Most importantly, however, that time will witness the return of Jesus the Messiah, the Son of Man; and his identity as the DIVINE King will be completely revealed. " 'For as lightning that comes from the east is visible even in the west, so will be the coming of the Son of Man…When the Son of Man comes in his glory, and all the angels with him, he will sit on his throne in heavenly glory" (Mt 24:27; 25:31). As mentioned earlier, the King's purpose at this time will be to judge all those living on the earth.

> All the nations will be gathered before him, and he will separate the people one from another as a shepherd separates the sheep from the goats. He will put the sheep on his right and the goats on his left (Mt 25:32).

Thus, Matthew completes his exposition of Jesus as the DIVINE Messiah: a man of great authority; the Way of Righteousness; King of a realm greater than Caesar's; Lord of David who sits at the right hand of the Creator God; Judge of the unbelieving nation of Israel; and the Resurrected One who returns to earth to judge all nations.

Both Matthew and Mark conclude the activities of Passion Week Tuesday with the story of Jesus' anointing at Bethany. John places this incident prior to Passion Week at the home of Mary, Martha and Lazarus (see Jn 12:1). In John's version Judas Iscariot was quick to object to the seemingly wasteful act. Matthew and Mark indicate that a number of the disciples questioned Mary's extravagant use of the expensive, perfumed oil.

It was an act of worship on Mary's part and symbolic of the Jewish rite of anointing the body prior to burial. Apparently Jesus' disciples missed the beauty and symbolism, but Jesus was quite moved. " 'I tell you the truth,'" he said " 'wherever this gospel is preached throughout the world, what she has done will also be told, in memory of her'" (Mt 26:13). Differences in the timing and location of the story are probably stylistic. John's account, for example, may be more factual while Matthew and Mark likely sequenced Mary's act of worship as a prelude to Jesus' impending death.

Jerusalem, Wednesday of Passion Week, c. A.D. 30

Unlike Tuesday, almost nothing is written about Jesus' activities on Wednesday of Passion Week. Matthew does mention that He warned his disciples that Passover was two days away, " 'and the Son of Man will be handed over to be crucified'" (Mt 26:2). And apparently it was on Wednesday that the plot to kill Jesus took its final form. Mark writes:

> Now the Passover and the Feast of Unleavened Bread were only two days away, and the chief priests and the teachers of the law were looking for some sly way to arrest Jesus and kill him. "But not during the Feast," they said, "or the people may riot" (Mk 14:1-2).

The plot had the obvious involvement and sanction of the highest Jewish officials. "Then," Matthew records "the chief priests and the elders of the people assembled in the palace of the high priest, whose name was Caiaphas, and they plotted to arrest Jesus" (Mt 26:3).

Around this same time Judas Iscariot, one of the twelve apostles, came to the aid of the plotters. Luke notes that, "Satan entered Judas…And Judas went to the chief priests and the officers of the temple guard and discussed with them how he might betray Jesus" (Lk 22:3, 4). This sinister turn of events has raised countless searching questions over the course of history. How did Judas come under the control of Satan? Was God somehow controlling the situation and thereby causing Judas to betray Jesus? Once again these questions directly involve the WILL of God as He relates to man.

According to the Synoptics' accounts, Judas, on his own volition, acted to turn over Jesus to those seeking to kill Him. In Matthew's narrative the common interest of Judas and the Pharisees becomes clear—Mammon, i.e. wealth or money. Judas was willing to accept money as an idolatrous substitute for Jesus, and the Pharisees were willing to pay it to be rid of Him. " 'What are you willing to give me if I hand him over to you?'" Judas asked. "So they counted out for him thirty silver coins. From then on Judas watched for an opportunity to hand him over" (Mt 26:15-16).

CHAPTER EIGHT--BACKGROUND ON HOLY THURSDAY AND GOOD FRIDAY: CONSCIOUSNESS, MATERIALISM, AND EVOLUTION

Plaque marking the "Way of the Cross," i.e. the route believed to have been taken by Jesus from the Praetorium to the site of His crucifixion at Golgotha (Calvary)

As events move toward the trial, crucifixion and death of Jesus it is difficult to escape a sense of dread. His physical suffering and death raise disconcerting questions and remind us of our own mortality. Probably the single biggest issue is the "why" question. Why did Jesus have to die? And closely related is the question of why He died the brutal death of a common criminal. These questions relate more directly to the ATONEMENT and WILL paradoxes and will be addressed more fully in future writings. Questions more pertinent to DIVINITY—particularly the death of a DIVINE being—tend more toward the following: If Jesus was really God, how could He actually die? What actually happened when Jesus died? How is Jesus' death different from (and similar to) that of other human beings? These are questions that look back at the very nature of Jesus as both God and man.

Answers about Jesus' nature, and the implications of death for Him, are wrapped up in basic concepts of the physical and non-physical. Insight into the relation between the physical self (body) and the non-physical (mind, soul, spirit, etc.) can be both reassuring and faith-building. It can, for example, help provide a clearer interpretation of what was happening as Jesus' life ebbed away on the cross.

On Consciousness: Subjective Experience of the Objective

Ponder for a moment how the body relates to the soul and what the soul has to do with the spirit. And how does the mind relate to any of these? How does death affect them? The term "body" seems straightforward enough; it refers to the physiology of a person, the living organic matter that comprises the physical individual. Terms dealing with the non-physical "parts" or attributes of people are not quite so easy to define. The relative ease of describing and defining the physical self is largely a function of its physicality; physical reality in general is easy for people to directly observe and describe.

The dichotomy between our physical and non-physical selves is such that terms used to define one have always failed when used to precisely define the other. As a result of the split, separate language developed over time to distinguish the physical person from his or her non-physical attributes. Since antiquity each has been assumed to be unique and, therefore, not reducible to terms used to describe the other. For example, one may attempt to describe "intellect" in more physical terms such as brain mass or I.Q. points; or a long list of non-physical characteristics such as quick-witted, perceptive, incisive, etc. can be used to convey its meaning.

As time passes, the gap between our separate constructs of physical and non-physical self will likely diminish. Science is moving toward more *meta*-physical explanations of what constitutes the physical universe. The assumed dichotomy between our physical and non-physical selves may actually be an inaccurate result of our limited observational tools and ability to comprehend broader reality. In the meantime, however, we must recognize the self-imposed division between the two.

There are also problems *within* the construct of the non-physical self. It is a complex composite of many concepts—personality, spirit, emotion, will, intellect—to name a few. Possibly the best way to avoid definitional problems of the non-physical self is to substitute a single term that subsumes the others under a key characteristic which they have in common. The term "consciousness," for example, can be used to partially capture the essence of most of these terms.

If we think of human consciousness as overall self-awareness, i.e. awareness and knowledge of oneself in *whatever dimensions that may be possible for created human beings*, there is no need to labor through distinctions between soul and spirit, mind and emotion and so forth. What the subsumed terms have in common are their various aspects of self-awareness or consciousness. For example, the individual has a certain self-awareness of intellect, spirituality, physique, relationship with others, etc. The *totality* of this awareness is defined here as "consciousness."

When broadly defined as above, consciousness is important as a theological and philosophical concept because it, along with our physiology, defines the human experience. Consciousness and physiology are what we are. There are two basic streams of thought regarding the *origin* of consciousness. Epiphenomenal teaching (also referred to as promissory materialism or materialism) argues that consciousness is a secondary phenomenon of physiological processes. All self-awareness, in other words, is a by-product of normal, physical functions. In the strict epiphenomenal sense, metaphysical awareness, i.e. awareness of anything beyond the physical, is not possible (or is illusory) since all awareness is an adjunct of the physical.

Virtually all theistic philosophical systems postulate *relationship* between physiology and consciousness rather than *causality*. Consciousness does not rise spontaneously from our physiology but occurs separately; it is a concurrent phenomenon in its own right. One of the principal tasks of theistic systems is to explain this body/consciousness relationship. Pantheism, incidentally, straddles the line between epiphenomenal and phenomenal explanations by suggesting that all matter (not just humans, animals and organic matter) is infused with a sort of divine consciousness or spirituality. All matter and divine spirit are said to be co-extensive.

Perhaps the single, experiential event shared by

humans that best differentiates theistic constructs of body/consciousness relationship from the epiphenomenal is physical death. Theistic views allow for a separation (and an implicit independence) and continuation of consciousness at the point when physiological function ceases. Epiphenomenalism argues that consciousness terminates at physical death. So, the epiphenomenal position has a certain conclusiveness and simplicity about it that appeals to tidy minds.

Continued existence independent of the physical, by comparison, seems a bit cumbersome and speculative. But despite its intellectual messiness, it also has great *teleological* appeal. It promises fuller satisfaction of that great inherent yearning of consciousness itself: what is my purpose? Epiphenomenalism's reply of transient pleasure seems obvious but unconvincing. Its purpose is much too small, too inconsistent with the beauty and gravity of the questions that consciousness poses. Conversely, theological answers tend toward the extremes of being convoluted and complicated or rote and simplistic.

Epiphenomenalism/Materialism

It is important to recognize epiphenomenalism for what it is and avoid the pitfalls of over-philosophizing. Unfortunately, epiphenomenalism—or as it has been widely accepted in scientific circles, "promissory materialism"[24]—runs so counter to the notions of free will, conscience, soul and spirit that Christians need to seriously consider its implications for their beliefs. For an informed and very readable explanation of why the epiphenomenal argument for the material nature of human consciousness is untenable I would recommend D'Souza's *What's So Great About Christianity.*[25] Mario Beauregard and Denyse O'Leary provide a more detailed, neuroscientific accounting of human spirit separate from the brain in their book, *The Spiritual Brain.*[26]

Promissory materialism, or just plain "materialism" posits that the non-physical experiential reality that we refer to as mind, consciousness, free will, spirit, etc. derives *solely* from the physical brain and is, therefore, actually physical. Free will in the materialist view is thought to be an illusion because there is no mind independent of the brain that has the ability to make effective choices. Choice is an illusion generated by the brain as it responds slavishly to the rules of biophysics. Personhood and personality are interesting but unnecessary spin-offs of extant brain mass.

The reduction of personhood, mind, free will, etc. to brain matter, however, contains an inherent, fatal flaw. If free will—the facility to effectively make decisions on the basis of the awareness that consciousness presents—is illusory, then science itself is an illusion as it is based on long series of decisions made in precisely that manner. In other words, free will is a necessary condition for scientific thought to have any validity.

If scientific thought is predetermined by the brain biomass of the scientist, the scientist has no effective input into any conclusions that are drawn, including any testing he or she may perform to validate those conclusions. Since free will and personhood are merely illusions incidental to brain activity in the materialist scheme, there can be no real capability (e.g. a person) apart from the brain to decide upon the validity and reality of what the brain experiences (e.g. in testing scientific hypotheses).

One possible rejoinder to this argument is that the brain effectively acts as its own, decision-making person and draws the correct scientific conclusions. But if that is the case, how are the brain's auto-decisions brought to reality so that other brains can share them? Decisions that cannot be shared are hardly scientific. To my knowledge, there is no such thing as direct brain-to-brain transference of conclusions—except, perhaps, in sci-fi thrillers.

Consciousness remains as the requisite intermediary, but in the materialist view it is useless because it is an illusion. It cannot be trusted as the means of transferring notions about reality. The no-free-will assumption of materialism, incidentally, is similar to one made by several strains of Christianity which hold that effective free will (from the moral standpoint) does not exist.

Disregarding the above line of argument, many have concluded that the mind is totally under the control of the laws of physics. According to materialist thought all science is merely the knowledge that matter has about itself—or in the case of the brain, the knowledge that what is essentially fat tissue has about other forms of matter. We can push this thinking further and conjecture about what knowledge the mountains may have of the stars or what your tulip garden may think of Shakespearean sonnets. Materialist thinking often leads to the conclusion that *all* matter has intelligence because matter (and energy) is all that exists. Material generates the non-material; ergo, matter effectively *is* intelligence, mind, free will, and all those other non-material qualities we associate with people.

"Higher" forms of consciousness and intelligence—if we assume, for example, that nature reveals itself more clearly to people than to rocks—must simply be a function of the kind of material and the form it takes, i.e. how it is organized. As suggested, fat tissue, and especially "living" fat tissue may be a particularly smart form of matter. But, alas—I have raised the issue of life and whether matter has to be "alive" to have consciousness and intelligence.

If life is *not* necessary, we must encounter smart rocks on a daily basis without even knowing it, and therefore putting to the lie the epithet "dumb as a box of rocks." On the other hand, if matter must be organic (alive at one time or another) to be intelligent—as the brain surely is—the smartness equation is completely changed.

If life *is* a prerequisite, it becomes necessary for the materialist to sharply define it and differentiate its various forms to understand the various levels of intelligence (and consciousness) that may exist. To be credible the devout materialist must define precisely how consciousness is produced and how the "subjective" experience of reality is only an impersonal "objective" expression of matter. Just promising to do so at some future date is nothing more than an expression of the materialist's faith in his or her own personal intelligence (which, to be consistent, he or she would have to contend, is an illusion). Unlike evolutionary theory, which suffers somewhat from an inability to replicate conditions in the lab due to the time dimension, consciousness constantly exhibits itself.

But in reality the ardent materialist's task is an insuperable one. He places himself in the position of having to explicitly demonstrate how physical properties and mechanics produce the non-physical phenomena we experience as subjective consciousness (thought, emotion, volition, etc.) No one can stand outside his own subjective experience of reality (or inside anyone else's) in order to make observations and measurements concerning the actual generation of that experience.

The only possible direct observations of subjective consciousness are introspective, but these take the form of consciousness describing *what* it experiences. *How* those experiences are generated cannot be examined by consciousness looking upon itself. Likewise, it is impossible for one subjective consciousness to directly examine how someone else's consciousness is generated.

Ironically, for the materialist, even if the workings of subjective consciousness could be directly observed, the observer's conclusions could not be admitted as scientific evidence due to their subjective nature. According to the materialist's own logic they would have to be deemed as only the by-product of the observer's brain activity, and therefore irrelevant to any true measure of reality.

Evolutionary Theory and the Randomness Bugaboo

As it relates to the relationship between God and man the question of Darwinian evolution by natural selection (EBNS) is something of a red herring. The biological detail of how God may have produced the physical corpus of man is very interesting but of secondary importance to what makes man "special." Man is special in creation not so much because he has physical representation which is "fearfully and wonderfully made" (Ps 139:14), but because his consciousness (non-physical or metaphysical characteristics) were created in the image and likeness of God.

Nevertheless, God's possible use of a "law" or process to produce physical man has been a source of bitter controversy since Charles Darwin put it forth. Many if not most believers in God (myself included) have strongly resisted the notion of EBNS at some point in their faith journey. Most often they take this view because they believe EBNS to be antithetical to God. But is it truly? By definition the only thing actually antithetical to God is atheism, i.e. the absence of God and the argument for that absence.

The single greatest objection that most people of faith have against EBNS is that it posits a truly random process resulting in the production of the human species with no involvement of a divine Creator. Ergo, EBNS is atheistic. This is a faulty conclusion, however, because it is impossible to demonstrate that true or *absolute* randomness is an operating principle in the space-time that we inhabit. In order to validly draw the conclusion that the selection process is absolutely random, the observer would have to demonstrate with certainty that there is nothing *outside* space-time (our universe) that could be affecting the selection process. If that possibility exists, the process may have the appearance of being random from the space-time perspective but may actually be non-random.

The simple truth is that neither believers nor non-believers can actually (physically) project themselves outside of space-time to ascertain the absolute magnitude and composition of reality. It is impossible for atheists to use *any* natural process to prove the absence of a God who may exist outside the universe.[27] Believers in God need not be concerned that God may choose to express His WILL concerning the biological development of man as one of the many principles that regulate His universe. In this sense the theory of EBNS is really no different than the theory of gravity or the theory of relativity. EBNS takes no position on whether or not God may choose to express His WILL in *other* ways—such as direct intervention in His universe.

Believers' often-unfriendly attitude toward EBNS may well trace to the manner in which God has exerted His will on creation rather than the actual design of the principle. Believers cherish the concept of a *personal* God, one who is like their own person in all respects, including their personal physiology. There is a sense of being closer to God when we conceive of Him as more like us. But this gets back to the notion that man's real "specialness" is his likeness of spirit with that of his Creator not his physiology.

Atheists, on the other hand, seem to have developed strong confidence (some would say overconfidence) in the belief that the *apparent* randomness of EBNS is absolute, and therefore becomes a reasonable substitute for God. This thinking is interesting because it is an expression of human WILL to interpret incomplete (and incomplete-able) data as proof of God's non-existence. It is an expression of will to separate from a personal God, and it is accompanied by the positive feeling (for them) of confidence that He does not exist. Their reasoning and emotion, as would be expected, is opposite that of believers. The motivation behind the atheistic exercise of human will seems to be a strong desire not to be beholden to a personal Creator. In the absence of such a Creator the WILL of man becomes paramount.

The atheistic argument that apparent randomness in a limited universe removes the need for a God makes two totally unfounded assumptions: (1) nothingness can "cause" something (e.g. the universe) to happen and sustain what it causes to be; and (2) the changes that everything brought into existence undergo occur in a completely ("absolutely") random fashion, i.e. without purpose. If both assumptions can be clearly demonstrated, there is obviously no need for a creating, sustaining God. Unfortunately (for atheists) neither can be.

In his book *The Last Superstition: A Refutation of the New Atheism*, Edward Feser uses Aristotle's and Thomas Aquinas's classic logic to demonstrate convincingly that *all* things and events (effects) stem from a sequence of causes, and that a First Mover (God) is necessary to initiate and sustain the sequence.[28] Aristotelian logic is also diametrically opposed to the notion of absolute randomness. For example, equal *ex ante* statistical probabilities for any given population of *possible* occurrences (the numeric—and theoretic—concept of randomness) does *not* imply that each specific, *actual* occurrence does *not* have a "final cause" or purpose in the Aristotelian sense. If one searches deeply enough, a cause (or causes) can be assigned to any event on an *ex post* basis.

Theists enjoy the great advantage of not having to transit outside the universe to experience cause and effect, and to draw logical, metaphysical inferences about it. Atheists, on the other hand, cannot demonstrate the validity of their assumptions about causation from nothingness and absolute randomness without full knowledge of what lies beyond the universe. They are in the untenable position of having to prove a negative assertion (the non-existence of God) without having access to *all possible* existence—while simultaneously denying the strong positive evidence (causative purpose within the universe) to which they do have access.

Believers who accept the notion of EBNS as a "law" of nature also assume that God is the originator of nature and all its laws. For their part, non-believers have the insurmountable task of explaining how *all* the laws of physics and biophysics that provide for the support of complex life forms came to be. This web of interrelated laws (and the underlying "constants") is sometimes referred to as the *anthropic principle.* With regards to EBNS, non-believers must answer the puzzle of why nature would "favor" survival over non-survival. In other words, if it cannot be demonstrated that nature operates in an absolutely random fashion, what is *nature's* nature that it would consistently promote life?[29] The very notion of such a preponderant bias in favor of life smacks strongly of some sort of intelligent external force.

The other big objection that believers in God have to EBNS is that the results of the process seriously *exceed* expectations. This objection questions that if the selection criterion behind EBNS is singular, i.e. if it can be accurately expressed as selection *solely* on the basis of an organism's improved probability of survival, how do highly complex organisms with characteristics unrelated, unnecessary, and even antithetical to survival get selected? Man is a good example of such an organism. His huge brain (and consciousness) is associated with qualities such as aesthetic appreciation, moral discernment, and empathy for his fellow man.

It stretches credulity to argue that these capacities

developed *totally* as a means of forwarding and dispersing genetic material. It seems that Occam's razor may have been too assiduously applied, resulting in a simple, elegant theory but one that is not quite internally consistent. For example, EBNS would seem more convincing if it resulted in species whose complexity aided in making them progressively more indestructible (e.g. super-intelligent bacteria and super-brainy cockroaches). Instead, the increasing complexity seems associated with species more vulnerable to their environment and themselves (e.g. dinosaurs and man).

There is, of course, no reason that an enormous variety of species could not be brought to exist contemporaneously, but the argument that the trend toward complexity is driven entirely by survivability may be overly simplistic. The game of which survival traits appeared in which sequence to produce diversity and complexity can be played almost *ad infinitum* and not satisfy the complexity issue. If, for example, mankind uses its intelligence to destroy itself and other complex life forms, what is the bio-*logic* of progressively greater complexity? Would EBNS have made a "mistake" or would mankind simply have misunderstood nature's selection criteria?

Mankind's self-destruction is a hypothetical—but not implausible—outcome of EBNS. Since the "nature" in Darwinian EBNS is neither theistic nor atheistic but essentially an operating principle, we would have to conclude that the principle is flawed (or at least incomplete) if the complexity of life forms resulted in their biological termination. The concurrent drive for survivable organisms to gain in complexity would have led to destruction, not survival.

And presumably (a theistic presumption) no one but God and His saints would remain to bear witness exactly how the theory was faulty or incomplete. Committed materialists would seemingly be indifferent to such an outcome, since the total destruction of human consciousness would represent nothing more than the elimination of illusion. From their viewpoint, doing away with illusion may even be a net positive given that illusions are generally considered *false* impressions of reality.

CHAPTER NINE

HOLY THURSDAY AND GOOD FRIDAY

Center right: Basilica of the Agony (Church of All Nations) at the site believed to be the Garden of Gethsemane on the Mount of Olives. Looking northeast from outside the eastern wall of the Old City

Physical death is a critical juncture for all people including non-Christians and Christians, but its mystery and threat are greatly diminished by the teachings and actions of Jesus. When the body quits working...well…the body quits working and nothing more. This is the flip side of the epiphenomenal view that when the body quits working the complete individual self shuts down.

For the Christian believer, consciousness (remember the broad definition) does not shut down. It co-exists with the body but is not dependent on it for definition and meaning. Or, to think of it another way, the body is a physical representation of consciousness, not vice versa. It provides physically discernable presence in the space-time universe but does not totally define the individual person. Reality is greater than what we experience as our physical selves and the physical universe. That which is not physically discernable, including consciousness, is as real (and arguably much more real in an absolute sense) as the body with which it co-exists in the space-time realm. Death interrupts this coexistence but marks only the demise of the original, incarnate body, i.e. the physical self.

Setting aside for the moment the more important questions about the purpose of Jesus' death, what can we conclude happened when He gave up His life? Physical and non-physical separated. The flesh and blood of the man Jesus, no longer able to survive physiologically without supernatural intervention, ceased functioning. His DIVINE, non-physical self continued its existence apart from the body with which it had co-existed. Use of the term "co-existed" may seem a bit sterile, and begs the question whether it is the non-physical that animates and gives life to the physical. The short answer is yes, but the exact interaction of the two cannot now and never can be completely explained in empirical terms in the space-time we inhabit. Our knowledge of the non-physical while on this earth will remain far from complete.

Given this view of death, when we lament that Jesus the Christ died we can also take solace. Certainly the non-physical, DIVINE consciousness (or spirit) that animated the man Jesus did not perish. That consciousness which had subjected itself to co-existing with created matter (or body) also permitted itself to be separated from it. In other words, the DIVINE consciousness which created all matter subjected itself to the same experience that *created* consciousness (or spirit of man) ultimately has been condemned to undergo. As suggested above the "whys" associated with this sovereign choice are much more intriguing than the "whats."

Jerusalem, Thursday of Passion Week, c. A.D. 30

By all accounts Thursday of Passion Week was a time of preparation. "On the first day of the Feast of Unleavened Bread, when it was customary to sacrifice the Passover lamb, Jesus' disciples asked him, 'Where do you want us to go and make preparations for you to eat the Passover?' " (Mk 14:13). They arranged for a large upper room in the city and, "When evening came, Jesus arrived with the Twelve" (Mk 14:17).

John's Gospel captures most of the detail of what transpired that evening, though several significant events are mentioned only by the Synoptics. Before considering this momentous meeting with the twelve, it may be helpful to answer questions that often come up regarding its timing. Specifically, if Jesus and His disciples observed the Passover on Thursday evening as indicated by the Synoptics, what does John mean when he says that the next morning, as Jesus was led to the palace of the Roman governor: "...to avoid ceremonial uncleanness the Jews did not enter the palace; they wanted to be able to eat the Passover." (Jn 18:28)? Was not the time for the Passover meal already past? And did Jesus actually observe the Passover, or did the Synoptics simply record it as though He had for their own purposes?

Northern Palestinian Jews (including Jesus and His disciples) measured each day from sunrise to sunrise while those in southern Palestine (including the priests and Sadducees in Jerusalem) marked days from sunset to sunset. Any given "day" for the combined groups covered the period from sunrise on one day through sunset of the *next* day, incorporating two sunsets and two evenings. Due to this difference in timekeeping, the northern Palestinian Jews observed Passover twenty-four hours ahead of the Jews of Jerusalem, i.e. immediately following the first sunset of the elongated day mentioned above. Thus, Jesus and His disciples were able to partake of the Passover meal on the evening before His trial and crucifixion, while the Jews of Jerusalem would not observe it until Friday evening following His death. That second sunset also marked the beginning of the Sabbath for the Jews of southern Palestine.[30]

According to John (13:4-5) Jesus got up and began to wash His disciples' feet fairly early in the evening as the Passover meal was being served. His action may have been prompted by the dispute that arose among the disciples noted by Luke (Lk 22:24). They were still concerned with questions of who would be the "greatest," i.e. have the highest position and greatest recognition among men. Jesus' willingness to perform one of the most menial of tasks was an effective antidote to their bickering and a demonstration of His own DIVINE character. There was no question among the disciples that He was their "Lord and Teacher" (Jn 13:14). Yet, despite His superior position, He was willing to serve them because of His love for them. Love is the essence of the relationship between Father, Son and Holy Spirit. And, as Jesus demonstrated, it is the way they choose to relate to mankind and expect Jesus' disciples to relate to each other.

As the Passover meal progressed, Jesus did something that changed the significance of the entire feast. Building on the rich historical context of Passover and all its attendant symbolism, he instituted a new "covenant" (or "testimony" or "contract") with His followers. His new covenant would share the blood symbolism of the Mosaic covenant at Sinai and the sacrificial blood of the Passover lambs, which protected the Israelites from the Lord's wrath. Jeremiah the prophet had spelled out the terms of the new covenant in some detail.

> "The time is coming," declares the Lord, "when I will make a new covenant with the house of Israel and with the house of Judah…I will put my law in their minds and write it on their hearts. I will be their God and they will be my people…For I will forgive their wickedness and will remember their sins no more" (Jer 31:31-34).

Jesus used wine at the Passover meal to represent his own blood that would soon be shed, formally sealing his new covenant. Luke says it this way:

> And he took bread, gave thanks and broke it, and gave it to them, saying, "This is my body given for you; do this in remembrance of me." In the same way, after the supper he took the cup, saying, "This cup is the new covenant in my blood, which is poured out for you" (Lk 22:19-20).

Matthew's equivalent of "poured out for you" is "poured out for many for the forgiveness of sins" (Mt 26:28).

Though brief in comparison to written covenants of His day, the content of what Jesus said is absolutely mind-boggling. The bread and wine were symbols of his body and blood, which would be offered up to effect the forgiveness of sins. His disciples, Jesus said, should, " 'do this in remembrance of me,'" i.e. break and share bread (and by implication at least, share the cup) as a memorial to the covenant He had instituted (Lk 22:19). Incidentally, that the bread and wine were *symbols* of the covenantal body and blood is clear, since Jesus was present in physical form. He would have contradicted Himself had He intended to indicate that the bread and wine were His *physical* body and blood.

Who, we must ask, is capable of bringing about forgiveness? Who can cover over or wash away the offenses of the many against the Creator God, so that He will remember them no more? ATONEMENT in this sense is only within the purview of the DIVINE Creator Himself. And what are the obligations of the other parties to the covenant? Jesus preached consistently throughout His ministry about His disciples' obligations: to accept and follow Him as the initiator of the new covenant and enabler of the promised forgiveness.

Having likely completed the meal but while still in the upper room, Jesus entered into a lengthy and intimate discourse with His disciples. (Judas Iscariot had exited by this time.) His comments were aimed at comforting His closest followers and preparing them for future events. They also served as a review and synopsis of His basic theology. Central to the message of Jesus' final discourse and the following prayer to His Father is His relationship with the Father and Holy Spirit. Together they are the clearest presentation of the Trinitarian God in the New Testament. Jesus also explained similarities between the Trinitarian relationship and His own relationship with the disciples (and all believers), and their relationships with each other. Finally, Jesus contrasted Himself and His relationships with the rejectionist world. Each section of this powerful discourse, as well as Jesus' prayer at Gethsemane, deserves close examination.

Thursday of Passion Week: Jesus' Final Discourse--The Trinity

Jesus began the conversation by saying: " 'Now is the Son of Man glorified and God is glorified in him. If God is glorified in him, God will glorify the Son in himself, and will glorify him at once'" (Jn 13:31-32). Here Jesus is speaking of how intimately His own glory is tied to that of God the Father. Glorification of God is a key Biblical concept. It is the very purpose of creation; and it has to do with the recognition and appreciation of God for who He is. Glorification is the coming into consciousness of the true character and worth of the Creator. Jesus said He will be glorified *in* the Father and the Father will be glorified *in* Him by the action He was about to undertake, i.e. the crucifixion. It will occur "at once," or "straightway" as the KJV puts it, again stressing the inseparability of Father and Son.

John's use of the preposition "in" here and throughout the discourse may seem a bit unusual to modern readers. It has the normal meaning of inclusion within a prescribed space or time period or within something immaterial. Examples of each would be *in* the building, *in* the nineteenth century, and *in* politics. "In" also denotes the *sharing* of space, time or something immaterial. When I am in a building, for example, I share the space defined by the building; when I am in the nineteenth century I share in existence during that period; when I am in politics I share in an intellectual endeavor with others. Being "in," or "sharing" in this sense, means participating with, rather than dividing among (as in sharing an apple pie).

Thus, when John talks about one person being "in" another, as he does in chapters fourteen through seventeen, he is speaking of something shared by or in common between those persons. The most intimate sharing possible is that of shared consciousness, or communion of consciousness. When it happens there is a deep and mutual empathy of consciousness between the persons "in" one another. Such sharing or communion can exist between equals such as between the Father, Son and Holy

Spirit.

It can also exist between beings who are not equal, such as between God and man. When it exists between non-equals it is incomplete and limited by the capacity of the subordinate participant. Thus, man can be completely "in" God because God can appreciate the consciousness of man to its fullest potential. And God can be in man, but not completely, as man is subordinate to God and lacks the capacity to fully share in His consciousness. Jesus and the Father had perfectly shared consciousness of their own glory; what the crucifixion would help bring about is the revelation of that glory to the consciousness of man.

Still unclear about Jesus' relation to the Father, and why Jesus was returning to the Father, Philip said: " 'Lord, show us the Father and that will be enough for us'" (Jn 14:8). Jesus' reply revealed a great deal about the Father-Son relationship.

> "Don't you know me, Philip, even after I have been among you such a long time? Anyone who has seen me has seen the Father. How can you say, 'Show us the Father'? Don't you believe that I am in the Father, and that the Father is in me? The words I say to you are not just my own. Rather, it is the Father, living in me, who is doing his work. Believe me when I say that I am in the Father and the Father is in me…'" (Jn 14:9-11).

Father and Son are separate, and yet to see one is to see the other. They are so closely related as to be considered "in" one another. These statements of relationship are not primarily references to Jesus' physical body. The Father and Son being *in* one another are allusions to the sharing of DIVINE consciousness mentioned above. It is a sharing between equals so complete and perfect as to provide true unity of purpose.

Jesus went on to explain more about the DIVINE nature to the apostles, a nature that was later dubbed "Trinitarian" or "Triune" in Christian circles. He spoke of a third person or spirit.

> "And I will ask the Father, and he will give you another Counselor to be with you forever—the Spirit of truth. The world cannot accept him, because it neither sees him nor knows him. But you know him, for he lives with you and will be in you" (Jn 14:16-17).

Though previously mentioned elsewhere (e.g. at Jesus' baptism), here the Holy Spirit's critical role in the plan of salvation is set forth. His nature and purpose are *truth*, and he will be "another Counselor" to those who follow the teachings of Jesus. Use of the phrase "another Counselor" is significant for two reasons. It clearly distinguishes the Holy Spirit as a separate person; and the Greek translation specifically denotes another of the *same kind*, i.e. of a DIVINE nature like Jesus and the Father. His purpose would be to help believers comprehend the truth of Jesus and His teachings.

Following His description of the Father-Son-Spirit relationship, Jesus spoke of Himself as an incarnate personification of spirit. " 'You heard me say, "I am going away and I am coming back to you." If you loved me, you would be glad that I am going to the Father, for the Father is greater than I'" (Jn 14:28). Jesus called the Father "greater" than Himself in this context because He was still restricted by His physical form, i.e. by His unresurrected body. Upon death, when He would leave His disciples to go to the Father, His DIVINE spirit nature would be unencumbered. For that the disciples were to be "glad."

The idea of a self-imposed, temporary subordination to the Father while Jesus remained incarnate is repeated a few verses later. " 'I will not speak with you much longer, for the prince of this world is coming. He has no hold on me, but the world must learn that I love the Father and that I do exactly what my Father has commanded me'" (Jn 14:30-31). Faithful subordinates obey the commands of their superiors. Through the exercise of His DIVINE WILL, Jesus had consciously placed Himself in a subordinate position; He had assumed human form. But He had not abrogated His own DIVINITY or DIVINE WILL while incarnate. For this reason, unlike other men, "the prince of this world" (Satan) had no hold on Jesus.

Because His spirit was (and is) DIVINE and completely shared the consciousness of the Father, He was able to follow the Father's will "exactly," i.e. without sin. Though subject to the earthly conditions of temptation, Jesus' will was diametrically opposed and impervious to it. As the perfect subordinate, so to speak, He expressed His love for the Father by keeping His will in complete conformity with the Father's. This is true obedience and demonstrates the unity of spirit and consistency of will between the persons of the Trinity. The world, and particularly Jesus' followers who are in the world, must learn to emulate this example.

Seeking to comfort His disciples, Jesus again spoke of His departure and reminded them that they would not be alone. " 'But I tell you the truth: It is for your good that I am going away. Unless I go away, the Counselor will not come to you; but if I go, I will send him to you'" (Jn 16:7). Taken with the quote from John 14:16 where Jesus talks about asking the Father to send the Counselor, it is quite obvious that Father, Son and Holy Spirit are separate persons working in close harmony.

There is really no evidence that Jesus' references to distinct "persons" are merely some kind of linguistic or literary conceit. It remains difficult, however, for many to conceptualize a Trinitarian God. In part, this is due to the great and long-standing emphasis given by Judaism to the singularity of Yahweh. Also, in more modern times, there has developed a huge cultural emphasis on the physical aspects of personhood. Unifying three physical persons seems impossible. As mentioned earlier, it may be easier to envision the Trinity as personalities. These personalities have such complete awareness and sensitivity to the consciousness of one another that they operate as one. This is oneness of spirit, which is not violated by the Son indwelling a human body.

Jesus then elaborated on the truth to be revealed by the Spirit. " 'All that belongs to the Father is mine. That is why I said the Spirit will take from what is mine and make it known to you'" (Jn 16:15). Jesus was not speaking of material things that belong to the Father, but the characteristics that define His nature. He and the Father share the same DIVINE nature. The KJV says that Jesus "hath" all things that are the Father's, where "hath" (or *skheho* in the Greek) places particular emphasis on power. The Spirit, intimately familiar with the essential nature of Father and Son, will "take from" that truth and make it known to Jesus' disciples. Revelation of that truth, it may be inferred, would have to be consistent with God's purpose.

Ancient olive trees in the Garden of Gethsemane on the Mount of Olives

It should be noted that Jesus' physical body did not "belong to" the Father. It was unrelated to the essential character of the Father, and, therefore, to the essential character of the Son. Jesus' physical body did not "belong to" Himself in the same sense that the attributes of the Father do. As with all human beings, Jesus' unresurrected body was basically a means of manifesting physical presence in His created universe.

Transit to and from the world (or created universe) is touched upon directly in John 16:28. " 'I came from the Father and entered the world; now I am leaving the world and going back to the Father.'" Jesus' nature, being DIVINE, is to dwell "with" and "in" the Father. Such existence does not require physical space or *locus* as mankind knows it. When he "entered the world," Jesus took on the physical dimensionalities of his created universe in order to bring his message more directly to created man, to the physical context most familiar to man. Upon "leaving the world" he was leaving the place defined most clearly and most obviously by its physical attributes.

Physical bodies, as we know them, would be literally out of place if they were able to leave the created universe. Since physicality requires place (or space, or locus) to exist, the implication is that they would be *annihilated*, or returned to nothingness. As we will see, Jesus' physical body vacated the tomb following His death. But His resurrected body, which walked about the earth and ascended to the Father, was significantly different from the body that experienced death and entered the tomb.

Jesus' Final Discourse—Relationship With His Followers

While conversing with His apostles about the Trinity, Jesus interspersed thoughts about His relationship with them and their future proselytes. Early on John quotes one of the most famous, powerful and misunderstood lines in the Gospels: " 'I am the way and the truth and the life. No one comes to the Father except through me. If you really knew me, you would know my Father as well" (Jn 14:6-7). Often taken as exclusionary and sometimes even as harshly discriminatory, we need to better understand who the speaker is before drawing conclusions. If He is who He claims to be—the DIVINE Son of God—His statement about our possible relationship with God through Him points to the primary significance of God's nature, and only secondarily to the nature of what He has created.

In other words, *how* we might relate to God is not an issue of our sensibilities regarding fairness and open-mindedness. It is a function of the Creator's nature, specifically His power and love. Man enters God's creation totally dependent upon Him and ignorant of His love. The sole "way" *to* God must, of necessity, *be* God; man has no inherent power to establish or regulate real relationship with the One who created him. Christians believe that it is the DIVINE Christ who provides and personifies the "way."

The (moral) power of WILL given by God to man is limited to accepting or rejecting the relational way established by Christ. Mankind may desire and seek other ways for his own reasons. Or, man may choose to deny the need to relate to a Creator by assuming some sort of spontaneous or self-creation. But if man's WILL runs counter to the DIVINE WILL, his relationship with the true God will suffer. Jesus' statement in this regard is bold and unequivocal. Its weight and veracity derive precisely from His claim of DIVINITY—and entails man's total dependence upon Him. The only way around Christ's earth-changing statement, i.e. the only rationale for claiming some other access to God, is to deny the DIVINITY of Jesus.

Does God's provision for relating to Him imply that only God's WILL is important, and that mankind's role in the plan of creation is to unquestioningly "tow the line" and remain silent? Just the opposite is true. The apostle Paul exhorts us to: "Test everything. Hold on to the good" (1Th 5:21). Given in the specific context of examining prophecy, Paul's challenge applies to all Scripture and teaching associated with it. Honest and careful examination will lead to the truth about God's relationship with His creation.

Examining DIVINE revelation about creation—and to some degree creation itself—will yield the conclusions: (1) that mankind (and all Creation) is totally dependent on and subordinate to God; (2) that dependency upon and subordination to the Creator is a position of extreme privilege and value established by the Creator; (3) that mankind's ultimate well being (happiness, joy, understanding, fulfillment, etc.) can only be achieved in harmonious relationship with the Creator; and finally (4) that obedience to the Creator is a sign of strength, not weakness. With a better understanding of God's nature we gain a fuller appreciation of His creation, including our own human "self." Improved understanding brings the realization that God's way is the optimal one to follow.

Having explained Himself as the sole means of access to the Father, Jesus drew a parallel between His Father-Son relationship and His relationship to man. " 'On that day you will realize that I am in my Father, and you are in me, and I am in you' " (Jn 14:20). A fuller comprehension of his pivotal role as a bridge to mankind would be made clear to the apostles "on that day," a clear contextual reference to the time following Jesus' resurrection. Then it would be clear that as Jesus and the Father are "in" one another, so too will Jesus and the apostles (and their followers) be in one another. This sharing of consciousness, as mentioned above, parallels but cannot exactly duplicate the Father-Son-Holy Spirit relationship. Man's nature is limited and subordinate to God. Jesus alludes to this difference in John's next chapter (fifteen), his teaching on the vine and the branches.

> "I am the vine; you are the branches. If a man remains in me and I in him, he will bear much fruit; apart from me you can do nothing. If anyone does not remain in me, he is like a branch that is thrown away and withers…This is to my Father's glory, that you bear much fruit, showing yourselves to be my disciples" (Jn 15:5,8).

Though frequently used in Scripture as a symbol of Israel, Jesus used the well-understood agricultural reference of vines and grape-growing here to graphically illustrate relationship. Those who follow His teachings are branches that remain "in" Him, attached to the life-giving vine. The relationship is direct, one-on-one, subordinate and completely dependent. Nothing and no one stands between the vine and its branches. Life giving sustenance flows in one direction from the vine to the branches. When a man and Jesus remain in one another, the man will have the life that Jesus brings, and will bear the fruit of that life. Being alive in Jesus is to be saved from being "thrown away," and withering. It is to share true intimacy of spirit, intimacy of consciousness with Father, Son and Holy Spirit. It is a life initiated in the earthly domain and unaffected by physical death.

Most people like to think of themselves as self-starters and initiators of actions that get things accomplished. And so it is with relationships. It gives a greater sense of participation and control to conclude that we can start and stop relationships at our own choosing. Relationship through Jesus to God does not fit this template very well. Both DIVINE and human WILL are involved, but it is Jesus who establishes the terms of relationship with the Creator. Throughout His ministry Jesus indicated that His followers must have and express faith in Him. " 'I tell you the truth, anyone who has faith in me will do what I have been doing. He will do even greater things than these, because I am going to the Father'" (Jn 14:12).

Is Jesus saying that we must work hard and "make up our minds" to put our trust in Him? That we should try with all our might to get something going with Him, as we sometimes do with other people? His emphasis at the conclusion of the vine-and-branches teaching seems to be the opposite. " 'You did not choose me, but I chose you and appointed you to go and bear fruit—fruit that will last'" (Jn 15:16).

It was unusual in Jesus' time for rabbis to choose their followers. Nevertheless, He specifically chose each of the twelve, thereby establishing the precedent and pattern for how relationship with Him would be initiated. What are the implications of this for being "in" Jesus and being "saved?" Perhaps they are not as threatening as some would suggest. Part of the thesis of this book is that the invitation to relationship with God has been opened to *all* mankind. We will need to set aside, at least temporarily, thoughts about those who lived and died before Jesus' saving work, those completely denied access to the Gospels, etc.

Beyond the initiation of relationship with God is the development and continuation of that relationship. This is the point at which many who are influenced by Jesus' teachings fail to follow His way. For one reason or another, they are unable to follow His explicit and oft-repeated instructions concerning obedience.

> "If you love me, you will obey what I command...Whoever has my commands and obeys them, he is the one who loves me. He who loves me will be loved by my Father,

> and I too will love him and show myself to him…If anyone loves me, he will obey my teaching. My Father will love him, and we will come to him and make our home with him. He who does not love me will not obey my teaching" (Jn 14:15,21,23-24).

The connection seems simple and straightforward: meaningful relationship with Jesus, the Father and Holy Spirit is contingent upon obeying (or "keeping" as the KJV puts it) His commands, which are laid out in His teachings. But if relationship with God is so simple, why did Jesus give the following warning? " 'Enter through the narrow gate. For wide is the gate and broad is the road that leads to destruction, and many enter through it. But small is the gate and narrow the road that leads to life, and only a few find it'" (Mt 7:13-14).

Ironically, *love* seems to be the first great obstacle in the path to relationship with God—not love per se, but mankind's restricted consciousness of the broad scope of that phenomenon. We too easily tend to become obsessed with the sentimental, romantic and erotic aspects of love. These ingratiating and appealing characteristics are captured fairly well by the Greek notions of *phileo* and *eros*. What is often overlooked is the more challenging reality of *agape* love.

We get hints of what *agape* love is about from love's other aspects, but it truly adds its own dimension. In speaking of relationship with the Trinity, Jesus is speaking primarily of *agape* love. *Phileo* and *eros* are legitimate and beautiful in their own right, but in the sharing of consciousness with the Creator they are more of a precursor to relationship than fulfillment of it.

What is this *agape* love that Jesus is talking about? Hold onto your hats because it is one of the truly *revolutionary* parts of His teaching. Agape love is nothing less than a defining characteristic of the essential nature and consciousness of God. It is integral to who God is. It is the very essence and nature of God to express deep and constant concern for and interest in His creation, particularly humankind. Agape love is not necessarily devoid of feeling or emotion. It may best be exemplified, however, as the deliberate choice of DIVINE WILL to benefit someone (or some consciousness) without assignable cause other than witnessing to the very nature of the Lover Himself. In other words it has all the flavor of *grace* and *mercy*—the projection of benefit and kindness onto a recipient irrespective of the worthiness of the recipient, but illustrative of the nature of the giver.

Modern culture has pretty well convinced itself that agape love is not possible. And not only is it not possible, it's not even "cool." What's cool is self-fulfillment and self love in the Ayn Rand mode. Truly altruistic behavior, she would argue, is not possible because all human behavior is ultimately motivated by the desire to improve one's own position.[31] We should accept the fact that people are fundamentally selfish and revel in it; selfishness is cool, selfishness is intellectually "honest," you can (and should) have everything, survival of the fittest…blah, blah, blah. This thinking misses the critical point: agape love is reflective of, not beneficial to the giver.

One who demonstrates agape love is doing so because of something they have and are (i.e. some defining characteristic) not because of something they need. Unquestionably, the "something they have" is enormous internal strength—the kind of strength that enables them to benefit others without requiring reciprocal payment. Humans do not naturally posses strength (call it power if you choose) of this sort. God does. The wisdom of obedience to the WILL of God is that it harmonizes the WILL of man to His WILL, and allows His power to flow through us. Thus, man out of sync with God is not capable of agape love. But as he aligns his consciousness with that of the Creator, strength and love abound.

Obedience is not necessarily easy; and disobedience can readily become an obstacle in relating to God. The natural inclination to not obey—which from the obverse perspective is the inclination to obey our own thoughts and motivations—is simply an aspect of human will and human consciousness. As humans, we naturally pay attention to and are guided by our consciousness as it develops and matures. There is nothing inherently wrong or immoral in the natural skepticism of human will, or its natural inclination to give credence to its own experience. Disobedience to the WILL of God becomes an issue, and potential roadblock to relationship, as human consciousness becomes more aware of DIVINE WILL and consciousness. This is not to imply in the least that we should "play it safe" by either remaining ignorant of the will of God, or attempting to totally neutralize our own will.

Obedience as an effective *modus operandi* is consistent with the structure of a superior-subordinate relationship. Being subordinate to Jesus and the Trinity, it makes sense that humans can best relate to them and benefit from the relationship by submitting to their will. They have something of inestimable value to impart to mankind, but mankind has to be in the proper frame of consciousness to receive it. Man has to be aware of the basic structure of the relationship.

It is then necessary to adopt an attitude that continually seeks to emulate their character—in short, to obey their will for us to be more like them. What it does *not* mean is a one-time assignment or relinquishment of will that would result in automatic, compliant behavior. In the view espoused here, the consciousness of man has been endowed with the ability to make real choices for the purpose of enabling him to actively seek the Creator. Obedience is the only effective way to do that.

Diminishing or negating the ability to make real choices diminishes or negates the ability to obey and the capacity for loving relationship with the Creator.

Jesus' Final Discourse: Relationship Between His Followers

Love, Jesus explained, is also to be the hallmark of relationship between and among His followers. " 'A new command I give you: Love one another. As I have loved you, so you must love one another. By this all men will know that you are my disciples, if you love one another' " (Jn 13:34-35). Again, love is at the center of Jesus' message. Love, agape love, is the essence of God; it is the basis of relationship between God and man. Here Jesus established it as the standard for relationship between His followers—an extremely high and magnificent standard.

Embedded within this standard for relating is an interesting subtlety. When one asks what Jesus means by "as I have loved you," the unconditional sense of "agape" stands out; it is love without respect to the prior standing of the recipient. The notions of sacrifice and servanthood are also clear. Though Jesus was the superior and true Lord of His followers, He was willing to become incarnate and then surrender that incarnate life for their benefit. As their Lord, however, Jesus was not in a position to obey His followers; rather, He demanded obedience from them. Thus, there seems to be a sort of "directionality" in relationship as Jesus explained it. Obedience flows up toward the superior (toward Jesus and God) but not vice versa. Love flows in both directions, but only upward when accompanied by obedience.

What, then, are the implications of Jesus' commands for relationship between his followers? Agape love is to flow between them, unconstrained by prior conditions on either end. Sacrifice and servanthood are emphasized, and

Jesus referred to them again later in the discourse: " 'My command is this: Love each other as I have loved you. Greater love has no one than this, that he lay down his life for his friends. You are my friends if you do what I command'" (Jn 15:12-14). Jesus' laying down of His own life for His friends set the high standard for sacrifice between His followers. Noticeably absent, however, is any mention of obedience, except in relation to Himself.

In their human nature, people are equal and not subordinate to one another. There are no inherent, distinct differences between human beings—as there are between God and man—that would argue for one to be superior and another subordinate. To the contrary, on those occasions where the disciples sought favorable position among themselves, Jesus chastised them and placed the emphasis back on sacrifice. Between and among believers there is no real basis for one to obey the will of another, not in the sense that Jesus expects His individual followers to obey Him.

Jesus' Final Discourse: Relationship to the "World"

In setting the standard for relationship among His followers, Jesus drew a sharp line between them and the "world." " 'If the world hates you, keep in mind that it hated me first. If you belonged to the world, it would love you as its own'" (Jn 15: 18,19). Hate, the opposite of love, expresses a strong, conscious preference against something and is usually accompanied by a strong sense of aversion. Implicit in the notion of hatred is the desire to be separate from (and sometimes to assail) the object of aversion. Jesus indicated that the "world" wants nothing to do with Him. It wants to be separate from Him as it would from a leper. His followers should expect this kind of reaction.

But what does Jesus mean by the "world?" In John's writings the term has several meanings, including the planet on which we live as well as the whole universe. Here it refers to humankind's self-generated system of moral values—an ethical system based solely on the consciousness of man, absent (or largely disregarding) revealed input from God. By nature, the world, or the world system of values, almost always runs counter to the DIVINE WILL and purpose because it consciously separates itself from God. Its behavior is internally directed, based on its own will and consciousness. It expresses a strong preference—in a sense love—for itself.

Exactly opposite the world system (or worldliness) is the concept of holiness. By definition, "holiness" (from the Greek *hageeos*) means separation; it is a separation based upon the truth, and teachings of DIVINE origin. It is focused on coming closer to God (and separate from the world) by moving toward Him. Holiness expresses a strong preference to be guided by and to act according to the will of God. In other words, it is the will of man attempting to obey the DIVINE WILL. Unlike worldliness, where the divine will is ignored or opposed, holiness involves the conscious attempt to harmonize with the will of God as man believes it to be revealed.

Thus, worldliness and holiness both involve conscious separation. Worldliness moves away from God toward the world (effectively toward itself) while holiness moves away from the world toward God. The worldly and the holy mutually and consciously end up moving away from one another. Holiness is not, as it is often misunderstood, some kind of arbitrary and forceful removal or exclusion of one group of people from another irrespective of individual consciousness and will. For example, God expressed His will (i.e. He chose) the Israelites to be His holy people. But many, if not most, consciously opposed His will and embraced idolatry. And they did so repeatedly. In the New Testament, Jesus chose His twelve apostles; but even within this extremely select group, not all twelve accepted His will to be faithful followers.

As Jesus explained it, the world system will hate, reject and persecute His followers. " 'They will treat you this way because of my name, for they do not know the One who sent me'" (Jn 15:21). The hatred will be intense, emotional, and justified by the world ethic. " 'In fact, a time is coming when anyone who kills you will think he is offering a service to God. They will do such things because they have not known the Father or me'" (Jn 16:2,3). The dichotomy is sharp: those who "know" Jesus and the Father, and those who do not "know" Jesus, and are consequently unable to know the Father.

Jesus clearly positioned Himself as the fulcrum upon which the most critical of choices must be made. Individuals can choose to accept His teachings (and guidance of the Spirit) in the pursuit of holiness; alternatively they can choose to reject Him in the pursuit of worldliness. There are no other real alternatives. Jesus the DIVINE, speaking as God for God, has laid out the singular path to holiness. Other paths to holiness put forward by man are the creations of man—in effect, other versions of the worldliness option.

Distilling the vast array of ethical possibilities that man is capable of generating into a simple choice of accepting or rejecting Jesus has come to be regarded as "harsh," "biased," "unfair," "simple-minded," etc. From the human perspective these descriptions may seem plausible. But in speaking of the world condition and His followers' relation to it, Jesus was not taking and not articulating the human perspective. His understanding and consciousness of reality was well beyond that of humans.

DIVINE perspective is accurate and true, and not really open to debate. The debatable part, i.e. how to *interpret* what He has said about His perspective, is challenging enough. Essentially, Jesus told His apostles that He had used His authority to lay down the truth in His teachings. Subsequent to His actions individuals have the option of accepting or rejecting what He said and did. It should be noted that *the option itself* is priceless. God Himself, in the body of a man, took special action to make the option available. In the absence of this real option to the path of holiness, mankind's desire to be holy was not, and could not be fulfilled.

Without question, the option of choosing or rejecting Jesus creates tension between those who do and do not come to have faith in Him. He foresaw this condition and spoke openly of it (see, for example, Mt 10:34-36). Is there any purpose or use in this often emotionally laden divide of consciousness? What are its implications for relationship between believers in Jesus and believers in the world? " 'In this world,'" Jesus said, " 'you will have trouble'" (Jn 16:33). And, as we have seen, the "trouble" will involve persecution, even to the point of death. " 'But take heart I have overcome the world'" (Jn 16:33). Jesus knew the end result of the tension and struggle beforehand. He will prevail.

In the meantime His followers are not to yield to the world—actions which might seem "inclusive," "accepting," and "cool" in its eyes, and helpful in lowering that pesky tension. Syncretism, however, runs directly counter to Jesus' very purpose of confronting the world with His stark choice. And it is antithetical to the "great commission" to make disciples of all nations (see Mt 28:18-20). The tension, it seems, is to remain as a stimulus, a prod to help world believers question their beliefs. Christians who actually live their faith and are able to bear valid witness can use that tension as leverage. Faithful witness can be a powerful influence in bringing about a reversal in peoples' worldly perspective, i.e. a turning toward holiness, which John the Baptist called "repentance."

Thursday of Passion Week: Jesus' Prayer to the Father

Relief of Jesus in prayer the evening before His arrest. Located adjacent to the Basilica of the Agony and believed to be the site of the Garden of Gethsemane

John's Gospel complements the Synoptics, a feature of his writing that becomes more obvious as the story of Thursday evening unfolds. He alone tells of the washing of the disciples' feet; but he leaves it to the Synoptics to explain the establishment of the Lord's Supper. All of the Gospel writers tell of Jesus praying fervently to the Father on the evening before His arrest. John provides the detail of that prayer, not mentioning exactly where it occurred. The Synoptics all speak of Jesus praying at Gethsemane, an orchard on the lower slopes of the Mount of Olives, near Bethphage. It is possible that Jesus prayed separately at two locations, but context suggests that John and the Synoptics wrote about the same event.

Much of what Jesus conversed about with the Father echoed His earlier discourse with the apostles. John 17:20-23 captures the basic content.

> "My prayer is not for them [the apostles] alone. I pray also for those who will believe

> in me through their message, that all of them may be one, Father, just as you are in me and I am in you. May they also be in us so that the world may believe that you have sent me. I have given them the glory that you gave me, that they may be one as we are one: I in them and you in me. May they be brought to complete unity to let the world know that you sent me and have loved them even as you have loved me."

Jesus was expressing his DIVINE WILL to the Father regarding His earthly mission. He prayed that His apostles would carry His message forward; that all His followers would be united in spirit, as He and the Father are; that the unity of His followers would serve to validate the truth of His message to the world; and that their unity would also confirm the Trinity's agape love for them.

The literary structure of Jesus' discourse with his disciples, followed by an intimate and private "discourse" (prayer) with the Father, mimics His pivotal role as interlocutor between man and God. He positioned Himself in the middle, where He could be the, "I in them and you in me." At this point in history, Thursday evening of Passion Week, Jesus stood between the Father and Holy Spirit and His followers. The purpose of His ministry had been to communicate the DIVINE WILL, and open new relationship with God. That purpose was about to be fulfilled.

Jesus prayed that His followers would, "be in us" and that He would be "in them." This would come to pass, mediated and empowered through His own actions. The Spirit of God—including the Son and Holy Spirit—would be shared by, or come to dwell "in" his followers. This sharing of spirit between God and man would be directly analogous to, *but not equivalent to,* the sharing of spirit within the Trinity.

As part of creation, human spirit cannot actually *become* God, i.e. it cannot take on His DIVINE nature. The sharing cannot be complete in the same sense it is between the persons of the Trinity, because human spirit is subordinate to divine spirit. However, human beings can be *brought to* perfection; they can be brought to eternal life through the initiative and actions of Jesus. Eternal life is an inherent quality of the Creator, which, at His WILL, may be imparted to His creation.

The events of Thursday evening clearly demonstrate Jesus' *unique* position as mediator. He was not simply a messenger; and the accepted notions of Messiah at that time had become inadequate. His role had been prophesied, but mankind's expectations of Him became faulty. Jesus was one with the Spirit of God; He spoke the truth directly to man, truth known only to God; and He used the physical form of a man to deliver that truth. It is, in fact, this unique combination of characteristics and actions that stirs the great controversy about Jesus.

The conclusion of Jesus' prayer to the Father is an excellent reminder of the position He assumed as God-in-man, acting as a bridge between God and man. Shortly before His arrest He conferred directly with the Father that the time had come to complete His earthly mission. That mission was in the midst of His temporal creation, but Jesus spoke as an equal to the Father, and expressed His own DIVINE WILL. " 'Father, I want those you have given me to be with me where I am, and to see my glory, the glory you have given me because you loved me before the creation of the world' " (Jn 17:24). He wanted His followers to be with Him, sharing eternal love with the Creator of the universe. For that to happen the created universe as we know it need not exist. Time need not exist. But His followers will exist in some recognizable form, and they will experience God's agape love to the fullest extent possible.

Jerusalem, Friday of Passion Week

Judas was familiar with the olive grove where Jesus and His disciples often met. Intent on fulfilling his deal with the Sanhedrin, Judas led a detachment of soldiers and some officials from the chief priests and Pharisees to arrest Jesus. Apparently those who had come to make the arrest anticipated trouble; they carried torches, lanterns and weapons. According to John it was Simon Peter who drew his sword and struck the high priest's servant (named Malchus), cutting off his right ear (see Jn 18:1-3,10). Luke adds that Jesus insisted, " 'No more of this!' " and then, "he touched the man's ear and healed him" (Lk 22:51).

As incredulous as instant healing in this situation may seem, it only begins to describe what must have been a surrealistic arrest scene for Jesus' opponents. John indicates that when Jesus identified Himself, "they drew back and fell to the ground," not exactly the typical response of armed soldiers and officials to a Galilean carpenter (Jn 18:6). And what went through their minds when Jesus asked Peter in their presence if he did not think His Father could, "at once put at my disposal more than twelve legions of angels?" (Mt 26:53). Could they have imagined doing battle with thousands of angels, just one of which could slay thousands of their own kind? Was there one last moment, one last little twinge when those who came to arrest Jesus glimpsed His true DIVINE character?

Friday of Passion Week: Jesus Before the Sanhedrin

Jesus was bound and paraded first before Annas, the deposed high priest and father-in-law of the then-current high priest Caiaphas. Following what was likely a preliminary examination by Annas, they moved to the home of Caiaphas. There, Matthew tells us, the entire

Sanhedrin including the high priest, teachers of the law and elders had assembled to put Jesus on trial (see Mt 26:57-59). Obviously the scheme to arrest, question and accuse Jesus required a fair degree of planning by the Sanhedrin. Co-ordination with Judas Iscariot and the Roman authorities was involved; and what appears to have been a secret meeting of the Jewish high court was convened in the middle of the night. As told by Matthew and Mark, the aim of the court was clear. They "were looking for evidence against Jesus so that they could put him to death, but they did not find any" (Mk 14:55).

When reading about the Sanhedrin's proceedings that evening, one gets the sense of a group of anxious men with a verdict already in mind, but wanting desperately to maintain at least a modicum of proper jurisprudence and court etiquette. A number of witnesses were called forward to testify, but nothing of substance could be strung together that could be used to impose the death penalty. Finally, showing some signs of frustration, the high priest directly challenged Jesus. " 'I charge you under oath by the living God: Tell us if you are the Christ, the Son of God'" (Mt 26:63).

Even though the phrasing ("Son of God" in Matthew and "Son of the Blessed One" in Mark 14:61) strongly suggests deity to the modern reader, Caiaphas was probably not making that inference. He was questioning whether Jesus actually claimed to be the Messiah, presumably as anticipated by Orthodox Judaism, which did not equate the Messiah and God. In posing his challenge, however, Caiaphas was soliciting an answer that could be labeled "blasphemy," something to justify his (and the Sanhedrin's) predetermined verdict.

Challenges to Jesus about his identity from representatives of the Sanhedrin were not new. But in this instance there is a new element. Caiaphas invoked the formal legal procedure of putting Jesus under oath ("under oath by the living God"). Legally obliged to answer, Jesus broke His silence. " 'I am,'" said Jesus. " 'And you will see the Son of Man sitting at the right hand of the Mighty One and coming on the clouds of heaven'" (Mk 14:62).

Caiaphas was undoubtedly informed that Jesus had been making similar claims (see, for example Jn 8:58). The "I am" phrasing affirmed Jesus' claim to be the Messiah. But to the Sanhedrin it was also the unmistakable "I AM," the assertion of the DIVINE Yahweh. And to help dispel any possible misunderstanding, Jesus elaborated on the claim. He used the familiar "Son of Man" reference to the Messiah (see Da 7:13 and Ps 110) and described His proper position as by the side (at the right-hand position of honor and power) of "the Mighty One." Sharing sovereignty with Yahweh in this sense has the same meaning as being at one with Him (as described elsewhere by Jesus), and having all of His attributes. This was the same claim of special relationship that had moved the Pharisees on other occasions to attempt stoning Jesus. Not unexpectedly, the entire Sanhedrin followed the lead of Caiaphas in denouncing Him as a blasphemer. "They all condemned him as worthy of death" (Mk 14:64).

Coincident with Jesus' trial before the Sanhedrin, Peter underwent questioning about his identity. " 'You are not one of his disciples, are you?'" he was asked twice as he warmed himself at a fire. And, more pointedly, " 'Didn't I see you with him in the olive grove?'" (Jn 18:17,25,26). Each time Peter's response was the opposite of that of Jesus'; he denied his relationship to God. And at that moment a rooster began to crow.

Jesus had DIVINE omniscience that Peter would show weakness and fail the test on this occasion. When Peter had boasted only a few hours earlier that, " 'I will lay down my life for you'" (Jn 13:37), Jesus answered him with certainty: " 'I tell you the truth, before the rooster crows, you will disown me three times!'" (Jn 13:38). Dramatic foretelling of events such as this one and the betrayal by Judas Iscariot often draws the conclusion that Jesus' certain knowledge about them caused them to happen.

Peter and Judas really had no other choice, it is sometimes argued; God (and Jesus) were following their plan and making things happen the way they chose. Assertion of WILL by God vis-à-vis man is always important; for the moment, however, we need to focus on the knowledge that accompanied Jesus' will. His certain knowledge enabled Him to proceed with total—call it DIVINE—resolve. Unassisted human knowledge cannot be certain in an equivalent sense. The human will flip-flops in compliance to momentary changes in knowledge and emotion.

Friday of Passion Week: Jesus Before Pontius Pilate and Herod Antipas

Shortly after daybreak the whole Sanhedrin rose and led Jesus off to Pontius Pilate, the Roman governor of Judea. Their apparent aim was to bring charges of treason before the civil authority (see Lk 23:2). John provides the greatest detail on the Roman phase of Jesus' trial. Some speculate that John may have been an eyewitness to the events that occurred at Pilate's residential palace in Jerusalem, called the Praetorium.

All four Gospels record that Jesus responded positively when asked by Pilate whether He was "king of the Jews." Potentially, such a claim could have been grounds for charges of subversion. But, as John records, Pilate listened to Jesus' explanation that, " 'My kingdom is not of this world…You are right in saying I am a king. In fact, for this reason I was born, and for this I came into the world, to testify to the truth'" (Jn 18:36, 37). From the

Pharisaic perspective these claims actually were subversive, i.e. tending to overthrow their established order. Jesus was claiming to be sovereign in some other world and a witness to the truth in this one—totally consistent with his statement to Caiaphas earlier that morning (see Mk 14:62). But, from Pilate's "worldly" perspective, Jesus seemed harmless enough. Somewhat dolefully he muttered his famous line: " 'What is truth?'" (Jn 18:38).

Upon learning that Jesus was Galilean, Pilate attempted to avoid ruling in His case. He had Jesus bound over to Herod Antipas, the tetrarch of Judea and Perea (see Lk 23:6-7). Herod happened to be in Jerusalem, keeping an eye on the large crowds gathered for the Feast of Unleavened Bread. "When Herod saw Jesus, he was greatly pleased, because for a long time he had been wanting to see him" (Lk 23:8; see also Lk 9:9). Finally the miracle worker stood before him; perhaps Herod thought some great entertainment was in store.

Herod asked many questions, but Jesus gave no answers and worked no miracles. Disappointed, but apparently also unmoved by the accusations of the chief priests and teachers of the law, Herod passed Jesus back to Pilate. He had made no ruling. Luke concludes the scene: "That day Herod and Pilate became friends—before this they had been enemies" (Lk 23:12). What was the basis of their newfound friendship? Disdain for the pretentious Jewish "king?"

"Then Pilate took Jesus and had him flogged" (Jn 19:1). This obvious attempt to please the crowd was both illegal and brutal. Roman flogging was sometimes fatal. No sentence had been passed and Pilate could still, "find no basis for a charge against him" (Jn 19:6). The age-old question of who bears the responsibility for Jesus' death is addressed (at least in part) in the next few verses of John's text. Jewish officialdom, the Sanhedrin, had concluded

Plaque at the Sanctuary of the Flagellation, marking the place where Jesus was scourged

that Jesus must die because he claimed to be the "Son of God." Apparently they were relying on the Leviticus 24:16 prohibition against blasphemy. Pilate continued avoiding the whole issue and became, "even more afraid" (Jn 19:8) when the "Son of God" term was invoked. For him, as a non-Jew, that term probably had strong deistic implications. He wanted nothing to do with a case involving the "gods."

Pilate huddled privately with Jesus and asked Him more questions. " 'Where do you come from…Don't you realize I have power either to free you or to crucify you?'" (Jn 19:9,10). Jesus answered that any power Pilate had was, "from above" (Jn 19:11). That was unnerving enough, but then He concluded: " 'Therefore the one who handed me over to you is guilty of a greater sin.'" The implication was that Pilate did indeed have guilt, but that the Sanhedrin (Caiaphas in particular) had greater guilt.

Growing more anxious, "From then on, Pilate tried to set Jesus free" (Jn 19:12). Again, Jesus' accusers shouted out civil charges of treason and subversion. " 'If you let this man go, you are no friend of Caesar. Anyone who claims to be a king opposes Caesar'" (Jn 19:12). Realizing he needed to make some kind of official pronouncement, Pilate brought out Jesus and sat down on the judge's seat at a place called the Stone Pavement. Matthew adds that while Pilate was sitting on the judge's seat his wife sent him a message. " 'Don't have anything to do with that innocent man, for I have suffered a great deal today in a dream because of him'" (Mt 27:19). Pilate must have become even more determined to avoid the issue as best possible. Things were growing more mysterious with each passing moment. Who really was this Jesus, "king of the Jews?" Therein lay his quandary.

By this time the crowd was screaming for Jesus to be crucified. Pilate, as Governor, felt the pressure to take action, but had real reservations about doing so. Proclaim Jesus innocent and he risked a riot; proclaim him guilty and he risked something else, but the exact "something else" was unclear. What was clear in Pilate's mind, however, was that Jesus was not guilty of any civil charges. Had he simply stayed within his authority and made that judgment, he would have remained guiltless. Instead, "he took water and washed his hands in front of the crowd. 'I am innocent of this man's blood,' he said. 'It is your responsibility!' " (Mt 27:24). Pilate was guilty of *not* exercising his authority and *not* following his conscience. Effectively, he ceded his civil authority to the crowd, to do as it pleased.

Friday of Passion Week, "The Place of the Skull" Outside Jerusalem

Anyone who has seen Mel Gibson's classic movie *The Passion of the Christ* has a reasonably accurate idea of the sheer torture called crucifixion. It was a form of Roman punishment reserved for the lowest of non-citizen criminals. And it was the punishment that the chief priests, the elders and the crowd that they incited insisted upon (see Mt 27:20-23). Crucifixion combined the physical agony of being suspended from severely wounded limbs along with the slow terror of suffocation as the body became incapable of supporting itself. Roman rulers used it most effectively as a means of deterring insurrection and revolt.

The distance from the Praetorium to the crucifixion site (called Golgotha, or "place of the skull") was only about a quarter of a mile. Seriously weakened by flogging, however, Jesus was apparently unable to carry the cross (or, more likely, the cross beam). To help things along a

Crucifix and altar on Mount Golgotha inside the Church of the Holy Sepulcher (located within the Christian Quarter of the Old City)

man named Simon from the North African city of Cyrene was forced to help Jesus. (see Mk 15:21). Two other men were also led out that morning to Golgotha (also called Calvary, from the Latin) to be executed (Lk 23:32). Mark describes these men as "thieves," an offense which was not punishable by death under Roman law. But in the Greek that term has a broad meaning, which may include insurrection or treason. Jesus' offense, on the other hand, was for living out the reality of His being. Written above his head in three languages was His "charge." "It read: JESUS OF NAZARETH, THE KING OF THE JEWS" (Jn 19:19). When challenged by the chief priests that the "charge" had more the appearance of a proclamation, Pilate answered, " 'What I have written, I have written'" (Jn 19:22).

The denouement of the plan of redemption was finally reached. Jesus hung ignominiously on a cross between two wretched thieves. How could this be? How could the king of the Jews, the Messiah, the Son of the Living God allow Himself to be mocked, tortured and murdered by His own creation? The immeasurable glory of the ATONEMENT, which culminated during these few hours in history, is truly breathtaking. Among the Gospel writers Luke makes the most direct references to this almost unfathomable happening. " 'Father, forgive them, for they do not know what they are doing,'" Jesus said of his tormentors and, ultimately, all mankind (Lk 23:34). For the repentant thief hanging by His side the DIVINE forgiveness was immediate: " 'I tell you the truth, today you will be with me in paradise'" (Lk 23:43). Forgiveness, as we will see, is the story of the cross and the nature of the Creator.

Approximately six hours after it had begun, the physical anguish of the God-man nailed to a cross came to an end. Exactly what Jesus said prior to His death was most likely reported "elliptically," i.e. not in its complete verbatim text, but piecemeal, with each author recording the words deemed most significant. Matthew and Mark contain slight variations of the famous "forsaken me" quote: " 'Eloi, Eloi, lama sabachthani?'—which means, 'My God, my God, why have you forsaken me?'" (Mk 15:34). This question is a puzzler for many believers and non-believers alike. Was Jesus really feeling abandonment? If he was really God and at one with the Father, how could God forsake or abandon Him?

The words on Jesus' lips at that moment were almost certainly a recollection of David's experience in Psalm 22: "My God, my God, why have you forsaken me? Why are you so far from saving me, so far from the words of my groaning?" (Ps 22:1). The "son" (or descendent) of David was suffering his same human emotion of despair and desertion. It is important to remember, however, that Jesus also had the DIVINE perspective voiced by David later in the same Psalm: "For he has not despised or disdained the suffering of the afflicted one; he has not hidden his face from him but has listened to his cry for help" (Ps 22:24).

Luke notes that at the very end: "Jesus cried out with a loud voice, 'Father, into your hands I commit my spirit' " (Lk 23:46). The crying out in a loud voice is consistent with the other Gospels, and was highly unusual for death by crucifixion. Usually the period of excruciating pain was followed by a gradual lapse into unconsciousness and death. Neither Matthew nor Mark specify what Jesus said in his final "loud cry," (see Mt 27:50 and Mk 15:37). John reports that Jesus said, " 'It is finished'" (Jn 19:30).

Luke's recounting of Jesus' last words is significant for at least two reasons. First is the distinction between body and spirit. It is obvious that Jesus did not consider His spirit to be dependent on His physical body for its continued existence. Jesus was not an epiphenomenalist. And, perhaps more importantly with respect to his DIVINITY, Jesus maintained control of the situation. He "committed" (or "commended" in the KJV) His spirit to the Father. "Commit," which, translated from the Greek *paratithaymee,* means to place alongside, is used only here in the Gospels. By an act of His DIVINE WILL, Jesus placed His own spirit "alongside" the Father.

It is interesting to compare Jesus' passage at death with that of natural man. What do we experience as death occurs—when the body is no longer functional—regardless of how it got that way? At physical terminus spirit and body can no longer co-exist; the body loses its capacity to manifest the spirit in the physical realm. In

Painting of Christ being taken down from the cross (inside the Church of the Holy Sepulcher)

other words, spirit does not simply vanish; it is not annihilated at death. Spirit remains imperceptible to physical sensation and may seem "unreal," but only because its observable physical counterpart ceases to function and then deteriorates.

Death is a result of the physical limitations of the body, but it is no argument for the destruction (or non-existence) of spirit. Rather, the reverse is true; destruction of the body results in the ascendancy (or dominance, if you prefer) of the spirit. This separation of body from spirit in natural man happens irrespective of his or her will. Unlike Jesus, man's created spirit does not have the power at death to will itself alongside the Father. Jesus had that power, as well as the power to continue His physical life at will. Though His body had been extremely abused by men, death did not occur until he "committed" (an act of will) His spirit to the position of honor by the Father.

Descriptions of Jesus' death scene are somber, seemingly foreboding, and yet promising. "From the sixth hour until the ninth hour darkness came over all the land" (Mt 27:45). Matthew also describes an earthquake that split rocks and broke open tombs. All the Synoptics provide the very important detail that, "the curtain of the temple was torn in two from top to bottom" (Mt 27:51, Mk 15:38, and Lk 23:45). Might this have been a result of the earthquake described by Matthew? Perhaps, but the curtain between the Holy Place and the Most Holy Place was extraordinarily heavy and durable. More likely, the Synoptics are describing a separate dramatic sign (miracle) that accompanied Jesus' death. The importance of this sign is huge for both Jews and Gentiles: Jesus' "passage" to the Father opened direct access and passage to His believers. Juxtaposed with this unusual event—possibly to lend it credibility—the Synoptics quote a more down-to-earth Roman centurion, shaken by what was going on around him: " 'Surely he was the Son of God' " (Mt 27:54, Mk 15:39, and Lk 23:47).

CHAPTER TEN

RESURRECTION AND ASCENSION

Easter Sunday, Near "The Place of the Skull"

Jesus' body was placed in a tomb near the site of the crucifixion late that Friday afternoon. It remained there through the rest of Friday and the entire Sabbath. On the third day, which came to be called "Easter" Sunday, it received new life and Jesus exited the grave. "Easter," incidentally, derives from the Anglo-Saxon *eastre* (referencing the east) and means to shine, to dawn or to spring forth.

Though He had predicted His resurrection on several occasions (see, for example, Mt 17:22-23), Jesus' followers were surprised when it actually happened. That it was a factual, historical occurrence is a central tenet of the Christian belief system, and sometimes a point of strenuous denial for those disinclined to believe. Why is this so? The answer comes back to the basic issue of DIVINITY. Actual, physical resurrection of the dead man Jesus stands as certain validation of His claims of being the Messiah and God. It is a clear demonstration of the awesome power behind those claims—the kind of power that satisfies the emotional, intellectual, and spiritual needs of mankind for a real savior.

Jesus' resurrection has many of the same persuasive

features as the raising of Lazarus at Bethany. As in the case of Lazarus, Jesus stated publicly prior to His own resurrection that death would not be the final result of affliction. In both cases the purpose of the predictions was to establish a basis of credibility. When something is predicted—literally "spoken before"—and the predicted event occurs as indicated, people tend to grant credibility to the speaker.

Obviously, for Jesus to be able to rise from the dead it would be necessary that He physically die first. The death of Lazarus usually goes unchallenged. Biblical conspiracy theorists are more likely to argue that Jesus did not die as a result of being flogged and crucified—that He was removed from the cross and resuscitated by His followers. There is ample evidence attested by all four Gospels to debunk this theory. John, for example, tells us that when the soldiers came to Jesus and found Him dead one of them pierced His side with a spear, "bringing a sudden flow of blood and water" (Jn 19:34). Most likely, the soldier wanted to leave no doubt that he had completed his job. The sudden flow indicates that the spear thrust ruptured Jesus' pericardium and heart.

All three Synoptics relate that Joseph of Arimathea made a personal request to Pontius Pilate for Jesus' body (see Mt 27:58, Mk 15:43 and Lk 23:52). "Pilate was surprised to hear that he was already dead. Summoning the centurion, he asked him if Jesus had already died. When he learned from the centurion that it was so, he gave the body to Joseph" (Mk 15:44-45). Women who had accompanied Jesus from Galilee assisted Joseph as he took care of the body. They "saw the tomb and how his body was laid in it. Then they went home and prepared spices and perfumes" (Lk 23:55, 56). Large quantities of spices and perfume were not used for embalming purposes in Jewish burials, but to help overcome the odor of putrefaction.

Differences in the Jesus and Lazarus resurrection stories begin to emerge after the confirmation of their deaths. Jesus lay in the tomb for a shorter period, less than two full days versus almost four days for Lazarus. More important, however, is the source of resurrection power. Lazarus was dependent on an external source, the power of Jesus, to raise him back to life. But, in describing Jesus' resurrection, Matthew, Mark and Luke all proclaim, "he has risen!" (Mt 28:6, Mk 16:6, Lk 24:6). Just as He had the power to resurrect Lazarus and to commit His own spirit to the Father, Jesus had the power to reunite His DIVINE spirit with His body.

The two resurrection stories continue to diverge as the disciples have more contact with their risen Lord. Lazarus seemed to be his old self after being resurrected. His body was restored to its normal, healthy, natural condition. But when Jesus rose back to life, it is apparent

Courtyard of Lutheran Church of the Redeemer, Christian Quarter, Old City Jerusalem

that something had qualitatively changed. What appeared so unusual to those who perceived the transformed, physical body of Jesus was that it possessed characteristics of both the physical and the non-physical (or meta-physical). Believers since that time have taken to calling the risen body His "glorified" or "spirit" body.

The "Glorified" or "Spirit" Body of Jesus

Early on Sunday morning Mary Magdalene, "turned around and saw Jesus standing there, but she did not realize that it was Jesus" (Jn 20:14). She had mistaken Him for the gardener. When Jesus responded with her name: "She turned toward him and cried out in Aramaic, 'Rabboni!' (which means Teacher)" (Jn 20:16). Jesus seemed real enough for Mary to speak with Him, but she did not recognize Him until He spoke. Did Jesus intentionally disguise Himself in some manner, or was His physical appearance changed?

Later that same day, "Jesus himself came up and walked along with" two of His disciples (one of them named Cleopas) as they traveled to a village called Emmaus, about seven miles from Jerusalem (Lk 24:15). In this instance the text is clear that, "they were kept from recognizing him," or as the KJV puts it, "their eyes were holden that they should not know him" (Lk 24:16). "Kept from" or "holden" in the Greek (*krateho*) denotes forceful restraint, and would seem to indicate that the disciples' inability to recognize Jesus was due to some limitation imposed on them.

It cannot be inferred one way or the other from the Emmaus incident whether Jesus' identifying physical characteristics had changed. But during the evening meal with the two men, as Jesus broke bread and gave thanks, the unusual took on the air of the supernatural. "Then their eyes were opened and they recognized him, and he disappeared from their sight" (Lk 24:31). "Disappeared" or "vanished" has its normal meaning and is particularly interesting here because it occurs immediately after the two disciples' eyes "were opened." Jesus totally disappeared from their then-unrestricted physical perception.

Reinforcing the notion that Jesus' disappearance from the two men was not some sort of slipping away or sleight of hand are Luke's following comments. "They got up and returned at once to Jerusalem" (Lk 24:33). Though they left Emmaus "at once," Jesus apparently arrived back in Jerusalem some time before them, and had met with Simon Peter in the interim. "There they [Cleopas and his fellow traveler] found the Eleven and those with them, assembled together and saying, 'It is true! The Lord has risen and has appeared to Simon' " (Lk 24:34). There is no indication that Jesus might have appeared to Peter prior to His journey to Emmaus. If not, how did He travel so rapidly from Emmaus to Jerusalem? Why did Jesus disappear at Emmaus? Is Luke speaking of Jesus traveling in the normal physical mode, or of some sort of "spirit" travel?

While the assembled group was still talking about Jesus' appearances, "Jesus himself stood among them and said to them, 'Peace be with you.' They were startled and frightened, thinking they saw a ghost" (Lk 24:36-37). The phrase "stood among them" and the disciples being "frightened" imply that Jesus suddenly appeared from nowhere, i.e. the reverse of what He had done at Emmaus.

John's text lends strong support to this interpretation. "On the evening of that first day of the week, when the disciples were together, with the doors locked for fear of the Jews, Jesus came and stood among them and said, 'Peace be with you!' " (Jn 20:19). Though the doors were locked, Jesus somehow gained entry into the room and stood among them. Did He walk through the walls of the room, drop through the ceiling or simply materialize in their midst? Context (and a very similar appearance one week later when Jesus appeared to Thomas) favors the latter rendering.

In all of Jesus' reported appearances following His resurrection there is some delay or hesitation on the part of His followers in recognizing Him. The delay is prolonged for the travelers to Emmaus, and we are told that they were "kept from recognizing him." In the other instances there is only brief hesitation, but no explanation is given why it occurs. Possibly, Jesus' resurrected body did not manifest itself to His followers in exactly the same manner as His flesh-and-bones body did. In other words, His "spirit" body may not have looked, sounded, etc. exactly the same as it did prior to death.

In the appearances subsequent to Emmaus there is no mention that the sensory or other capabilities of Jesus' followers were restricted; nevertheless, their perception of Him does seem to have been altered. For example, John writes that following the appearances in Jerusalem Jesus appeared again to His disciples by the Sea of Galilee. "Early in the morning, Jesus stood on the shore, but the disciples did not realize that it was Jesus. He called out to them, 'Friends, haven't you any fish?' 'No,' they answered" (Jn 21:4-5).

After both seeing and hearing Jesus, the disciples (including Thomas, who had only recently demanded physical verification) failed to immediately recognize Him. They were only about one hundred yards from shore. And, even after joining Him on shore, Jesus' appearance left some doubt about His identity. "None of the disciples dared ask him 'Who are you?' They knew it was the Lord" (Jn 21:12). They "knew" who He was but not entirely from visual or other perceptual clues.

"Spirit Body": An Oxymoron?

Scripture about the resurrected Jesus is fascinating and challenging, and easily produces reflections like "spirit body" and "body of Christ"—phrases that often leave the non-believer's head spinning. Isn't "spirit body" really a self-contradictory little locution, sort of a mini-paradox? On the surface it may seem so, but if one digs a bit deeper it begins to make more sense. "Spirit body" is, after all, just another way of combining the non-physical or metaphysical with the physical in one breath. Combining the two may seem like an unforgivable violation unless one takes the perspective that the physical and metaphysical are not unrelated opposites, but more like points on the same continuum. They may not actually be as contradictory as seems at first blush.

Take, for example, something that seems really physical—something hardcore, concrete physical—something really "solid," like solid steel. On closer examination, scientists tell us, "solid" steel is actually more than 99.999% *space*. And even the most weighty or mass-full portions of the solid steel—the protons and neutrons—are composites of smaller units that are not truly solid. Consciousness conveniently fills in the space, imparting a self-generated quality of solidness and reality. It collects numerous such images to form a standard (or context) by which it measures the solidness and reality of all experience.

There seems to develop an almost axiomatic, perfect correlation between experiences that are evaluated as solid and those considered real. Steel, rocks and ice are solid and real; air, viruses and gamma rays are not as solid and not so intuitively real. Reality becomes delimited by the focus (sensate or otherwise) and interpretation consciousness places upon it. Curiously, this diminished reality *is* reality for the individual, even though it may be accompanied by the gnawing sense that it is incomplete.

Defining reality in terms of what we are capable of experiencing at any given point in time is the ultimate in narcissistic humanism.

Aside from the nature of *what* we perceive as reality, exactly *how* we go about doing that is another limitation on the portion of reality that we can grasp. Sensory perception, for example, occurs indirectly. The senses do not immediately and inerrantly "know" physical reality. Or, to put it more colloquially, we never actually "wrap our heads around" anything, thereby gaining a deep and full appreciation of its true reality. Instead, our senses provide streams of data about what they perceive to the brain (and consciousness), which processes the data to form impressions. Our impressions about reality, which seem so real and concrete, end up being nothing more than processed data (or information, or intelligence, if you prefer) representing not-so-solid, undefined, elemental units. "Elemental" is used here to describe absolute base units, not components of the periodic table.

Perhaps one of the more interesting questions regarding the manner in which humans experience reality is whether *all* of it can eventually be subjected to sensate perception. Can it all be defined and proven through observational techniques? Can investigative tools be developed that will expand our powers of sensate perception to observe all of reality? Since seeing (i.e. part of sensate perception) is believing for many people, the development of such tools seems of paramount importance to them.

But again, the basic problem with this expectation (or hope) is how anthro-narcissistic it is. It makes the totally unfounded presumption that all of reality is reducible to phenomena that humans happen to be best equipped to observe. In fact, this confidence and hope in human observation (and deduction from observation) has all the qualities of religious faith. The only real difference is in whom (God or man) the faith and trust are placed. Narcissistic humanism places great faith in the powers of man based on a key initial presumption: mankind originated spontaneously in the absence of any extraneous design or power.

It is not surprising that people are most comfortable and most confident about *physical* reality. That is the band of reality that our physical senses can most directly perceive, organize and arrange into images that we can integrate into consciousness, and begin to understand. But the broader reality, the one that expands to include what we refer to as the "metaphysical," may well be variant arrangements of the same "elemental units" (whatever they may be—perhaps pure energy and/or intelligence) that comprise the physical. Consciousness has to draw abstractions about this part of reality because it lacks sensate data about it.

From the perspective of a "continuous reality", the spiritual or metaphysical is not the antithesis of the material or physical but its apotheosis, i.e. its elevation or re-arrangement into a higher form. The greater and more desirable reality is not the one constrained by the physical dimensionalities as we experience them on earth. As suggested earlier, the pure and full assimilation by consciousness of even physical reality—let alone the metaphysical—most likely cannot happen while we are constrained in the physical, and by time and space.

Of Ghosts, Spirit Bodies, and Resurrection

Most would agree that an actual encounter with a ghost would be pretty scary, mainly because it would be very unusual, not something our senses have to deal with every day. Luke indicates that the disciples were frightened when Jesus suddenly, "stood among them" (Lk 24:36). They thought they had seen a ghost, and Jesus

Mosaic inside the Church of the Holy Sepulcher, Christian Quarter, Old City Jerusalem

immediately attempted to set them at ease. " 'Why are you troubled, and why do doubts rise in your minds? Look at my hands and my feet. It is I myself! Touch me and see; a ghost does not have flesh and bones, as you see I have" (Lk 24:38-39).

The person who suddenly appeared before the disciples had physical characteristics at least similar to those of the teacher they had known. Jesus attempted to re-establish his identity with the disciples by manifesting in the physical realm those characteristics that could be most easily identified in the physical, (e.g. his pierced hands and feet). But the *resurrected* person whom the disciples beheld was obviously no longer constrained by the physical. How could this be?

Under normal, earthly conditions physically realistic traits do not accompany metaphysical activity. Flesh-and-bones people do not suddenly appear out of nowhere. It was this combination of physical similitude with completely unconstrained freedom of movement that frightened the disciples. Jesus' resurrected body apparently had the qualities of spirit bodies as discussed above. He convincingly manifested as physical to those still under the constraints of physical laws, while no longer under such constraints Himself. In other words, Luke's quote of Jesus (Lk 24:38-39) may indicate not simply that Jesus resurrected body was still unchanged "flesh and bones," but that the manifestation of it was just as *real* to physical perception as His physical flesh-and-bones body had been prior to His death.

After seeing the visual proof of His wounded hands and feet (along with the rest of His manifest body) one would expect the apostles to accept Jesus' identity. But "they still did not believe it because of joy and amazement…" (Lk 24:41). Joy and amazement? Why would joy and amazement inhibit belief? In the face of seemingly overwhelming sensory evidence, the disciples remained skeptical. In effect, what is recorded here is interaction between emotion and WILL. Their emotion (joy) was saying yes, believe. But their ability to think through and confirm what their senses perceived was short-circuited because they were "amazed," a word that denotes overwhelming surprise. The net result was to remain skeptical, non-committal until they received more evidence or could better evaluate it.

Jesus responded to their need by asking: " 'Do you have anything here to eat?' They gave him a piece of broiled fish, and he took it and ate it in their presence" (Lk 24:41, 42-43). This gesture was done not to help establish Jesus' identity, but to validate their perceptions of Him as a real person, to get them past the amazement. Only real people can consume fish. But this is not to say that only *physical* people—those who have not undergone resurrection and the transformation it brings—can consume fish. Jesus' spirit body, *manifesting physically*, could also consume fish.

Presumably, a being who has the power to manifest physically at will, as Jesus apparently did, could as easily de-manifest (or make imperceptible to the physical senses) a bit of fish. For those of us still bound in our physical bodies, this kind of activity seems to have all of the qualities of a miracle. The upshot of Jesus' appearances, words, and actions following his death and resurrection is that resurrection is accompanied by "miraculous" changes to our corporeal selves.

The Birth-Death-Resurrection Experience: Jesus and His Followers

Where does this view of Scripture and the DIVINITY of Jesus lead us? What do His death and resurrection tell us about our own prospects beyond death? First and foremost is the powerful and glorious message that His life and death here on earth provide the hope and promise of life with Him beyond the grave. Jesus has set the course through this world and beyond that we may now follow. His resurrection is also the climactic answer to the big philosophical questions about God and how He relates to people—the "who am I?" and "what am I doing here?" kinds of questions. At this juncture it may be helpful to review how our personal experiences in life, through death, and back to life are modeled and explained by those of the Creator-born-man.

Jesus' Birth into Earthly Life

In Scripture the terms "ghost" and "spirit" are used synonymously, as in the case of Holy Ghost and Holy Spirit. But it is helpful to differentiate the spirit of Jesus from the Holy Spirit and the Father as it relates to His earthly experience. Jesus' spirit, unlike those of men and women, did not change as a result of His incarnation, life on earth, death and resurrection. He, along with the Father and Holy Spirit remain perfect and eternal.

But His spirit did indwell human flesh, an

experience He shared in common with all mankind. This temporal sharing of physicality was Jesus' clearest point of *identity with* mankind, and the one sense in which He was *identical to* man. Jesus in-body experience did not change His spirit nor did the transformation of His body upon resurrection. His spirit (consciousness) completely understood the human experience *without* taking on human form. His purpose in doing so was an acting-out of agape love, not a developmental exercise.

To argue that God became man in the sense that DIVINE consciousness (or spirit) transformed itself into human consciousness is to argue the impossible. It is to argue that the Creator changed into His creation. "Becoming" in this sense is not a change or transformation that is possible within the terms used to define God's nature; it is a *re-definition* of His nature. It is analogous to arguing that a doll maker could actually *become* one of his or her dolls. Since any being's nature is defined by its inherent characteristics, that nature is immutable (given that the original definition is correct). Furthermore, if the characteristics that define the nature of a being are correctly established, they cannot contradict one another. They must be compatible in order to accurately define its nature.

Thus, when someone argues that if God is omnipotent, He could change His nature to actually *become* man, the logic is flawed. God is who He is—perfect, unchanging, and omnipotent. The separate characteristics that we use to define His essence are internally consistent and cannot be used in opposition to each other to prove an inconsistency. It is presumptive (and illogical) on man's part to infer that one character of God's nature (omnipotence) could be used to negate or alter another (unchanging).

In effect, the argument that God has the power to change His nature to assume the nature of man is a bit of sophistry. It fails to recognize the inviolable integrity and consistency defined by "nature." God is omnipotent and unchanging at the same time; that He cannot and will not use His power to change His nature is not a limitation on His power, but a more complete definition of His nature. His power is unlimited, but it is also His nature that He will not use that power to change His own nature. Attempts to use one facet of any being's nature to contradict another are nonsensical if the individual facets are accurate and true.

Human Birth into Earthly Life

As suggested earlier, when people are born into this world a created spirit is brought to "co-exist" with a created, physical body. The co-existence (or simultaneous existence in space-time), however, is not a schizophrenic one. Spirit and body are not split apart and incongruous. Rather, the body can be thought of as a representation (not a duplication) of spirit made manifest in the physical as physical. In this view the body is a sort of "physical reflection" of the spirit, not a complete conversion or transformation of it.

Man's body functions as a containment vessel and physical depiction of his created spirit while that spirit inhabits space-time. People remain "alive" in the physical realm as long as their bodies remain physically capable of "reflecting" their underlying spirits. The distinction between natural man (or mankind) and Jesus is that His life-giving spirit was not created; it existed "outside" of time, i.e. "before" the creation of the universe. As opposed to Jesus' in-body experience, normal, human, in-body experience can and does result in *change* to the human spirit.

Jesus' Resurrection Experience

Choices of men and the vagaries of time produce bodily changes resulting in the eventual termination of spirit/body co-existence. Death comes to man. Resurrection (*anastasis* in the Greek) is often thought of as the reversal of this process. *Anastasis* speaks literally of a "causing to stand up on one's feet again." Since before the time of Jesus the concept has always included a body of some sort. And the literal translation seems to imply the resuscitation of the original physical body—or what is left of it.

Gospel descriptions of Jesus' resurrected body,

Tombs of Jehoshaphat and Absalom in the Kidron Valley, ouside the southeast corner of the Old City wall

however, argue against a literal "standing up." His physical body (corpse) is described as having been transformed upon resurrection. Jesus did move about and interact with His disciples. However, His resurrected body was, by all eyewitness accounts, not exactly the same as it had been prior to death. And, most notably, He began displaying non-physical characteristics such as being able to appear and disappear, ultimately ascending into the heavens.

Implications of Jesus' Resurrection for His Followers

From the Gospel descriptions of Jesus' resurrection we may reasonably infer something qualitatively different than the simple death-reversal anticipated by the Pharisees. Given His resurrection as a template, it is not likely that our individual spirits are once again brought to co-exist with the physical bodies we knew on earth.

Our bodies have definite physical functionality in the space-time universe we temporarily inhabit, most notably reproduction. They, along with their interactions with the rest of the material world around us, also help define us as individual persons. They contribute to the total experience of human consciousness, which is only partially defined by what we call the "physical." But our physical existence does help generate a unique part of our greater identity and greater consciousness. In this sense, it becomes an integral part of the human "I am," a very real part of the "me" that God created—a person and personality sustainable beyond the physical world.

At resurrection our "glorified" or "spirit" bodies—presented here as the ongoing conscious awareness of our one-time physical existence—unite with our created spirits. Spirit bodies are the transformation of our identity and conscious awareness that physical existence has provided into a non-physical, but very *real* form that can be fully integrated with the spirit. In this view, upon resurrection the transformed human body would not persist as a physical entity, but would be capable of manifesting physically. The united spirit and spirit body could display its acquired physical identity to any being capable of physical perception.

Religious Challenges to the "Spirit Body" View of Resurrection

Of course the above argument raises the objection that a flesh-bones-and-blood body *must* be rejoined with spirit at the resurrection. Many also believe that the resurrection must occur at a particular time (e.g. after the rapture). To begin with, a literal interpretation of Scripture such as resurrection of the corpse misses the point that Christ's kingdom is not of this world. It is not of the world most easily seen, understood and valued by physical (material) man. It will probably be unlike the physical form to which we are most accustomed but even more real, since realness in the fuller sense is not in proportion to how physical something is.

The felt need for flesh-and-bones resurrection also misses the point made earlier. Male and female bodies as well as their companion spirits are all created—produced by their Creator from nothing. And physical bodies may well be transformable into the metaphysical, something that can truly unite with created spirit. Though the basics of that process are suggested above, precisely how the transformation is accomplished remains unknown to earth dwellers.

Is it important that the resurrection take place at a specific time? What happens to people between the time of death and resurrection? The short answer to these kinds of questions is that time after death is inoperative and without effect—primarily because time itself is a construct of the Creator. We "enter the eternal" because time is removed as a restrictive dimension, not because it is extended so that we can experience it forever as we have on earth.[32] If this is so, the critical question becomes: what precipitates our "entering the eternal?" Death? Resurrection?

Scripture indicates that faithful Christians join with

Christ in heaven immediately after death (see, for example Lk 16:22-26; 23:43 and 2 Cor 5:6-8). Prior to their resurrection, however, they are apparently disembodied from their "earthly tent[s]" (2 Cor 5:1). Thus, we can conclude that Christians who have undergone physical death have consciousness of eternality, but that consciousness is somehow altered by resurrection. The apostle Paul describes an intermediate state that "is better by far" than earthly existence but qualitatively different than Christ's post-resurrection Kingdom (Phil 1:23).

Given that resurrection is a critical aspect of the Christian belief system, it should be remembered that it is not a unique occurrence for Christians. Indeed, there is only one aspect of space-time experience that *is* unique to Christians. To understand this truly unique experience we need to first think of the key events in the life of a "saved" individual, i.e. one who will share eternity with God, versus an "unsaved" person. The saved person experiences (1) physical birth; (2) spiritual birth; (3) physical death; and (4) resurrection and transformation. For the unsaved individual the only life experience that is different is event (2). Instead of spiritual birth taking place, spiritual death occurs.

Now, consider each of these major "life-steps" for just a moment. In step (1) the physical body is made manifest in temporal reality—spirit and body are temporarily joined (or, as described above, spirit "reflects" body for a time). Step (2) for the Christian is the beginning of the spiritual perfection process, but for the "unsaved" this process never begins. The physical death of step (3) marks the separation of body and spirit and physical destruction of the body. The consciousness of temporal existence is apparently "frozen" in time until resurrection. In step (4) the resurrected body is transformed for existence in eternality, i.e. for existence with the Creator (saved) or apart from Him (unsaved). My personal view is that the resurrection and transformation represent an "unfreezing" or "reawakening" of space-time consciousness to make it suitable for eternal existence.

One of the more confusing Christian assertions for non-believers is that *eternal* spirits can exist independently of temporal bodies. Specifically, the question arises how any spirit other than God can be eternal. If human spirits are eternal, are they not also gods? This erroneous conclusion is basically a distortion that results from the limited perspective of the space-time reference frame. It also misses the point that eternal existence, like temporal existence, is totally dependent upon the Creator.

We need for a moment to imagine ourselves outside the constraints of time. I can imagine two sets of conditions that would qualify as "eternal." Situation (1) is existence with no beginning and no end. This existence describes a preexistent God who "always was" or a preexistent, uncreated reality that just happened to "always be." Situation (2) is existence with a beginning and no end; Christianity holds that human and other created spirits exist in this manner. A third situation, which is not eternal, has both a beginning and an end. It includes the physical bodies of all humans.

What we cannot imagine our way completely out of, of course, is our space-time reference frame. In my attempt to ignore time I have had to use words like "always" and "beginning" to convey the idea of the eternal. What we can start to understand, however, is that eternality is unbounded by the linear, sequential regimen of time. In this sense it is completely "open-ended" and temporally non-directional. Past and future have no meaning, leaving only an eternal present.

An "eternal present" may be conceivable in the abstract but it is not experiential in space-time. This is the case because as time dwellers we require a temporal reference point from which to measure. In other words, because in space-time I invariably experience myself at some particular point in time along the past-future continuum, I cannot actually experience myself "off" of the continuum or "outside" of time. But, at least conceptually, I can project an open-ended period of time preceding my present time reference and an open-ended period beyond it.

Thus, within the limits of our space-time reference frame we can begin to understand how human spirits were "eternalized" when they were created. Though they have a beginning, their "future" is infinitely open-ended. In terms of the eternal present experiential reality of God, one could say that God simply reifies them at will. The linearity of time, along with the other physical characteristics that we experience within space-time, are imposed by the WILL of the Creator operating outside of space and time. Under these conditions creation of human spirit need not happen at a particular "time" (as we experience it), but instead is a direct function of the will of a timeless God (as He experiences it). Obviously we cannot share more completely in God's consciousness of total reality until we are empowered with a perspective more similar to His, i.e. until we are "eternalized."

At physical death the human spirit separates from its companion earthly body and enters eternity, unbounded by space-time. The physical body degenerates physically. At the "resurrection of the righteous" the body is raised up and eternalized, i.e. God empowers it to live in the eternal realm. The perfected spirit body is united with created human spirit, resulting in the human being that will share eternity with its Creator. Thus, experiences in the non-eternal (temporal) space-time existence of the resurrected human being become integral to his or her eternal identity.

Resurrection marks the transformation into a *new*, eternal existence. That event will occur in time on earth and—what seems ironic to us as time dwellers—will mark the end of time. The specific point in time that resurrection occurs for those who have died prior to the "end times" will be insignificant, as they no longer have consciousness of time. For the "unsaved," who do not experience the "resurrection of the righteous," there will be resurrection into an open-ended "second death."

Secular Challenges to Resurrection

The more secular objection that resurrection is a myth or figment rests on the presumption that conscious awareness (including spirit) is coincidental to and totally dependent upon the physical. Where there is no body there can be no spirit. According to this line of thinking resurrection is literally a "non-starter" because there is no independent spirit outside the body to bring it back to life.

This is the old materialist/epiphenomenal line of argument constructed largely from the observation that we never experience conscious awareness apart from our physical bodies. Since the two seemingly always occur together (i.e. they seem perfectly positively correlated), it follows that conscious awareness is a totally dependent adjunct of the body (or physical).

To understand how consciousness might function *independently of* (but also in conjunction with) the brain, one can think of the brain as physiological "equipment" that allows for the production of conscious awareness in space-time reality. In this view the brain is not synonymous with or equivalent to consciousness. Rather, it is the physical device used by consciousness to produce awareness about and within the space-time reference frame we inhabit while in physical form.

An imperfect analogy can be made between computer hardware/software and brain/consciousness. Computer hardware, functionally analogous to the human brain, is necessary for decoding instructions and data stored electromagnetically in the software. Few would argue, however, that the hardware is intelligent or comprises intelligence. Patterns of electromagnetic fields constituting the software are analogous to the neural networks involved in producing human consciousness of physical existence.

Electromagnetic fields and neural networks, however, are only *representational forms* for expressing intelligence and consciousness, not intelligence or consciousness *per se*. All computer software that exists today—and the intelligence it represents—originated from a source extraneous to computer system hardware and software. Likewise, all human consciousness originates from a source extraneous to the human brain and its neural networks. We can think of these original sources of intelligence and consciousness as "pure" or "abstracted," i.e. not bound by any particular form used to express them in a particular manner.

Thus, pure or abstracted intelligence and consciousness are not dependent on any representational form for their existence. They are independent of the manner in which they are expressed in physical reality. For example, the word "justice" and the number "7" can be represented by patterns of electromagnetic fields and neural networks, but their actual content (i.e. their actual meaning and significance to the person using them) is extraneous to the mechanisms representing them physically. The analogical "software" of consciousness (neural networks) functions essentially as a physical "container" for the actual contents of consciousness.

Continuing the hardware/software analogy, there is no reason to presume that the consciousness experienced during space-time could not take on a new representational form in another reference frame. The new form need not require a physical brain, and there would be no loss of actual content. Although the brain is not determinative of consciousness in space-time, it may be contributory in the same way that more powerful computers can produce clearer images of physical reality by virtue of their increased processing capacity.

To sum up the computer analogy, computers (in combination with software) may give the impression of being very intelligent, but they are really only machines designed by human intelligence to simulate itself. Brains may give the impression of *being* consciousness, but I would argue that they are actually an organic medium designed by a superior consciousness. Brains (and their associated sensory equipment) provide the material structure for created human consciousness to experience space-time and matter as physical reality—and to interact with them and the superior consciousness that created them.

Epiphenomenal thinking leaves a host of questions about consciousness unanswered. What happens when we become un-conscious; i.e., how is it possible for the brain to *not* generate consciousness if consciousness is totally a function of the brain? By-products typically occur at all times the primary process is active. How does the "placebo effect" occur where measurable physiological changes are induced by non-physical or physically inert stimuli? How can people who have died (i.e. met all the medical criteria for death) continue to have experiences while dead? It is not uncommon for other persons to validate such experiences after the dead person is resuscitated and describes what happened while dead. What does it mean when prayer or meditation is followed by a reduction in blood pressure and physical pain? Psychosomatic relationships will likely never be completely explained through empirical study. Mental stimulus may result in physiological response or vice versa; that *either* may trigger the other is indicative that mind and brain/body are interactive—but by no means that they are equivalent.

Arguing that a mutual relation between observed phenomena implies causation (as epiphenomenalism does with respect to brain and consciousness) is fraught with problems. Simply observing current and past relationships and constructing correlations based on the observations cannot provide sufficient evidence that one phenomenon actually produces or causes another. A causal link—including a link between a physical cause (brain) and non-physical effect (subjective consciousness) must be explained in *physical* detail to have any scientific validity.

But such an explanation suffers essentially the same difficulty (some would say impossibility) as attempting to scientifically explain miracles: only one side of the cause-effect relationship is physically observable, (i.e. the effect with respect to miracles and the assumed cause with respect to the qualia of experiential consciousness). Epiphenomenalism, which has a purported physical basis, is required to establish empirically (i.e. physically) the precise "how" of brain-to-consciousness cause and effect. Correlations such as the simultaneity of functioning brain mass and subjective consciousness can be established between *any* observed phenomena, and can easily lead to false conclusions.

Improperly classifying Pluto as a planet, for example, involved the erroneous use of correlation. For many years when astronomers observed Pluto it looked and behaved just like a planet and was given official planetary status. On closer examination, however, it was seen to not correlate so well with other planets. Specifically, Pluto's moon Charon is much too large in comparison to the relative size of true planetary satellites. Pluto does not "dominate its neighborhood" as planets do[33]. Furthermore, unlike planets, Pluto does not "sweep up" asteroids, comets and other spatial debris. For those who preferred Pluto as a planet, do not despair. We may find new correlations and re-decide that it is one.

Ascension: The Return of Jesus to the Father

One of the most appealing testimonies of the DIVINITY of Jesus in all of Scripture is that of Thomas (the "twin"). Appearing for the second time to the disciples fearfully assembled behind locked doors, Jesus challenged Thomas's skepticism: " 'Put your finger here; see my hands. Reach out your hand and put it into my side. Stop doubting and believe'" (Jn 20:27). Thomas, the devout follower, but also a man with a high threshold of proof, was finally convinced.[34] "Thomas said to him, 'my Lord and my God!' " (Jn 20:28). His physical senses—in which Thomas placed so much confidence and used as the final arbiter of reality—were satisfied. Jesus mildly and lovingly rebuked him for this. "Then Jesus told him, 'Because you have seen me, you have believed; blessed are those who have not seen and yet have believed' " (Jn 20:29).

For the sheer drama of it, however, nothing eclipses Luke's description of Jesus' departure from the physical. "When he had led them out to the vicinity of Bethany, he lifted up his hands and blessed them. While he was blessing them, he left them and was taken up into heaven" (Lk 24:50-51). Luke expands on this in *The Book of Acts*.

> After he said this, he was taken up before their very eyes, and a cloud hid him from their sight. They were looking intently up into the sky as he was going, when suddenly two men dressed in white stood beside them (Acts 1:9-10).

Jesus' disciples stood staring as His resurrected, glorified body rose into the sky. The Pharisees would have loved it, but one wonders if even this spectacle would have engendered belief that He was returning to the Father as He said He would.

Ascension in this dramatic manner did help buttress

the faith of Jesus' disciples. It also repeats the notion of Jesus returning to the higher spiritual realm from which He descended to earth. In the midst of all this one cannot help but wonder where Jesus' physical body went and what He is doing. As suggested earlier, the testimonial evidence suggests that His body was transformed upon resurrection but was still capable of manifesting to human perception. And we are told that it ascended into heaven.

But how is it possible for a *created* body such as Jesus had to unite with an uncreated spirit, i.e. God? We need to remember that Jesus' body was always subject to His DIVINE spirit, and ultimately His DIVINE WILL. He never sinned as a result of the exercise of His will. Thus, even though His body was created, it remained perfect and not subject to death as a result of sin. It is theologically consistent, therefore, that His transformed, created body could unite with His DIVINE perfect spirit.

An Aside: Death—The Illogical Appeal of Atheism

Thinking of death and resurrection as transitioning events rather than existence terminating and initiating ones argues foursquare against atheism. Death, though it is covered extensively in Scripture, never takes on the meaning of going out of existence as it does in atheistic thinking. In the greater, metaphysical reality that Scripture deals with, it is nihilistic termination upon death (not an afterlife) that is considered illusory. Christian thought holds that people never "die" in the sense that the entirety of their personal being goes back to nothingness. Individuals transition between states of existence but none—even those condemned to the so-called "second death"—cease being. People are born into life on earth (a positive transition into the physical) and they die (a negative transition out of the physical). Some establish relationship with the Creator while on earth, but others do

Jewish cemetery on the Mount of Olives, outside the eastern wall of Old City Jerusalem

not (respectively the most profoundly positive and negative transitions).

Annihilation at death, by contrast, is literally a dead end. But its significance is dubious and even contradictory for the atheist. It is extremely negative in that it brings an abrupt halt to the pleasures of physical existence. On the positive side, it demands no accountability for one's activities while alive. Death automatically "forgives" all moral wrongs. The illogic of this conception of death is that it attempts to fulfill two impossibly disparate functions. It is both the annihilator and savior, the ultimate evil and the ultimate good. In any meaningful, consistent reality a single phenomenon cannot define itself and its exact opposite.

Atheists might respond that death viewed as ultimate evil *and* good is nonsensical only if one presupposes the "greater, metaphysical reality" as was done here. If the metaphysical is only a pipedream, annihilation at death would be a suitable end and not in conflict with either a "good," pleasure-filled life or a "bad," unpleasant one. In the atheistic version of physical existence (which ignores the metaphysical possibilities of after-life) "good" and "bad" are subjective constructs created in the minds of individuals. They have only temporary, personal meaning and demand no reconciliation once the mind that created them ceases.

This is a fair rebuttal but rests on the very shaky presumption that *all* of reality is what human consciousness defines it to be. Any part of reality that cannot be rationalized to human consciousness is assumed to not exist. Opposite this view is the Christian view that reality has no inherent limits of which man can have certain knowledge. In order to have such knowledge man would have to experience and fully comprehend all of reality.

At this point the atheistic argument for full knowledge of reality degenerates into a circular one that it is "full enough" to qualify as "full." It is obvious from our ongoing, accelerating pursuit of knowledge, however, that we do not have a comprehensive understanding of all reality. It is also obvious that we have no idea if, how, and when we might gain full knowledge. If these premises are true, human consciousness is in no position to define reality. Furthermore, the presumption that we will ultimately gain full knowledge of reality is no basis for assuming that what we do not currently know does not exist. The presumption of eventual omniscience, of course, is that human consciousness, on its own power, is in the process of becoming God.

The existence of a physical reality does not preclude metaphysical reality or impose any limits upon it. To the contrary, it is *prima facie* evidence of the possibility of something beyond itself. Because it exists, it opens the door to a much more expansive reality. Limitations on reality are imposed only by the capabilities of the one experiencing it. Atheists are ready, willing and, in some cases, emotionally driven to set those limitations based on their own limited abilities of perception and cognition. In effect, atheism generates its own reality by imposing limitations on what reality is. *Arguably, this is the single, greatest folly of mankind: denying everything beyond himself by assuming the self-appointed position of king of reality.* Tragically, and incredibly, for most atheists human sovereignty is the by-product of mindless, random chance.

For Christians death is a consistently negative, transitional event that diminishes the individual. Because it is only transitional, however, resurrection is capable of restoring the diminishment. Those resurrected to eternal life with and "in" the Creator are restored, but move beyond restoration to glorification and perfection. This transition to perfection begins at the time of being "reborn" into the spirit of Christ, i.e. before physical death occurs.

Those suffering the second death are also resurrected and their bodies are restored. However, for them the second death—the antithesis of being born again—is a transition away from or "out" of the Creator brought to effect at the end of time. Christian theology teaches that the "saved" are born twice (physical and spiritual transitions) and die once (physical transition). The "lost" are born once (physical transition) and die twice (physical and spiritual transitions).

CHAPTER ELEVEN

ACTS OF THE APOSTLES: THE JERUSALEM CHURCH

Development of Christ's Church After the Ascension

Gospel accounts of the life and teachings of Jesus come to a close with His ascension to the Father. He left His followers with an enormous challenge that has been called "the great commission."

> "All authority in heaven and on earth has been given to me. Therefore go and make disciples of all nations, baptizing them in the name of the Father and of the Son and of the Holy Spirit, and teaching them to obey everything I have commanded you" (Matt 28:18-20).

Jesus looked to His apostles to carry on His work and participate in His plan for the salvation of mankind. His personal, DIVINE authority was removed with Him at the ascension. Nevertheless, as we shall see, the Apostles exercised great power in fulfilling their commission.

Luke's second volume, *The Book of Acts*, relates the story of the early days of the followers of Jesus absent His physical presence. It is an elegantly written, historically precise and detailed account of the spread of Jesus' teachings from a small nucleus of believers at Jerusalem through Judea, Samaria, Asia Minor, Greece and to the "ends of the earth" (Rome). The Holy Spirit plays a central role as a guiding, empowering presence and worthy successor to the incarnate Jesus. Some have suggested that *The Book of Acts*, also referred to as *The Acts of the Apostles* might have been more appropriately titled *The Acts of the Holy Spirit Through the Apostles.*

Christianity's popularity seriously concerned the leaders of Orthodox Judaism. Many Sanhedrin members considered Jesus' teachings heretical and contrary to their own faith rather than a continuation and fulfillment of it. They sought to put the apostles to death on the same basic charges brought against Jesus. But Gamaliel, a Pharisee and the most famed teacher of his time, suggested a test to measure the truth of the apostles' teachings.

> "Leave these men alone! Let them go! For if their purpose or activity is of human origin, it will fail. But if it is from God, you will not be able to stop these men; you will only find yourselves fighting against God" (Acts 5:38, 39).

Gamaliel's assessment proved correct. Despite severe persecution the good news of the Gospels was embraced passionately wherever it was preached. Its growth was not the result of human conquest. Christianity, rooted in love and salvation, was carried forward on the basis of those precepts under the watchful guidance of the Holy Spirit.

Jerusalem, the Day of Pentecost, c. A.D. 30

Ten days after Jesus ascended into the heavens the apostles and other disciples, assembled together in one place (possibly the temple precincts), "were filled with the Holy Spirit and began to speak in other tongues as the

Spirit enabled them" (Acts 2:4). Jewish visitors from foreign lands, celebrating Pentecost, recognized the "wonders of God" being spoken in their native languages by the group of Galileans (Acts 2:11). They became curious and began asking questions. Peter used this occasion to deliver one of the clearest expositions of

Eastern wall and Golden Gate of Old City Jerusalem

Christology found in Scripture outside the Gospels.

His expository form and sequencing follow the same pattern used by Jesus. Peter first proclaimed that the anticipated Messiah had come. " 'Men of Israel, listen to this: Jesus of Nazareth was a man accredited by God to you by miracles, wonders and signs, which God did among you through him, as you yourselves know'" (Acts 2:22). The Jewish people put this humble Nazarene to death, " 'with the help of wicked men,'" i.e. Gentile Romans (Acts 2:23).

Peter then crossed into theological territory that was both familiar and unfamiliar to his Jewish listeners. Many had been taught and believed in the literal resurrection of the dead, but were unclear about its timing and connection to salvation. " 'But God raised him from the dead,'" Peter continued, " 'freeing him from the agony of death, because it was impossible for death to keep its hold on him'" (Acts 2:24). Men killed Jesus, but only with His consent, and even then death had no real power over Him. As Jesus Himself had indicated, the power of this world (and ultimately death) had no "hold" on Him (see John 14:30). Death could not possibly "keep its hold on him" because, as Peter would proclaim in his later teachings, He is the DIVINE author of life.

At this point in his sermon Peter referenced the revered patriarch David to remind his listeners of their own Messianic tradition. Rejoicing, David had prophesied, " 'my body also will live in hope, because you will not abandon me to the grave, nor will you let your Holy One see decay'" (Psalm 16:10 quoted in Acts 2:27). Peter explained that David was not speaking of himself as the Messiah (Holy One), but of one of his promised descendents. David's decayed remains still lay buried in a tomb in Jerusalem, a fact universally accepted by the Jews.

In contrast to David, Peter and the apostles bore personal witness that: " 'God has raised this Jesus to life,'" and His resurrected body ascended into the heavens to be, " 'exalted to the right hand of God'" (Acts 2:32,33). The witness of the apostles was given some additional credibility because Jesus' physical remains were nowhere to be found, though attempts were likely made to locate His body by those seeking to disprove His resurrection and ascension. Since He had died only fifty days earlier (i.e. fifty days prior to Pentecost) and had been a very public figure, this should have been a simple task. But no mention is made in Scripture (or other reliable histories) of finding Jesus' corpse subsequent to the recorded date of His ascension.

Through his personal witness and teaching Peter effectively redefined resurrection for his Jewish brethren. Resurrection is real, but it precedes rebirth into a new life, and is not a restarting of the old one. The power of resurrection and new life lies in the one who raised

Himself from death, the originator and sustainer of life. Jesus submitted to death (in part) for the purpose of demonstrating that death could not contain Him. His body was raised from death under His own power to rejoin in eternal life with the Father. Peter preached that the same power of salvation and resurrection to new life was available to his Jewish listeners and their children and,
" 'for all who are far off—for all whom the Lord our God will call" (Acts 2:39). Those who are "far off" is an allusion to the Gentile nations.

Toward the end of his sermon Peter emphasized the critical point of the Messiah's DIVINITY. Using Psalm 110:1 in the same manner Jesus had (see, for example Matt 22:44-45) he explained Jesus' human relationship to David and his DIVINE relationship to "the Lord" (God). " 'Therefore let all Israel be assured of this: God has made this Jesus, whom you crucified, both Lord and Christ" (Acts 2:36). Peter concluded with an invitation to salvation and resurrection: " 'Repent and be baptized, every one of you, in the name of Jesus Christ for the forgiveness of your sins" (Acts 2:38).

At the Temple in Jerusalem, c. A.D. 30-35

The ministry of the apostles was accompanied by powerful signs and wonders, as was that of their master. Luke writes of one occasion where Peter and John approached the temple by the gate called Beautiful. A crippled beggar who had stationed himself there asked them for money. Peter responded with the same mercy and power so often demonstrated by Jesus. He healed the man's afflictions: "Taking him by the right hand, he helped him up, and instantly the man's feet and ankles became strong. He jumped to his feet and began to walk" (Acts 3:7,8).

Following Jesus' example, Peter used the

Western wall of the Temple Mount (Hakotel or "Wailing" Wall) located within the southeast corner of the Old City wall

demonstration of power to evangelize his people. His message was essentially the same as that delivered on Pentecost. But this time he made additional Old Testament references to help the crowd trace Messianic prophecies to their fulfillment in Jesus. Understanding how that prophecy was fulfilled involved a new understanding of the nature and purpose of the promised Messiah.

" 'Men of Israel,'" he asked the gathering crowd at Solomon's Colonnade, " 'why does this surprise you? Why do you stare at us as if by our own power or godliness we had made this man walk?'" (Acts 3:12). This was an obvious disclaimer that Peter and John were the source of healing power. Peter then attempted to explain Jesus in the context of their Messianic heritage. " 'The God of Abraham, Isaac and Jacob, the God of our fathers, has glorified his servant Jesus'" (Acts 3:13). "Servant" was a widely recognized Old Testament reference to the Messiah (see, for example Isa 42:1,19). Peter thus began his lesson with the bold statement that Yahweh, the God of Israel, revealed the nature of His Messiah, Jesus through the healing they had just witnessed.

Peter then drew closer to a description of Jesus as DIVINE. " 'You disowned the Holy and Righteous One and asked that a murderer be released to you'" (Acts 3:14). "Holy" and "Righteous" (from the Greek *dikahyos*) denote conduct that is blameless or "right" regardless of the standard being used, i.e. whether human or DIVINE. He then completed his exposition of the DIVINE nature of Messiah Jesus. " 'You killed the author of life, but God raised him from the dead. We are witnesses of this'" (Acts 3:15). "Author of life" unequivocally identified Jesus as the Creator God of the Jews. Peter and the apostles had personally observed that the Jews "killed" the Creator God, i.e. the physical man Jesus in whom the Creator God had been incarnate. But God, who obviously cannot be killed and was never dead, raised the (transformed) body of Jesus to eternal life.

At this point Peter reaffirmed that Jesus was the power behind the physical healing of the crippled beggar. " 'By faith in the name of Jesus, this man whom you see and know was made strong'" (Acts 3:16). His listeners, Peter warned, were also in need of a kind of healing—a spiritual healing or salvation which could only be effected by that same Jesus. " 'Repent, then, and turn to God, so that your sins may be wiped out, that times of refreshing may come from the Lord, and that he may send the Christ, who has been appointed for you—even Jesus'" (Acts 3:19-20).

It may seem that the requirements laid down by Peter to be spiritually healed were modest: repent and receive the Messiah Jesus. But for the "men of Israel" it remained questionable whether Messianic prophecy had actually been fulfilled. Neither the Messiah of whom Peter spoke nor the salvation that He brought were what they had come to expect. And feelings of guilt about their complicity (or active involvement) in Jesus' death complicated the issue for many. Dramatic signs such as healings helped overcome some of these obstructions to belief. Peter was also successful in continually harkening back to the most revered prophets of Israel in his attempts at portraying Jesus as the Messianic prophet of their forefathers (see, for example Acts 3:22-26).

Luke writes that following Peter's message at Solomon's Colonnade the number of men who believed in Jesus, "grew to about five thousand" (Acts 4:4). That was an increase of about two thousand since Pentecost and is indicative of the tremendous power and popularity of the very early Christian movement. Sadducee members of the Sanhedrin were sufficiently riled by its growth and the apostles' teachings regarding Jesus' resurrection that they had Peter and John arrested and brought before the court. The proceedings before the Sanhedrin illustrate the perceived threat of the early church to Orthodox Judaism. They also show the apostles' faith and their reliance on Jesus and the Holy Spirit.

" 'By what power or what name did you do this?' " they (possibly Caiaphas or Annas) asked Peter and John (Acts 4:7). Peter, "filled with the Holy Spirit" responded: " 'It is by the name of Jesus Christ of Nazareth, whom you crucified but whom God raised from the dead, that this man stands before you healed' " (Acts 4:8,10). The point that God had raised Jesus from the dead was critical to the Sadducees who did not believe in resurrection.

Peter then immediately connected resurrection to the greatest promise of the risen Messiah: " 'Salvation is found in no one else, for there is no other name under heaven given to men by which we must be saved' " (Acts 4:12). Luke indicates that the Sanhedrin members were "astonished" at Peter's message and his "courage" in delivering it. They noted that, "these men [Peter and John] had been with Jesus," recognizing that the force of what they said flowed from their great teacher (Acts 4:13).

In defiance of the miraculous evidence brought before them, the Sanhedrin rejected Peter's message of salvation. " 'Everybody living in Jerusalem knows they have done an outstanding miracle, and we cannot deny it,'" they admitted (Acts 4:16). Led by their own self-interests they again chose to reject the Messiah and, " 'stop this thing from spreading any further among the people.'" Fearful of the peoples' reaction if they punished the apostles, the Sanhedrin released them with a stern warning to not speak to anyone " 'in this name,'" i.e. the name of Jesus (Acts 4:17). Once again tragedy and irony abounded: Jewish men, reaching out to their own people with personal witness of their long-awaited Messiah, were rejected on the basis of keeping "this thing" from spreading.

Increase in Miraculous Power Among the Apostles: Jerusalem, c. A.D. 30-35

Resistance and hostility of the Sanhedrin to the message of Jesus and His apostles were nothing new. Having directly encountered the court, Peter and John became more aware of the opposition they would face as they continued proselytizing. They petitioned God for an increase in miraculous power to help achieve His purpose.

The apostles' prayed to the Sovereign Lord who, "made the heaven and the earth and the sea, and everything in them" (Acts 4:24). They asked for Jesus' intercession: "Stretch out your hand to heal and perform miraculous signs and wonders through the name of your holy servant Jesus" (Acts 4:30). After they prayed, "the place where they were meeting was shaken...and they were all filled with the Holy Spirit and spoke the word of God boldly" (Acts 4:31).

Their prayer and the Holy Spirit's response to it validate Jesus' earlier descriptions of how the plan of salvation would be fulfilled (see, for example John 14:25-26). Father, Son and Spirit are all directly involved and play distinct roles. The unity of their purpose in originating and executing the plan, however, should always be borne in mind when contemplating how and when each DIVINE personage takes action.

Surprisingly, the first sign given the apostles following their plea for miraculous power was a severe warning, not a generous healing. Like others in the early Christian community of Jerusalem, Ananias and his wife Sapphira sold a piece of property to benefit their group. Apparently they had pledged the entire proceeds from the sale but secretly held back part for themselves. When questioned about withholding some of the money, they lied and were immediately struck dead. Peter concluded that Satan had led them to lie to the Holy Spirit, i.e. to God Himself.

The judgment of Ananias and Sapphira may seem harsh, particularly when imposed by the God whose defining character is love. This sentiment, however, may miss the point that God's love is the absolute prerequisite, the *sine qua non* of spiritual relationship with Him. Ananias and Sapphira's great sin was to subordinate the love of God to their concern for the praise of men; they did so by deceiving the church and attempting to deceive God. The primacy of God and His love was an important lesson for the early church. It comes first—and it shuns hypocrisy.

Luke records that great power did then begin to flow through the apostles. They "performed many miraculous signs and wonders among the people" (Acts 5:12). Reminiscent of the desperate crowds pursuing

Jesus' help, the sick were brought into the streets on beds and mats, "so that at least Peter's shadow might fall on some of them as he passed by" (Acts 5:15). The sick were also brought to the apostles from the towns surrounding Jerusalem, and all of them were healed. Many men and women came to believe in Jesus—the result that the apostles had prayed for, and that the Sanhedrin feared.

The Sadducees viewed increases in the ranks of those accepting Jesus as the risen Messiah as losses to their party. They "were filled with jealousy" and began a systematic persecution of the apostles and their followers (Acts 5:17). Without charges, the high priest and his associates had the apostles thrown into jail and brought again before the Sanhedrin. It was during this second inquisition by the court that Gamaliel put forth his famous test for measuring the genuineness of the apostles' claims. Gamaliel was able to calm the Sadducees, but the court had the apostles flogged. By that time, however, the apostles' will and spirit had been forged into an instrument of the Lord. They had become the "sword of the Spirit" (see Eph 6:17).

"The apostles left the Sanhedrin, rejoicing because they had been counted worthy of suffering disgrace for the Name…they never stopped teaching and proclaiming the good news that Jesus is the Christ" (Acts 5:41,42). As they had patiently explained to the Sanhedrin for a second time, this Christ (Messiah) was the "Prince and Savior" exalted by God, "to his own right hand…that he might give repentance and forgiveness of sins to Israel" (Acts 5:31). In other words He was the Christ that the Sadducees and Pharisees awaited, and He was DIVINE.

Continued Growth and Persecution of the Church: Jerusalem c. A.D. 30-35

Luke is almost ebullient about the growth of the

church in the first few years following Jesus' ascension. Jews from foreign countries and varied backgrounds were won over in large numbers to the teachings of the apostles. Of special interest (and likely concern to the Orthodox establishment) is the mention that, "a large number of priests became obedient to the faith" (Acts 6:7).

As is typical of rapidly expanding groups, the Christians experienced growing pains. From early on the apostles were concerned with meeting the everyday material needs of the community (such as food for widows) without neglecting their primary calling of teaching and evangelizing. They asked the church for help, and it responded by selecting from among its members seven men, "known to be full of the Spirit and wisdom" (Acts 6:3). The term "deacon" (from the Greek *deeakoneho* meaning to wait upon or serve) would later come to describe the administrative duties assumed by these seven (see 1 Ti 3:10). Some, and possibly all of the original seven, were also actively involved in teaching and evangelizing.[35]

Stephen, like the apostles, was "a man full of God's grace and power" and he, "did great wonders and miraculous signs among the people" (Acts 6:8). His upbringing was likely Greek, and his activities aroused the opposition of other Hellenistic Jews. Those opposing him were one-time slaves or descendents of slaves from Cyrene, Alexandria, Cilicia and Asia. They argued with Stephen about his teachings but were unable to best him in open debate. "They could not stand up against his wisdom or the Spirit by whom he spoke" (Acts 6:10).

Luke indicates that Stephen's opponents (the "Freedmen") conspired to have charges of blasphemy brought against him. There is no mention of the Sanhedrin being involved in the conspiracy, but that body did accept Stephen's case when brought before it. The charges were false and very similar to those brought against Jesus.

Witnesses for the Freedmen testified that they had heard Stephen say, " 'that this Jesus of Nazareth will destroy this place [the temple] and change the customs Moses handed down to us' " (Acts 6:14).

Stephen was unmoved by the trappings of the Sanhedrin. His face looked "like the face of an angel," i.e. unruffled and totally confident as he delivered a rather unusual defense of the false charges against him (Acts 6:15). In effect it was more of a précis of Israelite history. He reviewed Jewish tradition starting with the departure of Abraham from Mesopotamia through the construction of Solomon's temple. The learned members of the Sanhedrin were unable to seriously dispute anything he put forward.

It was the conclusion of Stephen's speech—a cutting summary of his own people's reaction to prophetic leadership in the past and their denial of the Messiah—that excited emotion. " 'Was there ever a prophet your fathers did not persecute? They even killed those who predicted the coming of the Righteous One. And now you have betrayed and murdered him…' " (Acts 7:52). Stephen then saw a vision. He "looked up to heaven and saw the glory of God, and Jesus standing at the right hand of God" (Acts 7:55). And he shared the vision with the court. "'Look,' he said, 'I see heaven open and the Son of Man standing at the right hand of God'" (Acts 7:56).

Blasphemy! Oh Blasphemy! The insolent proselyte was spewing forth the same evil that his blasphemous teacher used to insult the court (see Matt 26:64). Heightened emotion exploded into violence. "At this they covered their ears and, yelling at the top of their voices, they all rushed at him [Stephen], dragged him out of the city and began to stone him" (Acts 7:57, 58). Stephen had dared to link the "Son of Man," Jesus' self-description as the Messiah, to "the right hand of God." For the Sanhedrin members this phrasing could mean only one thing: Jesus had the power of Yahweh God. Stephen repeated the same claim that Jesus had made before them: the Son of Man is DIVINE.

Saul of Tarsus was reported to be present at the stoning of Stephen, “giving approval to his death” (Acts 8:1). It is possible that Saul, or Paul as he was later named, had been involved in the plan to silence Stephen from the beginning. Paul’s hometown was located in the province of Cilicia, and he could have easily had ties with the Synagogue of the Freedmen. He is also known to have had close ties with members of the Sanhedrin, and may himself have been a member. His exact involvement is not known, but his zealous opposition to the early Christian movement does cast suspicion.

CHAPTER TWELVE

THE CHURCH BEYOND JERUSALEM

Sorcery: More Opposition to the Early Church, Samaria c. A.D. 35

On the same day that Stephen was stoned to death a "great persecution" broke out against the church in Jerusalem. Saul's active participation in it became public. "Going from house to house, he dragged off men and women and put them in prison" (Acts 8:1,3). Possibly overstating the case a bit, Luke indicates that *all* the church members except the apostles were scattered from Jerusalem throughout Judea and Samaria. Rather than discouraging interest in Christian teachings, however, the increased persecution helped stimulate its spread.

Philip, for example, one of the original seven "helpers" chosen by the church fled north to a city in Samaria, probably its capital (then called Sebaste and now known as Nablus). He preached the good news of the kingdom of God. There was great joy in the city as, " many paralytics and cripples were healed" and many were baptized in the name of Jesus (Acts 8:7). But Philip's success was met with a new form of opposition not previously encountered by the young church: sorcery.

Philip became acquainted with a man named Simon who had practiced sorcery in the city for some time. Luke indicates that Simon boasted "he was someone great," leading many in the city to say, "this man is the divine power known as the Great Power" (Acts 8:9,10). These remarks suggest that Simon had been either claiming to be God or something close to it. Apparently Simon recanted, at least temporarily, from his claims to great power; and even Philip may have been deceived by the professed change in heart. It is recorded that "Simon himself believed and was baptized" (Acts 8:13).

The root word for sorcery in the Greek is *magiah*, meaning magic or magic art. In modern usage it has gained a Disneyworld/Harry Potteresque connotation of an innocent character waving a starry wand and causing fun things to happen. Its historical associations are broad and ancient, and almost always relate to the mystical or supernatural. Astrology, witchcraft and Gnosticism, to name a few, all fall under the rubric of sorcery. In practice it is usually a combination of scientifically oriented observation (such as astronomy) and superstition aimed at controlling the natural or supernatural. The supposed control is exercised through various techniques such as incantations and spells.

Early Christian condemnation of the "magic arts" stems from the most basic of issues: DIVINITY itself. Sorcery is inimical to the Christian belief system because it consciously obfuscates the supernatural (or metaphysical) as a means of materially benefiting the practitioner. This is in direct and total opposition to the purpose and teachings of Jesus. His aim was to clarify mankind's relationship to the Creator; and his motivation was to benefit mankind with eternal, spiritual life.

Simon convinced the people of Samaria that he had DIVINE power for the purpose of making himself rich. The claim was obviously bogus as is shown by his offer to purchase the real spiritual power demonstrated by Peter and John (see Acts 8:18-19). Simon was willing to deceive everyone around him about the very nature of God in order to satisfy his own self-interest. His false claims and practice of the "magic arts" were an attempt to arrogate unto himself the power of the DIVINE.

Peter, upon visiting Philip in Samaria, recognized the gravity of Simon's deceit. He ordered Simon to repent of the "wickedness" of sorcery and warned him that he could have no part in the ministry of Jesus, "because your heart is not right before God" (Acts 8:22,21). Early Christian literature also voiced Peter's condemnation of sorcery, labeling Simon the "father" of Gnosticism.

Philip Evangelizes South and West of Samaria, c. A.D. 35

At the direction of "an angel of the Lord" Philip traveled south from Samaria toward Gaza (Acts 8:26). On his way he met an important official (and eunuch) of the queen of Ethiopia. Their encounter was an unconventional one. Sitting alone in his chariot, the official read aloud from the book of Isaiah, but was puzzled at its contents. Most likely a convert to Judaism, he was returning from a trip to Jerusalem where he had gone to worship. Philip, following explicit instructions from "the Spirit," approached the queen's official and asked: " 'Do you understand what you are reading?'" (Acts 8:29,30).

It was a passage in Isaiah where the prophet describes

someone who is, "led like a sheep to the slaughter, and as a lamb before the shearer is silent" (Isa 53:7). Experts in the Scripture had argued about its meaning; the "someone" could describe several persons including Isaiah himself. When asked for an explanation by the Ethiopian official, Philip "told him the good news about Jesus," that He was the "lamb" prophesied by Isaiah (Acts 8:35). The official apparently accepted Philip's teaching and asked to be baptized.

When they came up out of the water something extraordinary happened: "the Spirit of the Lord suddenly took Philip away, and the eunuch did not see him again, but went on his way rejoicing" (Acts 8:39). Is this merely picturesque speech, perhaps a way of saying that Philip was extremely busy and had to hurry on to his destination? Or is this an actual witness of powerful intervention by the Spirit of the Lord for some specific purpose?

The verb used in the KJV to describe what happened to Philip is "caught away" (*harpadzo* in the Greek). It denotes a sudden taking or plucking away by force. Thus, the most straightforward reading of the text indicates that sudden physical force was exerted on Philip to transport him away from the baptism toward the city of Azotus. Such a display of power is consistent with the personal involvement of the Spirit in the whole Ethiopian eunuch incident. Indeed, it is apparent throughout *The Book of Acts* that the Spirit provided powerful, and sometimes detailed guidance to the early church. Philip being "caught away" was dramatic confirmation to the Ethiopian official of his newfound faith, and inspiration to his whole entourage.

On the Road to Damascus, Syria, c. A.D. 35

Luke's narrative about the spread of the Christian Gospel takes another important turn at this point. As in the case of Philip's encounter with the Ethiopian eunuch, the account of Saul's conversion while enroute to Damascus has all the markings of the direct involvement of the Spirit of God. Saul had set out to Damascus with the avowed purpose of rounding up Christian believers and bringing them to trial in Jerusalem. In one of the greatest plot twists of all time, he ended up becoming Jesus' key spokesman to the non-Jewish world.

God did not deal gently with Saul, however, and the challenges He set before him proved extremely arduous. Luke relates that as Saul drew near to Damascus, "suddenly a light from heaven flashed around him" (Acts 9:3). The light was accompanied by a voice that asked: " 'Saul, Saul, why do you persecute me?'" (Acts 9:4).

Saul's brief interaction with the stunning presence formed the basic message to which he devoted the remainder of his earthly life. "'Who are you, Lord?' Saul asked" (Acts 9:5). He knew at once that he was in the presence of the "Lord," a term which in the New Testament Greek (*kooreeos*) almost invariably denotes the supreme authority, God. And at once his recognition was confirmed. " 'I am Jesus, whom you are persecuting,' he replied. 'Now get up and go into the city, and you will be told what you must do'" (Acts 9:5-6).

Saul was changed, both spiritually and physically. He got up from the ground totally blind, and he was unable to eat or drink anything for three days. While recuperating in Damascus Saul was visited by a disciple named Ananias. Both Saul and Ananias had received visions in which Jesus personally instructed them as to the purpose of Ananias's visit. Ananias was to minister in restoring Saul's sight and imparting the Holy Spirit.

As Ananias placed his hands on Saul: "Immediately, something like scales fell from Saul's eyes, and he could see again. He got up and was baptized..." (Acts 9:18). Saul's physical healing was accompanied by birth into a new life and the ability to see in a brand new way—spiritually. His Pharisaic misinterpretations about the Messiah were gone. Luke reports Saul's recognition of the importance of this new insight: "At once he began to preach in the synagogues that Jesus is the Son of God" (Acts 9:20).

Saul's brief, personal encounter with the glorified Jesus would lead him to become one of the boldest, most persistent, and most effective expositors of that remarkable proposition: Jesus the Christ is DIVINE.

Peter Evangelizes Outside of Jerusalem, c. A.D. 35-44

Not much is written about Saul covering the seven or eight years after his conversion. Moving from Damascus he ministered in Nabatean Arabia for about three years. He then visited the church in Jerusalem but was threatened by the Grecian Jews, likely the same group that had opposed Stephen. Fearing for his life, the church took Saul, "down to Caesarea and sent him off to Tarsus" (Acts 9:30). He ministered in the provinces of Syria and Cilicia, his home turf, between the years 38-43 A.D. During this period of Saul's relative obscurity Luke shifts the narrative focus back to the apostle Peter.

Of special interest to Luke were Peter's efforts to spread the Gospel into Samaria, north and west of Jerusalem. Peter continued to minister with power, as is evidenced by the miraculous cure of a paralytic man named Aeneas in the town of Lydda (see Acts 9:34), about 12 miles east of Joppa, now called Jaffa, a southern suburb of Tel Aviv. Hearing that Peter was nearby, some disciples in Joppa urgently requested that he visit them. One of their members, a woman by the name of Tabitha (Dorcas in the Greek), died and had been prepared for burial. Her fellow believers may have been seeking guidance and consolation from Peter, or they may have been hoping for something greater.

Luke's description of Peter's handling of Tabitha's situation at Joppa is very similar to Matthew's account of Jesus raising Jairus' daughter from the dead (see Matt 9:23-26). Peter was present on that occasion and the other

Jaffa (Joppa, Yafo) on the Mediterranean; southern suburb of Tel Aviv

two times that Jesus exercised this awesome power. He obviously knew of the possibility of restoring physical life, and he understood that the Spirit was working with power through him. Peter prayed before taking any action; he must have sensed that the timing and circumstances were correct. "Turning toward the dead woman he said, 'Tabitha, get up.' She opened her eyes, and seeing Peter she sat up" (Acts 9:40). This was not sorcery; this was the exercise of DIVINE power for the purpose of strengthening and building the church. "This became known all over Joppa, and many people believed in the Lord" (Acts 9:42).

Peter was actively following the commission of his master to, "make disciples of all nations" as he traveled about Samaria. It is apparent at this point in his ministry, however, that he did not understand the full scope of that directive. He was not clear about whom the new covenant included and how it should be implemented. In typical *Book of Acts* fashion God intervened directly to assist Peter in accomplishing His purpose, i.e. the extension of salvation to all mankind. He sent an angel to Cornelius, a Gentile Roman centurion in Caesarea to have him arrange a meeting with Peter who was still in Joppa. Peter, meanwhile, was given personal instructions while in a trance about how to proceed.

Luke gives a vivid description of what Peter experienced. "He saw heaven opened and something like a large sheet being let down to earth by its four corners." In the "sheet" were all kinds of animals, reptiles and birds. "Then a voice told him, 'Get up, Peter. Kill and eat'" (Acts 10:11,13). Steeped in Jewish dietary law regarding clean and unclean food, Peter's immediate reaction was to challenge the voice. " 'Surely not, Lord'! Peter replied. 'I have never eaten anything impure or unclean'" (Acts 10:14). The great dissonance Peter felt illustrates the binding force of Jewish law and the extreme reluctance of the Jewish people, including Jesus' own apostles, to set that law aside.

Peter's brief response highlights another reason for his discomfort. He knew immediately that the voice was that of the "Lord." Unlike Saul, Peter did not need to ask who the person behind the voice was. Peter had known Jesus personally. Why would the Lord instruct him to consciously disregard age-old Jewish law prohibiting the consumption of unclean meat? Peter needed clarification on that issue and, ultimately, on the much bigger issue it raised concerning the new covenant between God and His people. How do Jesus and his teachings change that relationship? For Jew and Gentile alike this issue always has been and remains enormously important and divisive.

Cobblestone street in Old Jaffa (Joppa, Yafo)

Clarification and instruction were forthcoming. “The voice spoke to him a second time, ‘Do not call anything impure that God has made clean’” (Acts: 10:15). In Moses’ time the God of the Israelites had established restrictions about what was clean and unclean. They were basically a means of separating the Israelites as a holy people with a special purpose. That same God had fulfilled His purpose and removed the restrictions. God had “made clean” food previously deemed unclean. He has the complete freedom to make changes at His discretion.

The difficulty that many people have with changes in God's law and covenant as spoken by Jesus (see, for example Matt 15:11) is simple but highly significant: they conclude that Jesus did not have the DIVINE authority to make them. Peter's vision strongly challenges that conclusion. He was communicating directly with the Lord God (most likely in the person of Jesus), and God told Peter that He Himself made the changes. To make certain that Peter understood the lesson, Luke writes that the vision "...happened three times" (Acts 10:16).

"While Peter was still thinking about the vision, the Spirit said to him, 'Simon, three men are looking for you'" (Acts 10:19). Peter accompanied the men back to Caesarea where he met with Cornelius and his household. By this time Peter recognized the fuller meaning of his vision. He announced to the rather large gathering: " 'God has shown me that I should not call any man impure or unclean...I now realize how true it is that God does not show favoritism but accepts men from every nation who fear him and do what is right'" (Acts 10:28,34). Peter had come to understand the plan that Jesus had spoken of so often. The Messiah had come through the Israelite nation to bring about the salvation of all nations. In this sense *all* barriers between Jew and Gentile had been removed.

Peter instructed Cornelius and his household in the basics of Jesus' ministry and how forgiveness of sin is available to everyone who believes in Him. Though Cornelius and all his family were "devout and God-fearing," they had previously been unable to make the connection between Jesus and salvation (Acts 10:2). While Peter was still speaking, "the Holy Spirit came on all who heard the message" (Acts 10:44). This was confirmation to Peter and the "circumcised believers" (i.e. Jewish believers in Jesus) who had come with him, "that the gift of the Holy Spirit had been poured out even on the Gentiles," and that they should be baptized (Acts 10:45).

Word spread throughout the church in Judea that Gentiles were being baptized into the body of believers. When Peter returned to Jerusalem the circumcised believers there criticized him for even coming into contact with Gentiles (see Acts 11:2-3). The stage was set for a showdown on the critical issue of salvation: to whom was it available and under what terms? Luke does not describe the exact venue, but it is likely that a major church assembly convened to hear Peter's account of his activities. Resolution of the matter was needed and Peter was accepted as an influential leader.

Essentially, Peter allowed events to speak for themselves. He explained the Joppa-Caesarea episode, "precisely as it had happened" (Acts 11:4). From this chain of events Peter drew a simple but, for his Jewish brothers, a shocking conclusion. " 'So if God gave them the same gift [i.e., the gift of being filled with the Holy Spirit as John the Baptist had foretold] as he gave us, who believed in the Lord Jesus Christ, who was I to think that I could oppose God?' " (Acts 11:17). "Them" was a reference to Gentile believers and "us" identified the audience of circumcised Jewish believers. What the two had in common was obviously not their lineage. The Holy Spirit indwelled and saved those "who believed in the Lord Jesus Christ." Peter interpreted any denial of the Holy Spirit's action as opposition to God, the Jewish Yahweh.

The reaction of the assembled church at Jerusalem to Peter's theological message is of monumental importance to all seekers of the truth. "When they heard this, they had no further objections and praised God, saying, 'So then, God has granted even the Gentiles repentance unto life' " (Acts 11:18). For the church that had made this conclusion—comprised almost, if not entirely of Jewish brothers at the time—the message was truly revolutionary. Going forward God would save Jew and Gentile on the same terms, belief in Him and His Son,

Jesus the Messiah.

Other efforts were made to convert Gentiles to belief in Jesus at about the same time that Peter was evangelizing in Samaria. For example, Luke writes that believers from Cyprus and Cyrene went to Antioch "to speak to [Gentile] Greeks" about the good news (Acts 11:20). Antioch would have been a likely choice given its large population (estimated at 500,000) and relative proximity. Despite its long pagan history, "The Lord's hand was with them, and a great number of people believed and turned to the Lord" (Acts 11:21). The church at Jerusalem dispatched Barnabas to assist the growing number of believers in Antioch.

Luke brings Saul back into the narrative at this point. Barnabas traveled northwest from Antioch to Tarsus to meet up with Saul, who was pursuing his own commission to proselytize Gentiles. Together they returned to Antioch and became active in the church, teaching there for a whole year. Antioch became famous in church history for several reasons. The first sizeable group of predominantly Gentile believers was located there. Saul's three, well documented missionary trips to the Gentiles originated from Antioch. And, of course, "The disciples were called Christians first at Antioch" (Acts 11:26). "Christian" was a term ridiculing believers and meant "of the party of Christ."

The Dispersal of Christianity Accelerates: Transition from Peter to Saul—Jerusalem, c. A.D. 44

Political reality of the time placed the church at Jerusalem in peril. King Herod Agrippa I had James the apostle (and brother of John) put to death by the sword. Seeking to further placate the Jewish population, he had Peter imprisoned. The story of Peter's escape is a prelude to the account of Saul's work in expanding the boundaries of Christianity. And it is another dramatic example of the power and protection given to the nascent church. As with many events in *The Book of Acts*, supernatural intervention was involved.

The evening before Peter was to be brought to trial an angel of the Lord, "struck Peter on the side and woke him up" (Acts 12:7). Chains attached to Peter's wrists fell away, and he and the angel walked past two sets of guards. The iron prison gate leading to the city then opened for them and they passed through it. Voila! Peter was out of prison and his captors had no idea what had happened. Is this story just a little too much for the average modern reader to accept as true? Perhaps it is just a literary device that Luke used in switching to a new protagonist.

Readers are always placed in the position of gauging the credibility of documents that purport to be historically accurate. In this instance there is no real evidence that Luke is attempting to deceive his readers or merely entertain them. Quite the opposite, it has all the traits of a well thought out, historical piece striving for accuracy and authenticity. For example, Luke provides interesting and important details: "After arresting him, he [Herod] put him [Peter] in prison, handing him over to be guarded by four squads of four soldiers each" (Acts 12:4). From this description one can ascertain how concerned Herod was that Peter not escape. The four squads served on shifts to provide round-the-clock protection.[36] By assigning the four soldiers on each shift to keep watch on a single prisoner the protection was made redundant. Multiple, armed soldiers would also have been effective against potential breakouts initiated by Peter's fellow believers.

A sense of genuineness is also given to Luke's writing by his refusal to gloss over the confusing aspects of supernatural events. Peter followed the angel out of prison, "but he had no idea that what the angel was doing was really happening; he thought he was seeing a vision"

(Acts 12:9). If Luke were attempting to fabricate a case, it would be much simpler to avoid comments such as this. Conversational exchanges between other individuals mentioned in regard to Peter's escape have this same realistic flow. Rhoda, a servant girl exclaimed, " 'Peter is at the door!'" when he arrived at Mary's house. The reaction of those inside is that of shaken, disappointed people, not supermen: " 'You're out of your mind,' they told her" (Acts 12:14,15).

Corroboration with historical facts from other sources can also lend credibility. Luke mentions that following Peter's escape Herod had a thorough search made for him but could not find him. Thereupon, Herod "cross-examined the guards and ordered that they be executed" (Acts 12:19). Punishing guards in this manner for allowing their prisoners to escape was common practice under Roman rule. It later became codified under emperor Justinian.

Interestingly, Herod's own death became an historical marker for Peter's escape. It is known from other sources that Herod Agrippa I died in 44 A.D. According to Luke, Herod traveled from Judea (Jerusalem) to Caesarea shortly after Peter's escape. At Caesarea he was stricken and died because he "did not give praise to God" (Acts 12:23). This is Luke's way of saying that God struck down Herod because he persecuted the church and allowed his subjects to recognize him as divine. Herod, like many kings, knowingly failed to draw the distinction between earthly power and DIVINITY.

CHAPTER THIRTEEN

PAUL'S MISSIONARY JOURNEYS

Paul's First Missionary Journey, c. A.D. 46-48

Capital of Corinthian column, Caesarea on the Mediterranean, about 25 miles north of Tel Aviv

On their return to Antioch, Barnabas and Saul received direction from the Holy Spirit to be set apart, " 'for the work to which I have called them' " (Acts 13:2). Since Luke makes note that there were prophets and teachers in the Antioch church, it is likely that the communication came in the form of a prophetic message. Years earlier the Lord (Jesus) had announced to Ananias what Saul's "work" would be. " 'This man is my chosen instrument to carry my name before the Gentiles and their kings and before the people of Israel' " (Acts 9:15).

Barnabas and Saul traveled from Antioch in Syria to Cyprus and its capital, Paphos. There, Luke speaks of an early encounter with sorcery, similar to Philip's experience as he set out to evangelize in Samaria. Sergius Paulus, the Roman proconsul to Cyprus, sent for Barnabas and Saul because he wanted to hear their message. But a Jewish sorcerer named Bar-Jesus (also Elymas) "opposed them and tried to turn the proconsul from the faith" (Acts 13:8). The antipathy of Bar-Jesus to the work of Barnabas and Saul was more direct than Simon's had been in Samaria. Simon used sorcery for personal material gain, whereas Bar-Jesus took his involvement in the magic arts a step further. It appears that he defended sorcery as a superior, alternative belief system.

Saul, like Peter, was quick to recognize the severity of the situation. Filled with the Holy Spirit, he charged that Bar-Jesus was, " 'a child of the devil and an enemy of everything that is right!' " (Acts 13:10). To put an immediate stop to the " 'deceit and trickery' " Saul then invoked the " 'hand of the Lord' " to temporarily blind Bar-Jesus (Acts 13:10,11).

Saul's action may seem harsh and may strike some as a "negative" miracle. But like all of the direct involvement of the Holy Spirit mentioned by Luke it had the decided positive effect of encouraging belief. "When the proconsul saw what had happened, he believed, for he was amazed at the teaching about the Lord" (Acts 13:12). Incidentally, it is in connection with the Bar-Jesus event that Luke mentions Saul's other name, Paul. Use of this second, Roman name may indicate that Saul had entered the Gentile phase of his ministry in earnest. Paul, which translates as "little," may also have been descriptive of his physical stature.

From Cyprus Paul and Barnabas traveled to Antioch in Pisidia, over 300 miles north and west of Paphos and approximately that same distance west of Antioch in Syria. The town was an important commercial hub and had a large Jewish population. Though Paul's primary goal was to evangelize Gentiles, it was his custom to preach the Gospel first among his Jewish brethren. Besides showing his love and concern for his own people, this arrangement had the practical benefit of providing an entrée into otherwise foreign, and sometimes hostile communities. Paul's heavy emphasis when he preached in the synagogue setting was usually on Jesus as the fulfillment of the Messianic promise. That was the case at Antioch as he concluded the first part of his address: " 'What God promised our fathers he has fulfilled for us, their children, by raising up Jesus'" (Acts 13:32,33).

But the Messiah Paul preached to his Jewish audiences always had a very special character, something new to them. Jesus himself, Paul explained, effected the forgiveness of sin, thereby justifying man in God's sight. Man, regardless of how conscientiously he tried to obey the law given by God to Moses, could not become righteous before God. Paul put it this way: " 'Therefore, my brothers, I want you to know that through Jesus the forgiveness of sins is proclaimed to you. Through him everyone who believes is justified from everything you could not be justified from by the Law of Moses'" (Acts 13:38-39). The "belief" Paul spoke of was belief in Jesus and his ability to accomplish something that man could not. Being DIVINE, Jesus Himself could be the ATONEMENT, the means of covering over the results of all mankind's innumerable bad choices.

Antioch was aroused by the message proclaimed by Paul and Barnabas. Luke writes that when they preached on the Sabbath following the initial meeting, "almost the whole city gathered to hear the word of the Lord" (Acts 13:44). Many members of the synagogue, however, greeted their success with resentment and abusive language. It was the same reaction Jesus received among His people—plain jealousy. Tragically, many of the Jews perceived the Messiah and salvation portrayed by Paul as undermining their power and privilege. Becoming more incensed, they "stirred up persecution against Paul and Barnabas and expelled them from their region" (Acts 13:50). Gentiles in the region had the opposite reaction: "they were glad and honored the word of the Lord; and all who were appointed for eternal life believed" (Acts 13:48).

Traveling east and south, Paul and Barnabas came to Iconium. Their reception was similar to what it had been at Antioch in Pisidia. Many listened to their message, and some believed, "But the Jews who refused to believe stirred up the Gentiles and poisoned their minds against the brothers" (Acts 14:2). Eventually a plot developed among the Gentiles and Jews to take drastic action to get rid of Paul and Barnabas. Instead of chasing them out of town, the non-believers of Iconium planned to stone them to death.

Repeated attempts to execute Paul by stoning took place as his missionary trips progressed. Severe reaction of this sort among several groups who rejected the Christian message was not coincidental. Among Jews, stoning was a prescribed punishment for blasphemy. Paul's claim that Jesus was the Messiah, of itself, would not have been sufficient grounds to incur such punishment. It seems clear that it was his further characterization of Jesus as the DIVINE savior that resulted in demands for death by stoning. Paul's message and the reaction of Jewish non-believers directly parallels Jesus' own attempts to explain who He was.

Fleeing south about 20 miles to the Roman colony of Lystra, Paul and Barnabas were received as gods. The population's overzealous response stemmed from a misinterpretation of the exercise of DIVINE power. Paul had ordered a man crippled in his feet since birth to, " 'Stand up on your feet!'" When the man jumped to his feet and began to walk the crowd shouted: " 'The gods have come down to us in human form!'" (Acts 14:10,11). They saw the healing in terms of local folklore and Greek theology. Paul and Barnabas were taken to be the Greek gods Hermes and Zeus revisiting their town incognito. Townspeople were so moved that they wanted to offer sacrifices to them.[37]

Grief stricken at the people's behavior, Paul managed to use the occasion to contrast Christian monotheism with Greco-Roman polytheism. He first denied any supernatural power of his own. " 'We too are only men, human like you.'" He then implored them to turn from " 'these worthless things,'" i.e. the many false gods they sought to appease, toward " 'the living God, who made heaven and earth.'" The time for all nations going " 'their own way,'" Paul suggested, had ended (Acts 14:15,16). The miraculous sign that the people of Lystra had witnessed was testimony to the good news of the one God.

Paul's first missionary efforts at Lystra conclude on a very unusual note. Nothing is said concerning the acceptance or rejection of his admonition. But one does get a sense of the mounting opposition Paul and Barnabas were leaving in their wake. Irate Jews from outside Lystra (Antioch and Iconium) came "and won the crowd over." They stoned Paul, drug him out of town and left him for dead (Acts 14:19). It is highly improbable that Paul was not seriously injured, or at least gave the appearance of being mortally wounded. His opponents wanted him dead and must have been convinced that they had accomplished their mission. Without much fanfare Luke finishes up by noting: "after the disciples had gathered around him, he

[Paul] got up and went back into the city" (Acts 14:20). Wow! Luke may not be describing a resurrection, but the power of the Spirit seems obvious.

The next day Paul and Barnabas traveled east and south to Derbe where they "won a large number of disciples" (Acts 14:21). At Derbe they reversed course and returned to Lystra, Iconium and Antioch for the purpose of, "strengthening the disciples and encouraging them to remain true to the faith" (Acts 14:22). They then moved directly south toward the Mediterranean, stopping to preach at Perga and Attalia. From Attalia they set sail back to Antioch, Syria where they reported to the church how God had, "opened the door of faith to the Gentiles." They remained with the disciples at Antioch "a long time," usually taken to mean more than a year (Acts 14:27,28).

The Council at Jerusalem, c. A.D. 50-51

Men from Judea came to Antioch and began teaching: " 'Unless you are circumcised, according to the custom taught by Moses, you cannot be saved'" (Acts 15:1). They were converts to Christianity and likely from the party of the Pharisees. The salvation these men spoke of was the eternal life with the Father taught by Jesus. In their minds Christian salvation was linked to obedience as taught in Old Testament, Jewish Scripture. Paul and Barnabas immediately challenged their teachings and, at the direction of the Antioch church, traveled to Jerusalem to confer with the apostles and elders.

The first ecumenical council of the church was thus a response to the very basic doctrinal issue of how salvation is achieved. Some of the Christian believers (who were also members of the party of the Pharisees) made an assertion to the assembly supporting what the "men from Judea" had been teaching in Antioch. They said: " 'The Gentiles must be circumcised and required to obey the Law of Moses'" (Acts 15:5). There are two important parts to their statement, one explicit and one implicit. The explicit requirement being proposed was that Gentiles must become full converts to Judaism before they can be true Christians. This appears somewhat self-serving, since those setting forth the requirement were raised in the Jewish tradition. Implicit in the requirement is the *priority* of converting to Judaism before salvation is possible. Making conversion to Judaism an *a priori* condition of salvation implies that salvation is dependent upon and impossible without it.

Judaism's rock-solid foundation and claim to uniqueness as a theocratic system has always been its line of covenants (or formal agreements) with the Creator God. Of key importance were the Abrahamic, Sinaitic, Davidic, and the so-called "new" covenant prophesied by Jeremiah. The covenants were established by God and formed the basis of relationship between Him and the Israelites. Perhaps their most significant feature is their promissory nature: one party (God) typically promised something to the other party (the Israelites), and in some instances He made the promise conditional on performance by the other party. Generally speaking, covenants are stand-alone agreements in the sense that the validity of each is established by the terms of that specific agreement. In other words, one covenant does not depend on another for its authority, though they may have a common theme.

When Jesus spoke of the "new covenant" in His blood (see Lk 22:20) He was referring back to God's promise delivered by the prophet Jeremiah over six hundred years earlier.

> "The time is coming," declares the Lord, "when I will make a new covenant with the house of Israel and with the house of Judah…I will put my law in their minds and write it on their hearts. I will be their God, and they will be my

people" (Jer 31:31,33).

Jesus proclaimed Himself (i.e. His first appearance on earth) as the beginning of the fulfillment of Jeremiah's promise. His new covenant was in line with and succeeded prior covenants with the Israelites, but it and its promise of eternal life (see Jer 31:34 and Jn 6:40,47) were separate from them.

Those teaching that salvation as taught by Jesus required prior conversion to Judaism were making one of two possible mistakes. They may have assumed that the "new" covenant was linked to (and ultimately derived its force from) prior covenants, particularly the Abrahamic and Sinaitic covenants. Therefore, to be saved as described in the new covenant, one needed first to be circumcised and to obey the Law of Moses. One needed to take on at least the outward signs of "being Jewish." Or they may have incorrectly assumed that the new covenant prophesied by Jeremiah was for the exclusive benefit of the Israelites because it was made with the house of Israel. The covenant did specify the "house of Israel" as the only named beneficiary (see Jer 31:33). From the stated covenantal terms it can be easily inferred that the benefits were to be limited solely to the Jewish nation. Under normal conditions such an inference would hold true, but there is one major exception that it ignores.

When the *fulfillment* of a covenant with God (e.g. the "new" covenant) is in the person of God Himself, the terms of the covenant are not necessarily fixed. They are dynamic in response to His ongoing WILL. Jesus, as the DIVINE Son of God, had the power to define Jeremiah's prophecy regarding who can be saved, and He did so as "everyone who believes in him [Jesus]" (Jn 3:15). To deny that Jesus had this power is simply to deny that He was God. Assuming that those raising the salvation issue at the Jerusalem Council were true converts to Christianity (and therefore believing that Jesus was God), one almost has to conclude that they were incorrectly linking compliance to the terms of "old" covenants with eligibility for benefits of the "new" covenant.

It is no exaggeration to suggest that the Jerusalem Council was concerned with a question critically relevant to Orthodox Judaism. It was a council initiated by Jewish converts to Christianity (Paul, Barnabas, et. al.), presided over by Jewish leaders of the party of the Christians (Peter,

Jewish men in the Jewish Quarter of Old City Jerusalem

James, et. al.), and dealt with the fundamental Jewish issue of salvation taught by a Jewish rabbi who claimed to be the Jewish Messiah (Jesus). The decisions of the council formalized a singular tenet of Christian belief that many in the Orthodox community continued to reject. Members of the council, predominantly Jewish in background, took the definitive position that salvation is achieved solely through belief in Jesus. Despite differences on this doctrine, which resulted in the Jewish-Christian schism, their origin underscores the extremely important commonalities in Judeo-Christian belief about the One God.

Luke writes that the apostles and elders met, most

likely separate from the assembled Jerusalem church as a whole. After much discussion, Simon Peter, the apostle of Jesus and probably the most authoritative figure in the church, got up and spoke. Peter recalled his experience with Cornelius the Roman centurion in Caesarea. " 'Brothers, you know that some time ago God made a choice among you that the Gentiles might hear from my lips the message of the gospel and believe'" (Acts 15:7). The Gentiles (Cornelius and his household) received his message and the Holy Spirit was given to them. From this personal experience Peter was able to illustrate the connection between faith and salvation. " 'He [God] made no distinction between us [Jews] and them [Gentiles], for he purified their hearts by faith…We believe it is through the grace of our Lord Jesus that we are saved, just as they are'" (Acts 15:9,11).

"Grace" (*kharece* in the Greek) usually indicates unmerited favor, as it does here in Peter's statement. The particular favor that Jesus extends in this context is the forgiveness of sins. It is this forgiveness of sins—more specifically Jesus' DIVINE power to forgive, and his DIVINE character to WILL forgiveness—that purifies hearts (removes sin) and saves sinners. Peter's comments summarized and formalized what was known by the apostles and taught by Jesus. The one path to salvation is the forgiveness of sin freely given by the Son of God, and it is available to all (Jew and Gentile) who believe in Him.

As if to validate what Peter had just spoken, Luke relates that Paul and Barnabas then addressed the whole assembly. They told of, "the miraculous signs and wonders God had done among the Gentiles through them" (Acts 15:12). And then James, the familial half-brother of Jesus and influential figure in the Jerusalem church, continued Peter's argument. His comments were aimed at old covenant provision for the salvation of Gentiles. Quoting the prophet Amos, James reminded the church that the restored kingdom of David will include, "all the Gentiles who bear my name" (Amos 9:12 as quoted in Acts 15:17). Though not mentioned by James at the time, Jeremiah's prophecy of a new covenant was widely known. He probably chose the text from Amos as an historic Jewish reference of Gentile inclusion in the new covenant.

James concluded that, " 'we should not make it difficult for the Gentiles who are turning to God'" (Acts 15:19). To help keep Gentile believers from offending Jewish sensitivities regarding certain customs, he proposed that they abstain from four pagan practices. The Jerusalem Council then drafted a letter to the Antioch church regarding its findings. Of special note in this communication is the attribution of authority. There was agreement among the apostles, elders and the whole church of Jerusalem, but the letter cites the involvement of the Holy Spirit as the primary basis for its acceptance (see Acts 15:28). Paul, Barnabas and others from Jerusalem delivered the letter. "The people read it and were glad for its encouraging message" (Acts 15:31).

Paul's Second Missionary Journey, c. A.D. 50-52

Column ruins at Caesarea on the Mediterranean

Following a relatively brief stay in Antioch, Paul and Silas, a leader in the Jerusalem church and a prophet, set out for the region of Cilicia. Paul was intent on strengthening some of the churches established on his first missionary trip and spreading the Gospel westward and northward. At Derbe, Timothy, a young disciple who would become Paul's faithful companion, joined them. "As they traveled from town to town, they delivered the decisions reached by the apostles and elders in Jerusalem for the people to obey" (Acts 16:4). Their direction of travel at this stage of their journey came under the control of the Holy Spirit, the Spirit of Jesus, and a visionary figure, the "man of Macedonia" (see Acts 16:6-9). They headed to the port city of Troas in the northwestern corner of Asia Minor where Luke, the author of *The Book of Acts*, apparently joined them. The famous "we" passages indicating Luke's personal involvement begin at Troas.

From Troas the small group sailed to Neapolis in Macedonia and then moved overland to the Roman colony of Philippi. Luke mentions the visit to Philippi primarily because of Paul's encounter with a slave girl, "who had a spirit by which she predicted the future" (Acts 16:16). In some respects the incident is similar to Paul and Barnabas's earlier one with the sorcerer, Bar-Jesus. Both disrupted Paul's efforts, but the slave girl, at least on the surface, seemed to support him. She kept following him around and shouting out: " 'These men are servants of the Most High God, who are telling you the way to be saved' " (Acts 16:17). Such an endorsement might appear helpful, but, as in the case of Bar-Jesus, Paul was more concerned with an underlying problem.

Paul became "troubled" and cast the spirit out of the girl in the name of Jesus Christ. His objection was the source of the girl's "future-predicting" or "soothsaying" power, not the message itself. That source was a spirit of "divination" (see KJV, Acts 16:16), i.e. an evil spirit opposed to the true God, which traced back to the cult of Apollo for its authority. As an opposing force, divination is very similar to sorcery. It is distinct, however, in that it focuses on speaking out or foretelling the future. This sort of opposition was particularly troubling to Paul and Silas, given their own mission of speaking out or prophesying the DIVINE truth.

Prophecy (from the Greek *profaytiah*) emanates from the true God and concerns the speaking out of His WILL. Divination, by contrast, is the speaking out or foretelling of something for man's own purposes. It is powered by either total deception or by spirits in opposition to God. Paul and Silas were well aware of this distinction and acted accordingly.

Owners of the slave girl realized that the loss of the divining spirit meant the loss of a source of income, since she could no longer be used for telling fortunes. They hauled Paul and Silas before the local magistrates who ordered that they be flogged and thrown into prison. In a scene reminiscent of Peter's imprisonment at Jerusalem, they were put in "the inner cell" and their feet were fastened in stocks to provide extra security. Once again there was direct intervention to free Paul and Silas, but in their case it took a less personal form than Peter's angelic visitation. "Suddenly there was such a violent earthquake that the foundations of the prison were shaken. At once all the prison doors flew open, and everybody's chains came loose" (Acts 16:26).

Some might conclude that Luke is describing a fortuitous natural event that resulted in *all* the prison doors flying open and *everybody's* chains coming loose. Perhaps, but earthquakes are much better known for massive, indiscriminate destruction. A "natural" one sufficiently strong to shake the foundations of the prison would likely not be selective enough to go about opening doors, loosening chains and injuring no one.

As is so often the case in New Testament writings, there is an ironic twist to the ending of the imprisonment story at Philippi. The jailer in charge of Paul and Silas and his entire family (or household) became Christian believers and were baptized! The description of how this occurred is an extremely concise rendering of the doctrine of salvation, which had only recently been agreed upon at the Council of Jerusalem. The jailer asked: " 'Sirs, what must I do to be saved?'" Paul and Silas answered simply: " ' Believe in the lord Jesus, and you will be saved—you and your household.'" (Acts 16:30,31) The inclusion of "your household," incidentally, does not imply that salvation on their part was a direct result of the jailer's personal belief, but rather an indirect result of him introducing the requirements for salvation to his family.

Traveling westward on the Egnatian Way, Paul and Silas passed through Amphipolis and Apollonia and stopped at Thessalonica, capital of the province of Macedonia. Thessalonica was a large city (approx. 200,000) with a Jewish population of sufficient size to support a synagogue. Paul spoke at the synagogue on three Sabbath days, attempting to reason with the Jews from Scripture that Jesus was the long-anticipated Messiah. Specifically, he attempted to explain and prove that, "the Messiah had to suffer and rise from the dead" to provide for their salvation (Acts 17:3).

Response to Paul's message was good, but as on previous occasions some of the Jews became "jealous" of his success. They instigated a riot in the city and searched for Paul and Silas, but were unable to find them. That same evening the two evangelists who, according to their Thessalonian accusers, had "caused trouble all over the world" escaped westward to Berea (Acts 17:6). Timothy probably remained in Philippi for a short period.

Bereans were said to be, "of more noble character than the Thessalonians" (Acts 17:11). Many members of the synagogue there received Paul's message and believed, as did a number of prominent Gentiles. Irate Jews from Thessalonica, however, followed Paul and Silas to Berea and began "agitating the crowds" (Acts 17:13). Immediately following the disturbance Paul set out for Athens, leaving Silas and Timothy in Berea. It may have been that Paul's intimate knowledge of Judaism along with his zealous outspokenness for Jesus caused some of his Jewish listeners (e.g. some of the Thessalonians) to focus their animosity on him. If so, it would have made sense for Paul to move on while others in his troupe continued the dialogue.

Athens, by its sheer prominence as a center of philosophy, art and science stood as a city of great potential for the Christian message. It was the birthplace of democratic governance and center stage for some of the greatest thinkers who had ever lived, including Socrates, Plato and Aristotle. It was ripe for a new way of approaching the metaphysical and a new way of thinking how man might relate to the metaphysical. Athens was both ribald and refined, proudly tolerant, and self-confident in its moral direction. "Little" Paul came onto this stage with a way of thinking and believing that would challenge to the core many of its ancient traditions and beliefs.

In Athens, as in most other cities, Paul "reasoned in the synagogue with the Jews and the God-fearing Greeks." His outreach to the Gentiles became more obvious as he went to the market place each day to speak with, "those who happened to be there" (Acts 17:17). Eventually, he became involved in a dispute with proponents of the two most popular schools of Greek philosophy, the Epicureans and Stoics.

Epicurean thought revolved around a sort of common sense materialism that considered the supreme good to be mankind's overall happiness. This could best be achieved through the avoidance of pain, and free will could be exercised to help achieve that end. By Paul's time its focus had become more sensual and hedonistic than originally conceived. Epicureans did not deny God's (or the gods') existence, taking what came to be called the "deistic" position of His (or their) non-involvement with man.

As an aside, it should be pointed out that in most respects the tenets of Epicurean philosophy live on in modern humanism, especially the deistic form that might be labeled "Darwinian humanism." Darwin did not attempt to disprove the existence of a Creator God. His basic premise is simply that God's direct involvement is not necessary to explain the development of life's numerous complex forms. Some have argued rather convincingly that Darwin's formulation of evolution by natural selection was theistically motivated. He was convinced that the derivation of earth's species was far too messy, inefficient and cruel to be the personal work of a benevolent God.[38]

Many proponents of Darwinian theory are perfectly satisfied with the possible existence of God as long as He (or anything that sounds like Him such as the "external causal agent" of the Big Bang) is not used to explain observable phenomena. Once God has been isolated in this manner, the preeminence of man and his happiness (however one chooses to define that) becomes totally logical. If God is so distant and impersonal, why in the world should anybody really worry about Him? And why not focus totally on physical human need and comfort?

Stoicism was almost the flip side of Epicurean thought. Its primary objective was self-mastery and self-sufficiency. This kind of control, as opposed to Epicurean indulgence, would result in an attitude of indifference toward pleasure and pain. Life's problems and difficulties, the Stoics believed, could best be handled by the application of pure reason unencumbered by human emotion.

Unlike the Epicureans, the Stoics held that all people are manifestations of the one universal spirit, basically a pantheistic view of nature. Since they believed all men are of the same divine spirit, Stoics arrived at some of the same moral imperatives as Jews and Christians, albeit from the opposite direction. They believed in brotherly love and coming to the aid of fellow human beings, ideas which are encapsulated in the Judeo-Christian "golden rule." Jews and Christians accepted this imperative as a function of being equal *creations* of a singular, personal God, not because they equally share in a divine nature.

The Stoics and Epicureans invited Paul to explain his new and foreign philosophy at a meeting of the Areopagus, essentially a city council concerned with the internal religious affairs of Athens. As noted earlier, when Paul preached the Gospel to Jewish audiences he typically used Old Testament Scripture as a common point of reference. And when dealing with Gentiles, such as the Athenians who were steeped in Hellenistic philosophy, he used their general acceptance of theism as a point of contact. The body of his address to the Areopagus, however, drew sharp contrasts between the Jewish Messiah who brings salvation and the Greek philosophical constructs of God.

" 'The God who made the world and everything in it is the Lord of heaven and earth and does not live in temples built by hands'" (Acts 17:24). His opening sentence distinguished God as the Creator who stands apart from His creation, and is sovereign over it. This God was not pantheistic as the Stoics envisioned Him, and being sovereign over His creation implied significant personal involvement. " 'From one man,'" Paul continued, " 'he made every nation of men, that they should inhabit the whole earth; and he determined the times set for them and the exact places where they should live'" (Acts 17:26). This level of God's involvement was well beyond what virtually all his listeners conceived it to be.

But Paul took God's interaction with man still further. " 'God did this so that men would seek him and perhaps reach out for him and find him, though he is not far from each one of us'" (Acts 17:27). Not only did God create man, and not only did He exercise sovereign control over man, but He also made it possible for man to relate to Him on a *personal* basis—for "each one of us" to find Him. Though his message was extreme in the context of philosophy then popular, it was not without Greek precedent. Paul quoted the beautiful line from the Cretan poet Epimenides (c. 600 B.C.) alluding to intimate relationship with God: " 'For in him we live and move and have our being.'" Likewise, he quoted the Cilician poet Aratus: " ' We are his offspring'" (Acts 17:28).

The Greeks of Paul's day drew inferences based on their philosophical systems that were in direct opposition to his teaching about God. Idol worship, in particular, was widespread among the Greeks, and it was completely unacceptable to Christian thinking and belief. Images of gold, silver, or stone were, " 'made by man's design and skill'" (Acts 17:29). In other words, idol worship tolerated the complete role reversal of Creator and creation. It was basically a stratagem by which man permitted himself to worship something he created (the idol), thereby paying homage to himself as creator. At the same time, man could go about feeling safe and secure because he had thrown at least some small sop to the "gods." The argument that idols were only representative of "greater spiritual beings" misses the point that the greater spiritual beings (gods) were also constructs generated by men.

Relationship with the DIVINE being of which Paul spoke has implications and consequences. " 'In the past,'" Paul went on, " 'God overlooked such ignorance [idolatry], but now he commands all people everywhere to repent'" (Acts 17:30). This is the great conclusion of the Christian message. Philosophy and mankind's insatiable thirst for knowledge is a good and noble pursuit. But ignoring the truth of the Scripture and its message of the Messiah results in a dangerous lack of knowledge of the most important kind—the Creator and mankind's relationship to Him. To turn from or "repent" of this headstrong, obsessive, self-gratifying fascination with making oneself the center of everything was Paul's plea to the Areopagus.

And why should they have listened? Because the great knowledge and capacities with which man has been endowed have further consequences. " 'For he has set a day when he will judge the world with justice by the man he has appointed.'" The man doing the judging will be Jesus, the Messiah of whom Paul spoke. And the convincing proof he gave the Athenians to accept his message was a monumental event that had transpired only about twenty years earlier. " 'He has given proof of this to all men by raising him [Jesus] from the dead'" (Acts 17:31).

Paul had given the thinkers of Athens a great deal to mull over. The idea of physical resurrection from the dead was especially challenging, even though most of them accepted the notion of an undying spirit or soul. Intrigued, but for the most part unconvinced, the Areopagus requested that Paul speak with them again. A few men did believe Paul's message, including one of the members of the Areopagus. Luke makes no mention of a second appearance before that body simply noting: "After this, Paul left Athens and went to Corinth" (Acts 18:1).

It was during his visit to Corinth that Luke writes of Paul's skill as a "tentmaker." There he met Aquila and his wife Priscilla who were also tentmakers, and he stayed and worked with them. For some time he taught in the synagogue, but the Jews opposed him and "became abusive" (Acts 18:6). Turning his efforts to the Gentiles, Paul received encouragement from the Lord (Jesus) in a night vision. " 'Do not be afraid; keep on speaking, do not be silent. For I am with you, and no one is going to attack and harm you, because I have many people in this city'" (Acts 18:9,10). It is likely that this promise of "many people" led Paul to continue teaching in Corinth for a full year and a half.

There is an interesting historical side note that the Jews of Corinth eventually mounted a "united attack on Paul and brought him into court" (Acts 18:12). Luke writes that this happened while Gallio was proconsul of Achaia, a period shown by archaeological evidence to have been A.D. 51-52. Thus, there is good reason to conclude that Paul's second missionary journey did not extend beyond this time frame. Upon departing Corinth Paul sailed eastward toward Ephesus and then on to Caesarea. He then "went up and greeted the church [at Jerusalem] and then went down to Antioch" (Acts 18:22).

Paul's Third Missionary Journey, c. A.D. 53-57

Paul spent "some time" in Antioch, apparently less than a year, before starting his third circuit of regions to the west. As on his second journey, he traveled overland through Galatia and Phrygia "strengthening all the disciples" (Acts 18:23). Moving directly westward, he came to Ephesus where he had stopped on the return leg of his second missionary trip. Paul had made the promise: " 'I will come back if it is God's will'" (Acts 18:21). Indeed, Ephesus did prove to be an important part of God's plan. Paul remained there for over two years, his longest stay anywhere as a missionary. Luke tells of the good work of Apollos at Achaia and Corinth while Paul was enroute to Ephesus.

As mentioned earlier, Paul's normal practice was to

teach first among the Jews and then carry his message to the Gentiles in any particular locale. Ephesus had a Jewish community large enough to support at least one synagogue. By the time of Paul's third mission, a number of Christian believers also resided there. The development of such nascent Christian groups resulted in Paul changing his procedure a bit. At Ephesus he first "found some disciples" (i.e. believers in Jesus) and ministered to them by baptizing them in the Holy Spirit (Acts 19:1). He then went to the synagogue and argued, "persuasively about the kingdom of God" for three months, which was much longer than usual (Acts 19:8).

Some of the Ephesian Jews became hostile to "the Way," a description that Jesus had used in reference to Himself, and publicly maligned it (Acts 19:9). Paul then began *daily* discussions with the general populace in the lecture hall of Tyrannus. Interest in the Way expanded, and Paul continued preaching, "so that all the Jews and Greeks who lived in the province of Asia [Asia Minor] heard the word of the Lord" (Acts 19:10).

Luke notes that, "God did extraordinary miracles through Paul" during his stay in Ephesus. Handkerchiefs and aprons that had touched him, "were taken to the sick, and their illnesses were cured and the evil spirits left them" (Acts 19:11,12). Such displays of power always had the underlying purpose of giving glory to the source of that power. Besides bringing comfort to the sick, it was a tremendous aid in helping Paul spread the word about Jesus.

Many were attracted to supernatural power and, as reported by Luke on past occasions, they desired to possess it (or at least the appearances of it) for their own purposes. This happened in Ephesus when the seven sons of a man named Sceva attempted an exorcism, " 'in the name of Jesus, whom Paul preaches' " (Acts 19:13). Seeing through their ruse, the evil spirit challenged them: " 'Jesus I know, and I know about Paul, but who are you?'" (Acts 19:15). Obviously the evil spirit had no fear of the seven sons because it knew they lacked real power and any real association with Jesus or Paul. Sceva's sons were engaging in a form of sorcery, using meaningless incantation to aggrandize themselves.

The sons-of-Sceva incident is another object lesson on the distinction between valid miracles and sorcery. Miracles are motivated by God's WILL, and sorcery is driven by the WILL of man. DIVINE power is behind miracles whereas no power (trickery) or evil power is behind sorcery. These distinctions become apparent in the conclusion of Luke's story. The man who had the evil spirit jumped on the feckless seven sons and, "gave them such a beating that they ran out of the house naked and bleeding" (Acts 19:16).

When the powerlessness of sorcery compared to divinely inspired, miraculous power became known to the Jews and Greeks living in Ephesus, "they were all seized with fear, and the name of the Lord Jesus was held in high honor" (Acts 19:17). Many who had practiced sorcery publicly burned their highly valued scrolls bearing magical formulas. "In this way the word of the Lord spread widely and grew in power" (Acts 19:20).

Luke further dramatizes the reach and power of Paul's work at Ephesus through another story, that of Demetrius the silversmith. As a businessman and leader of his trade, Demetrius was concerned that Paul's preaching was threatening demand for his product—images and shrines of the Greek goddess, Artemis. He argued before his fellow tradesmen that Paul's activity would lead to a loss of income, diminished status for the tradesmen, discrediting of Artemis and her temple, and a loss of the "divine majesty" attributed to her (Acts 19:27). The priority of Demetrius's concerns says a great deal about the importance of Artemis to the city of Ephesus and the province of Asia. She was a money-maker, made the artisans (and populace) feel good about themselves, and, lastly, she was a divine goddess who deserved to be worshipped.

What Paul had preached to the Areopagus in Athens was getting through to the people of Ephesus: "man-made gods are no gods at all" (Acts 19:26). Left unchallenged that kind of thinking could have had severe implications for the whole city, and especially for those directly involved in manufacturing the gods. As the crowd listened to Demetrius they became, "furious and began shouting: 'Great is Artemis of the Ephesians!'" (Acts 19:28). The crowd grew in size, seized Paul's traveling companions from Macedonia, and rushed into the city theater. Most of the people who gathered in the theater had no idea why they were there except, perhaps, to give voice to their feelings about Artemis. Paul was kept away out of his disciples' fear of mob violence. Excited Greeks in the crowd continued shouting their allegiance to Artemis for almost two hours.

Realizing his personal responsibility to Roman authorities, the city clerk (roughly equivalent to a modern-day mayor) attempted to placate the crowd. His line of reasoning—which worked—is notable for the faulty logic used in defending the supposed divine nature of Artemis.

> "Men of Ephesus," he asked the crowd, "doesn't all the world know that the city of Ephesus is the guardian of the temple of the great Artemis and of her image, which fell from heaven? Therefore, since these facts are undeniable, you ought to be quiet and not do anything rash" (Acts 19:35,36).

Essentially the city clerk was assuring the crowd that Artemis was the great goddess they claimed her to be because: (1) her image was revered by the people of Ephesus; and (2) their reverence for the image was widely known. The reasoning is completely circular and typifies the justification of any idol worship. People worship idols because they impute value to them. Idols have no inherent worth. The worship of some people is then accepted by others as evidence of the idol's value, thus reinforcing and perpetuating the worship. In the case of Artemis, special importance was given to the claim that her image (most likely a meteorite) "fell from heaven."

The clerk's surmise that the men whom the crowd seized had, "neither robbed temples, nor blasphemed our goddess" was correct (Acts 19:37). If anyone could have been accused of blaspheming Artemis, it would have been Paul, not his friends from Macedonia. The place for making such accusations would have been in a legal assembly sanctioned by Roman authority. Mob behavior, on the other hand, could have led to charges against the Greeks (especially the clerk) by Rome. In sympathy with the clerk, and with their indignation assuaged, the crowd dispersed.

Prior to the uproar over Artemis, Paul had planned to return to Jerusalem by way of Macedonia and Achaia, a considerable distance to the North and West of Ephesus. When the situation calmed down, he set out for Macedonia and then moved on to Greece, where he stayed for three months. Luke does not indicate exactly where Paul spent most of his time in Greece, but it was most likely Corinth. Some scholars have suggested that it was during this period that he wrote his most influential theological work, the epistle to the Romans. Paul changed his original plan of sailing from Greece to Syria (Antioch) upon learning of a plot against him. Instead of sailing east, he returned overland through Achaia and Macedonia and then by sea to Troas.

Paul and his companions stayed in Troas for a week. On the evening prior to his planned departure he spoke at length to a group gathered in an upstairs room.

Around midnight a young man named Eutychus, who was seated in a window, grew drowsy and fell to the ground three stories below. Luke, a physician by profession, was on the scene and writes that Eutychus "was picked up dead" (Acts 20:9). Assuming that Luke's evaluation was correct, what followed is the most low-keyed account of a resurrection recorded in Scripture.

Paul stopped preaching, went downstairs and put his arms around the young man. " ' Don't be alarmed,' he said. 'He's alive!'" (Acts 20:10). Is it possible that Luke was mistaken, and that the fall from the third story only knocked Eutychus temporarily unconscious? The very brief period between his fall and Paul's recognition that he was not dead does seem to leave this as an open question. Paul, for his part, does not refer to his action as a resurrection. He simply went back upstairs and continued preaching until daybreak. Other people present at the scene "took the young man home alive and were greatly comforted," but there is no mention of their astonishment at having witnessed a resurrection (Acts 20:12).

In order to reach Jerusalem by Pentecost, Paul and his companions bypassed Ephesus, sailing south from Troas to Miletus on the southwest corner of Asia Minor. His destination and timing were not a personal whim. Paul explained to the elders who had come from Ephesus to meet him at Miletus: " 'And now, compelled by the Spirit, I am going to Jerusalem, not knowing what will happen to me there'" (Acts 20:22). Not expecting to see the disciples from the region of Ephesus again, Paul sought to reinforce his basic message that both Jews and Greeks, "must turn to God in repentance and have faith in our Lord Jesus" (Acts 20:21).

Part of Paul's great attraction (and to some of his day, great repulsion) as an evangelist was his boldness in proclaiming what he called "the whole will of God" (Acts 20:27). He knew that he was breaking new ground for both Jews and Gentiles when he spoke of the DIVINITY of Jesus and the provision of God's grace through Him. Nor was he hesitant to warn the elders from Ephesus: " 'Even from your own number men will arise and distort the truth in order to draw away disciples after them'" (Acts 20:30). In other words, supposed leaders and overseers of the disciples would use their positions for their own purposes.

Of special concern to Paul, it seems, was the potential for church leaders seeking material gain to distort the message of Jesus. " 'You yourselves know that these hands of mine have supplied my own needs and the needs of my companions'" (Acts 20:34). Paul wanted to make certain that his listeners could not discredit his motives for speaking out passionately about his savior. He was not motivated by wealth, position or career.

From Miletus Paul set sail south and east. Passing on the south side of Cyprus, he and his companions landed at Tyre where they stayed with members of the local church for seven days. Several days later they reached Caesarea; here they stayed with Philip the evangelist and were met by Agabus the prophet. Agabus acted out a prophecy eerily reminiscent of the events leading up to Jesus' crucifixion. He took Paul's belt, bound his own hands and feet with it and said: " 'The Holy Spirit says, "In this way the Jews of Jerusalem will bind the owner of this belt and will hand him over to the Gentiles"'" (Acts 21:11).

Luke and others pleaded with Paul to stay away from Jerusalem. But Paul, like Jesus, was adamant about completing his mission and following the will of the Spirit. Finally, the group conceded that it was best that, " 'The Lord's will be done'" (Acts 21:14). Luke, Paul and several other disciples went up to Jerusalem and were given shelter by a man named Mnason, described as "one of the early disciples" (Acts 21:16).

Paul Arrested and Taken Before the Sanhedrin: Jerusalem, c. A.D. 57

Tile plaque at Jaffa Gate in center of western wall of Old City Jerusalem

Paul and his group were received warmly by the church at Jerusalem. The work of the apostles and elders was bearing tremendous fruit, as thousands of Gentiles and Jews became believers in Jesus. People who had previously opposed each other theologically came to believe in the same Messiah. But tensions over the implications of how their belief should be expressed in daily life continued to smolder. Many of the Jewish believers in Jesus mistakenly understood that Paul was teaching against the practices and traditions of Judaism. They were informed that, " 'you [Paul] teach all the Jews who live among the Gentiles to turn away from Moses, telling them not to circumcise their children or live according to our customs'" (Acts 21:21). Paul sought to set his Jewish brothers at ease by participating in the purification rites of four men who had taken a vow.

Apparently not satisfied with Paul's display of respect for Jewish rites, some Jews from Asia Minor seized him outside the temple and began shouting accusations.

" 'Men of Israel, help us! This is the man who teaches all men everywhere against our people and our law and this place. And besides, he has brought Greeks into the temple area and defiled this holy place'" (Acts 21:28). They were making two charges that may have been considered actionable by Jewish authorities: teaching "against…our law," and defiling the temple by bringing a Gentile into the court of Israel, i.e. closer to the temple than allowed by Jewish law. The latter charge can be easily dismissed, as it would have been virtually impossible to substantiate. Charges of teaching against the law were more substantive but false.

Upon a little closer examination, it becomes obvious that the Jews from Asia became incensed by something other than any actual breach of Jewish law. Paul taught that observant Jews could be good Christians. The single, relevant issue *within* Judaism separating the "party of the Christians" from the Pharisees and Sadducees was that of salvation. Jews belonging to the party of the Christians believed what Christ (and Paul) taught—that salvation was effected solely through Jesus and the grace of God. Jews not belonging to the party of Christ (such as the Jews from Asia) maintained that salvation was effected through adherence to the laws of Moses. Belief in Jesus as the source of salvation and as the Messiah was a *doctrinal dispute within Judaism*, not a violation of Mosaic Law.

Charges that Paul was violating Jewish law by teaching Jews to avoid circumcision rites and other customs were simply false. Most likely, some objected that belief in Jesus was blasphemous within Judaism because it necessarily implied that Jesus was God. That objection was the critical issue. But it could only be valid, and could only serve as grounds for accusations of violating the Mosaic Law, if Jesus' claims of DIVINITY could be disproved. The burden of proof rested with those bringing charges of a violation.

Jesus and his disciples had already given convincing evidence supporting His claims of being the DIVINE source of salvation. The fact that the evidence was not presented in such a manner as to forcefully overwhelm human reason and will did not reduce its validity. Nor did it justify the accusations brought by those Jews who were not members of the Christian party.

"The whole city [Jerusalem] was aroused" at the accusations bought by the Jews from the province of Asia (Acts 21:30). They seized Paul and proceeded to beat him to death. Acting swiftly, Claudius Lysias, the commander of the Roman garrison, moved to quell the riot by arresting Paul. The commander allowed Paul to address the enraged mob. His speech took place near the barracks in the Fortress of Antonia, adjacent to the northwest corner of the Temple Mount. Though it ended in near chaos and calls for Paul's destruction, it was an eloquent recounting of how a zealous Jew came to believe in Jesus as the Messiah of all mankind.

Unlike the first telling of Paul's conversion on the road to Damascus, Luke uses direct, first person quotations in the Jerusalem speech. Delivered in this manner it is even more convincing. Paul first established his *bona fides* as a highly educated, devout Pharisee who persecuted the followers of Jesus. He then gave a personal account of his stunning encounter with the resurrected Christ. Impressed by his story, the crowd grew quiet and remained that way until the explosive ending.

As they listened, many, especially the Pharisees and their sympathizers, may have had a sense of vindication about some of their own beliefs. Jesus was widely known to have died upon a cross, and was reputed by His followers to have risen from the dead. They also claimed that He ascended from the earth into heaven. The ascension part of the story was probably suspect to most since it was not required to fulfill Jewish expectations about resurrection.

Eyewitness accounts of the resurrected Jesus indicate that His body had been transformed from its natural physical state into a "glorified" form. But Paul's fully conscious experience of the resurrected (and ascended) Jesus was totally different from the glorified body of Christ that the other apostles and disciples had witnessed. Paul told the crowd: " 'About noon as I came near Damascus, suddenly a bright light from heaven flashed around me. I fell to the ground and heard a voice…'" (Acts 22:6-7). His companions saw the light and heard sound, but the sound was unintelligible to them.

Because the voice identified its person as " 'Jesus of Nazareth,'" Paul had no doubt that he was speaking with the resurrected Christ (Acts 22:8). As a Pharisee Paul accepted the doctrine of resurrection, but the person with whom he spoke was clearly not flesh, blood and bones. Jesus' only physical manifestation to him was as brilliant light and an intelligible voice. Still, the recognition of Jesus' person was so real and so intense that he considered himself personally commissioned by Christ as an apostle. Jesus' manifestation to Paul as light and sound supports the idea that resurrected bodies are no longer bound by the physical characteristics they have while on earth.

Presumably Jesus could have appeared to Paul in a more physically defined form as he did to Thomas (called Didymus). Paul's testimony that He did not suggests strongly that the resurrected body is transformed, and may or may not exhibit specific physical traits. Interpreting what resurrection may be like in this manner is consistent with Jesus' teachings on the subject. In his famous exchange with the Sadducees, who flatly denied any resurrection, Jesus corrected them saying: " 'At the resurrection people will neither marry nor be given in marriage; they will be like the angels in heaven'" (Matt 22:30). Angels are spiritual creatures that seldom manifest in the physical.

But there was a *non-doctrinal* issue that lay outside the bounds of Mosaic Law, and raised passions within the Jewish community. It became clear as Paul concluded his speech to the quieted mob that had seized and beaten him: " 'Then the Lord said to me, "Go; I will send you far away to the Gentiles"'" (Acts 22:21). With these words the crowd again immediately sought to kill him—not for a violation within Jewish law, but at the mere suggestion that salvation was possible *outside* or beyond it. Their passion, it seems, was fueled by the offer of salvation to a foreign people not under their law. Thus, the motivation for attacking Paul and the party of the Christians was pride and jealousy for the exclusiveness of the old covenant, rather than a legitimate defense of violations against it.

Jewish intolerance of Gentile salvation absent full conversion to Judaism indicates rejection of Jesus' teachings of a new covenant. Many who rejected what He said became defensive of the old covenant, and it appears that they simultaneously deemed the new covenant invalid for both Jew and Gentile. In order to preserve the status and privileges of the old covenant, some Jews (e.g. those from Asia Minor mentioned in Acts 21:27) sought to deny the new covenant to everyone. Ultimately, their denial stemmed from resistance to the new covenant teaching that the Mosaic Law was not adequate for achieving true salvation. Their rejection of Jesus led to impassioned and irrational accusations.

Paul's comments about taking his testimony to the Gentiles led to expressions of great grief and anger among the crowd. "As they were shouting and throwing off their cloaks and flinging dust into the air, the commander [Claudius Lysias] ordered Paul to be taken into the barracks" (Acts 22:23-24). In an attempt to discover Paul's identity and why the crowd was so upset, Lysias ordered that he be flogged. This would have been the same kind of brutal scourge that Jesus suffered had Paul not let it be known that he was a Roman citizen. Roman citizens were not subject to the scourge. Somewhat shaken at learning of Paul's citizenship, the commander released him the next day and ordered that the entire Sanhedrin assemble.

Still wanting to know why Paul was being accused, Lysias brought him to appear before the Sanhedrin. Rather than waiting for charges to be brought forth, Paul sought to assure the court of his innocence: " 'My brothers, I have fulfilled my duty to God in all good conscience to this day'" (Acts 23:1). For this comment Ananias, the high priest, ordered that Paul be punched in the face. Ananias's violent reaction was probably sufficient to make Paul realize that a fair trial, regardless of the charges that might be introduced, was highly unlikely. Following an exchange with the high priest about the blow he had suffered, Paul made a bold statement. It was intended both as a defense and as a means of reminding the Sanhedrin of its own doctrinal disputes.

" 'My brothers, I am a Pharisee, the son of a Pharisee. I stand on trial because of my hope in the resurrection of the dead'" (Acts 23:6). There is a beautiful honesty and irony in Paul's statement. He was aligning himself with the Pharisees in their acceptance of resurrection, while at the same time speaking out its greater truth—resurrection involved more than a corpse regaining physical life. Paul's "hope" was well founded in the resurrection of Jesus. But to deny that Jesus had risen from the dead, as many of the Pharisees did, was to deny strong evidence of what they believed. Paul's hope was in a kind of resurrection and salvation that could only be brought about by Jesus' divine intervention. Indeed, it was these further implications of resurrection—the ones regarding Jesus' claims of being the DIVINE Messiah—that were dangerous. As with Jesus, Paul's remarks could be construed as blasphemy.

His brief statement did prove inflammatory. The dispute among Sanhedrin members over the resurrection issue became so violent that Lysias ordered Paul to be taken back to the barracks at the Fortress of Antonia. A conspiracy to kill Paul developed quickly but was foiled by his nephew; this is the only mention in Scripture of any of Paul's family members.

Realizing that Paul could not get a fair trial before the Sanhedrin and that events could easily spin out of control, Lysias decided to pass jurisdiction to Antonius Felix, the Roman governor of Samaria and Judea. As a Roman citizen, Paul was entitled to the rights and privileges of Roman justice. Lysias determined that the accusations against Paul had to do with Jewish law, "but there was no charge against him that deserved death or imprisonment" (Acts 23:29). Under the cover of night and extremely heavy Roman guard, Lysias transferred Paul to protective custody under Felix, headquartered at Caesarea Maritima on the Mediterranean.

CHAPTER FOURTEEN

PAUL'S TRIALS

Roman aqueduct at Caesarea on the Mediditerranean

The Trial Before Felix, c. A.D 57

Paul's appearance before the Sanhedrin in Jerusalem was the beginning of an extensive courtroom drama dealing primarily with the jurisdiction of his case. Sanhedrin members, particularly the Sadducees, sought to have Paul returned for trial in their court. Roman authorities, beginning with Lysias, were wary of charges being brought by the Sanhedrin, and felt an obligation to give Paul protection and due process under their law. Lysias's letter of referral to Felix reflected this conflict of interests (see Acts 23:29). Lacking familiarity with Jewish law, Lysias acted promptly to serve Rome by moving jurisdiction, at least temporarily, to the Roman court at Caesarea.

A mere five days after Paul's transfer to Caesarea, a delegation of the Sanhedrin headed by Ananias presented its arguments before governor Felix. " 'We have found this man to be a troublemaker, stirring up riots among the Jews all over the world. He is a ringleader of the Nazarene sect and even tried to desecrate the temple; so we seized him'" (Acts 24:5-6). These were serious charges; first against the state of Rome for insurrection; secondly for leading a religious "sect" that had not been approved by Rome; and finally an offense against Jewish law (and God) for desecrating the temple.

Charge one was extremely dangerous for Paul since Roman authority was ruthless in stamping out incipient insurrection. But this charge was unsupportable and had little chance of gaining any traction as is apparent from Lysias's observations to Felix. The second charge also had possible serious consequences, but it too was difficult to validate. Ananias and his group would have had to demonstrate that the Christian "sect" was essentially unrelated to the Pharisee and Sadducee sects of Judaism. Charge three, desecration of the temple by bringing a Gentile into the court of Israel, was impressive as an oratorical point. This was obviously a matter of Jewish law and offered the greatest opportunity for the Sanhedrin to regain jurisdiction. Violent sectarian dispute within the Sanhedrin, however, is what had originally led Lysias to remove Paul from that court.

Because the charge of creating an unauthorized sect was spurious, and because it was so divisive of Christian and non-Christian Jews, it may be helpful to dig a bit deeper into its origin. The word "sect" is translated from the Greek *haheeresis* meaning a choice or opinion, especially a self-willed opinion; the term "heresy" derives from this same root. In portraying Christian Jews as members of the "Nazarene sect," Tertullus (Ananias's official spokesman) was attempting to distance them from the Sadducees and Pharisees, while at the same time suggesting that they were not genuinely Jewish. In point of fact, the three prominent sects (or "parties") of Judaism in Paul's time had the same common traditions and origin. There were, and always had been, doctrinal disputes between the parties but these were insufficient to deny common heritage. In other words, labeling Paul and his fellow Jewish believers in Christ as members of a totally distinct "Nazarene sect" was a legal maneuver with no real substance. Jewish believers in Christ did not then, and do not today, forfeit any of their ethnicity or tradition.

Paul's defense before Felix was straightforward and to the point. He had only recently returned to Jerusalem and would not have had sufficient time to mount any kind of meaningful insurrection. To the contrary, he argued: " 'My accusers did not find me arguing with anyone at the temple, or stirring up a crowd in the synagogues or anywhere else in the city'" (Acts 24:12). He admitted to being, " 'a follower of the Way, which they call a sect,'" but emphasized commonalities between the "the Way" (i.e. belief in Christ) and Judaism's other sects. " 'I believe everything that agrees with the Law and that is written in the Prophets, and I have the same hope in God as these men, that there will be a resurrection of both the righteous and the wicked'" (Acts 24:14,15). With respect to violation of the temple, Paul pleaded that he had been ceremonially clean and had not been involved in any disturbance. He added that Jews from Asia, the likely source of this charge, were not present at the trial but should have been to have any credibility. Paul summed up by challenging the Sanhedrin members who were present to state the crime of which they had found him guilty.

They had not been able to find Paul guilty of

anything. The closest they had come to an official verdict was the declaration by some of the Pharisee members: " 'We find nothing wrong with this man'" (Acts 23:9). They had wondered aloud that a spirit or an angel might actually have spoken to Paul. And they were willing to accept that his story of conversion could be true.

Felix, who was well acquainted with Christianity, almost certainly realized that the Sanhedrin had no real case against Paul. As a political expedient and a favor to the Jewish authorities, he adjourned the proceedings until Lysias could be brought to Caesarea to testify. Ostensibly, Lysias could have provided additional detail concerning possible infractions of Roman law. Most likely, Felix was simply buying time and hoping for things to cool down in his provinces. Nothing more is heard of Lysias.

Paul's Trial Before Festus, c. A.D. 59

Antonius Felix governed Samaria and Judea for another two years after Paul's trial and was recalled to Rome in A.D. 60. During his last two years as governor he kept Paul under house arrest in Caesarea, most likely in the Praetorium. Porcius Festus succeeded Felix and, at the insistence of the Jewish leaders in Jerusalem, promptly reviewed Paul's case. "When Paul appeared [before Festus's court], the Jews who had come down from Jerusalem stood around him, bringing many serious charges against him, which they could not prove" (Acts 25:7). Undoubtedly the charges were very similar if not identical to those brought before Felix. Regaining jurisdiction remained the apparent, primary objective of the Sanhedrin; but in reality their desire to get rid of Paul had taken a new turn. They wanted him transferred to Jerusalem, "for they were preparing an ambush to kill him along the way" (Acts 25:3).

Festus, seeking good relations with the Jewish

leaders, played into their hands. He asked Paul if he would be willing to stand trial in Jerusalem on the charges brought by the chief priests and Jewish leaders. Paul smelled trouble. He sensed that the Sanhedrin was still plotting to kill him, and he wanted to retain the physical protection provided by Rome. Paul still had many things to accomplish. Foremost in his mind was the directive he

I APPEAL UNTO CAESAR

"For if I be an offender, or have committed any thing worthy of death, I refuse not to die: but if there be none of these things whereof these accuse me, no man may deliver me unto them. I appeal unto Caesar. Then Festus, when he had conferred with the council, answered, Hast thou appealed unto Caesar? Unto Caesar shalt thou go". (Acts 25: 11-12)

"And on the morrow, when Agrippa was come, and Bernice, with great pomp, and was entered into the place of hearing, with the chief captains and principal men of the city, at Festus' commandment Paul was brought forth". (Acts 25:23)

In 58 A.D. the Apostle Paul, accused of having caused a riot, was sent to Caesarea to be tried by the governor. Being a Roman citizen, Paul demanded to be heard at the Emperor's court. He sailed to Rome from Caesarea's harbor. There he was tried and a few years later executed.
This hall may well be the "place of hearing" mentioned in The Acts of Apostles.

Plaque at the Promontory Palace, Caesarea National Park, Israel

had received as the Lord "stood near" him following his earlier encounter with the Sanhedrin. " 'Take courage! As you have testified about me in Jerusalem, so you must also testify in Rome'" (Acts 23:11). The opportunity to turn persecution into fulfillment was astounding and Paul immediately seized it. His response to Festus is famous: " 'I appeal to Caesar'" (Acts 25:11).

Festus granted the appeal, and in doing so put himself in a somewhat precarious position. He was referring a case to the emperor but was unable to clearly explain why he was making the referral. King Agrippa II, successor to his father who had been king of Judea, came with his sister Bernice to pay their respects to the newly installed Festus. Along with other business, Paul's case was discussed and Agrippa took an interest in it.

Agrippa, like Felix, was, "well acquainted with all the Jewish [and Christian] customs and controversies" (Acts 26:3). Festus convened a meeting of the high-ranking officers and leading men of the city, both Roman and Jewish, to further investigate Paul. It was not an official trial. As Festus explained to the assembly, the purpose for his bringing them together was so that, " 'I may have something to write [to the emperor]. For I think it is unreasonable to send on a prisoner without specifying the charges against him'" (Acts 25:26,27).

Paul's "defense" during the investigation took the form of a sermon on his Judeo-Christian beliefs. As before the Sanhedrin, he first set out to establish his credentials as a devout Jew. " '[The Jews] have known me for a long time and can testify, if they are willing, that according to the strictest sect of our religion, I have lived as a Pharisee.'" Zealous in his Judaic beliefs, Paul did " 'all that was possible to oppose the name of Jesus of Nazareth'" (Acts 26:5,9).

His opposition included trying to force Christians to blaspheme, putting them in prison, and voting for their executions. His mention of blasphemy is particularly interesting because it was the charge that had been used to convict Christ. Paul used it to execute Jewish believers in Christ and, if left unchallenged, the Sanhedrin would use it to put Paul to death. The specific, blasphemous offense in all of these instances was public acknowledgement that Jesus was the DIVINE Son of God.

Paul's central message to the elite assembly of Jews and Gentiles was a simple one. It was the story of his conversion—its third telling in *The Book of Acts*. And the focus of the conversion story is that Jesus is the DIVINE source of salvation. Paul knew that he was not guilty under Jewish law because the personal revelation of Jesus' divinity to him was not opposed to Jewish law, prophecy or teaching. " 'I am saying nothing beyond what the prophets and Moses said would happen—that the Christ would suffer and, as the first to rise from the dead, would proclaim light to his own people and to the Gentiles'" (Acts 26:22,23). Paul's references to the Messiah's suffering and resurrection include the Psalms and Isaiah (e.g. Ps 22; Is. 53; Ps 16:10). The Pharisees and Sadducees might challenge the genuineness of his conversion

Looking toward the Mediterranean Sea from the promontory on the southern end of Caesarea. Paul was likely kept under house arrest at Agrippa's palace on this site

experience and his scriptural interpretation of it. But they could not challenge the relevance of either to Judaism, and they could not honestly brand them as blasphemy.

Agrippa understood the force of Paul's arguments from both the Roman and Jewish perspectives. Following the interview, he said to Festus: " 'This man could have been set free if he had not appealed to Caesar'" (Acts 26:32). Paul's activities were clearly not a violation of Roman law. From the Jewish perspective, Agrippa was in agreement with Festus's earlier assessment: " '...they had some points of dispute with him [Paul] about their own religion and about a dead man named Jesus who Paul claimed was alive'" (Acts 25:19). In other words, Paul's profession of Jesus as the DIVINE Messiah was an intra-Judaic *dispute* and not a violation of Mosaic Law simply because one sect (Sadducees or Pharisees) claimed greater authority than another (Christians). Indeed, Paul was claiming the ultimate authority—personal direction from the risen Messiah.

Paul's Journey to Rome, c. A.D. 59-60

The final two chapters of *The Book of Acts* comprise one of the most exciting, detailed and harrowing of ancient sea adventures. Paul and other prisoners, accompanied by a centurion named Julius, set sail for Rome. They encountered hurricane force winds. They were adrift and battered by ferocious storms in the open sea until giving up hope of being saved. They were shipwrecked on the island of Malta for three months while Paul went about healing the sick. Finally, they reached Sicily and the Italian peninsula. "The next day the south wind came up, and on the following day we reached Puteoli. There we found some brothers who invited us to spend a week with them. And so we came to Rome" (Acts 28:13,14). Christianity had preceded Paul in that part of the world.

While awaiting trial in Rome Paul was allowed to live in his own rented house. Though under guard, he had relatively easy access to visitors. Shortly after his arrival he called the leaders of the Jews together and began explaining how he had come to be in Rome. " '…I was compelled to appeal to Caesar—not that I had any charge to bring against my own people' " (Acts 28:19). The Jews of Rome had not heard anything bad about Paul, but they wanted to know what he was teaching, " 'for we know that people everywhere are talking against this sect [Christians]' " (Acts 28:22).

Many members of the Jewish community did meet at Paul's house and he preached to them from morning till evening. His basic approach with this group was the same as he used in synagogues everywhere; he attempted to relate Christ to Judaism. " [He] tried to convince them about Jesus from the Law of Moses and from the Prophets" (Acts 28:23). As usual, there was some acceptance and some disagreement. And, as usual, there was a strong negative reaction when the inclusion of Gentiles in God's plan for salvation was mentioned. But Paul's extraordinary efforts and commitment to spreading the good news of the Gospel did not go unrewarded. He was positioned at the center of the civilized world. "Boldly and without hindrance he preached the kingdom of God and taught about the Lord Jesus Christ" for two years (Acts 28:31).

CHAPTER FIFTEEN

THE BOOK OF REVELATION:

FROM HERE TO ETERNITY

B-2 bomber flyover at airshow in Missouri

Introduction

We're little black sheep who've gone astray,
Baa-aa-aa!
Gentlemen-rankers out on the spree,
Damned from here to Eternity,
God ha' mercy on such as we,
Baa! Yah! Bah!

Rudyard Kipling: "Gentlemen-Rankers"

Kipling's rebellious lament about life as an officer in the British army provided the title and basic theme for a famous novel and movie in the early 1950's, *From Here to Eternity*. All three—poem, novel, and movie—seem to draw a connection between immoral behavior in this life and damnation in the next. Unfortunately, the connection was not clear enough for the characters to confront reality and change their behavior.

Kipling would have done well to examine the book of *Revelation* to learn what the "road" from here to eternity is all about. As the apostle John so eloquently and forcefully describes, it is a road of transition from the very familiar surroundings of this earth to a new, eternal state we can barely imagine. John guides and encourages us along that road, always reminding us that there is never reason to become despondent or unrepentant.

As with most narratives, including the four Gospels and *The Book of Acts*, the flow in *Revelation* is time sequenced. Christ instructed John to, "Write, therefore, what you have seen, what is now and what will take place later (Rev 1:19)." Because it deals with the conditions of Christ's church across a broad expanse of time (beginning in John's day), *Revelation* is highly regarded as both historical documentation and apocalyptic prophecy. Four basic interpretations of its contents reflect opinions about when specific events occurred or will occur relative to the time that John wrote of his experience.

Preterists, for example, argue that most of what John saw took place shortly after he saw it. *Historicists*, like the *Preterists*, take the historical viewpoint, but allow much more time (until the end of history) for the revelation to unfold. *Futurists* consider John's revelation primarily as prophecy about "end-time" events. *Idealists* pay little attention to when John's visions might play out. Their main concern is with the symbolic meaning of what he saw.

To some degree the basic interpretations of *Revelation* are mutually exclusive. A strict preterist interpretation is the most limited in this sense because it practically dismisses history beyond the first century A.D. as well as "the future." The other interpretations are more complementary and tend to reflect the interpreter's focus of interest as much as argument from historic facts. Multiple, well-developed interpretations not in direct opposition to each other are, of course, a great benefit to the reader. They add depth of meaning to the visions being revealed.

Though my personal bent is to give more weight to the futurist position, there is one aspect of that approach that seems to need greater emphasis. *Revelation* undoubtedly deals with the future from John's perspective, but it can be even more informative when viewed as going *beyond* the future. Towards its conclusion *Revelation* transitions the reader into a whole new reality, to a "new heaven and a new earth" (Rev 21:1) where the timeliness of "future" disappears. Pictures of that new reality—the metaphysical reality of eternal existence with the Creator—are its most exhilarating, demanding and rewarding disclosures.

Revelation as a Literary Piece

Though the greatest value of *Revelation* is not literary, it is worthwhile briefly examining its literary structure to help understand John's challenge in writing of his experience. The main plot of *Revelation* is the judgment of creation by the Creator and the transition of mankind into eternal reality. Beginning in John's own lifetime, the time-sequenced story line continues through the "end times" and into the eternal reality of the Creator.

Several interludes interrupt the flow of the main plot. They have two basic purposes: (1) to encourage the reader in contemplating the awesome subject of judgment from God's perspective; and (2) to reveal subplots that contribute to the exposition of the main plot. The subplots are almost freewheeling with respect to the basic timeline of the main plot. They can project all the way ahead to the end of the story (and into eternity) or look backward on history prior to John's time.

Movements back and forth in time and between the physical reality of earth and the metaphysical reality of God can be quite confusing. This confusion is part and parcel of John's enormous task of using the symbols of human language to represent an infinite, eternal reality in which it has no basis. Language by its nature is earthbound and is most effective in communicating about earthly phenomena.

Human consciousness depends on the Spirit of God and its own attributes (reason and emotion) to expand the symbolic content of language and to help bridge the physical-metaphysical gap. In effect John had to reduce his metaphysical experience to symbols in physical form. We, with the help of the Spirit, need to reverse that process, i.e. to interpret the symbols he wrote in order to share as fully as possible in his experience.

An Aside: The Physical, Metaphysical, and God

Generally speaking people tend to feel most comfortable with, and are most easily influenced by, things they can "get their hands on." Material things also provide other perceptual clues that confirm their realism. This is the world of the physical, the world of matter—and by way of its convertibility—the world of energy. Science devotes itself to the study of matter and energy and to the derivation of ideas, theories and models that attempt to

Painting inside the Church of the Holy Sepulcher, Old City Jerusalem

explain how matter and energy act and interact. In modeling the workings of the material universe, theories about how it came into being invariably bump into a roadblock called a "singularity." This is simply a point at which the model blows up and fails to give meaningful results. Most "Big Bang" cosmological theories, for example, extrapolate back in time to a condition of zero size in all spatial dimensions, infinite density, infinite temperature and infinite space-time curvature. Those are interesting conclusions, but does it really make sense to regress from a universe with measured, finite dimensions to a starting point that is immeasurably infinite? This sounds suspiciously like something arising *ex nihilo*. It also raises the conundrum of *how* the Big Bang was initiated.

Singularities are, in fact, an honest recognition by science of its inherent limits. When the limits are reached science simply acknowledges that its observations and logic (part of consciousness) have yielded apparently illogical conclusions. If this is true of physical reality, is there anything we can conclude about the metaphysical? One way to bridge this gap is to conceptualize the metaphysical as that which lies beyond the latest singularity. Shortcomings in the scientific explanations obscure metaphysical reality and result in it being "meta" with respect to our sensate-bound means of observation and cognitive proofs. Incidentally, the fact that man is constantly pushing the boundaries and attempting to solve the latest singularities is *a priori* evidence that metaphysical reality exists. However, it is a *non sequitur* to assume that man will eventually solve *all* the singularities that he constructs.

By definition an all-knowing being (God) would never confront a singularity. And it may be inferred that unless man were to become equal to God, he will always continue to bump up against them. This holds true in Christian theology regardless of how elevated man's consciousness may become because created beings—though capable of being perfected—lack the potential of becoming equal to God. In Christian thinking God is all-powerful and cannot replicate Himself *because* He is all-powerful. Logically, there cannot be more than one being that has *all* of anything. It is not a limitation of God's power to not be able to replicate Himself; rather, it is His own nature that precludes the possibility.

God provides any power that man experiences. When man's consciousness (including spirit) is perfected in metaphysical relationship with the Creator, it achieves the ultimate potential with which it was created. Man will enjoy unbridled intimacy with his Creator. This view of the distinctiveness of Creator and creation is antithetical to those of latter day scientist-philosophers such as Peter Russell. For example, Russell concludes that consciousness is not material, but is a fundamental constituent of a universe that has always existed.[39] Man and God are inseparable, he believes, because consciousness has always existed, and the highest form of consciousness (man) derives from it.

In summary, Christian theology recognizes clear and permanent distinction between Creator and creation. It also recognizes a distinction between the physical and metaphysical that is a function (and product or effect) of man's limited abilities as a created being. As has been true for many centuries, Christianity continues to encourage science to push forward the threshold of mankind's knowledge. That effort can proceed without limit and without threat to the truth of God.

The "Now" in Revelation

Any attempt at accurate exegesis of the book of *Revelation* depends on the point in time Christ referenced when he instructed John to write about "what is now" (Rev 1:19). If that point can be fixed somewhere along the timeline of history, it helps the reader ascertain when specific events revealed to John occurred or will occur. Most preterists argue that John wrote about his revelations in the early to mid A.D. 60's, during the latter part of Nero's reign. This dating is important to their interpretation because they consider much of what he saw, including the period of tribulation, to have been fulfilled with the destruction of Jerusalem in A.D. 70.

Church tradition and history, however, have consistently dated *Revelation* in the mid A.D. 90's, toward the end of Domitian's reign. John indicates within the text that the revelations were given to him while he was on the island of Patmos. It is widely believed that he was exiled there late in life, probably in the early A.D. 90's. If church tradition is correct, John could not have received his revelations nor written about them until many years after

Jerusalem had been destroyed. His prophecy, therefore, could not relate to its destruction and the hardships preceding the destruction.

It should also be noted that the preterist argument becomes moot if the SECOND COMING of Christ has not yet occurred. This is the case because most of the events described by John as happening in the future are closely tied in Scripture to the SECOND COMING. They are fixed in time as closely (some would argue more closely) with respect to that event as with respect to John's "now." Few would argue that Jesus' second advent on earth has actually taken place.

Besides providing a specific historical reference point, John's instruction to write about what he had "seen" and what is "now" has added significance. It led him to produce a fairly detailed record of: (1) how Christ's revelations were communicated to him; (2) how Christ appeared in the eternal state; and (3) what the material and spiritual conditions of seven churches located in Asia Minor were at the time of the revelations. Regarding the mode of communication, John testifies: "On the Lord's Day I was in the Spirit and I heard behind me a loud voice like a trumpet...(Rev 1:10)." Being "in the Spirit" describes a state of spiritual exaltation, not a dream. John's spirit (consciousness) was opened and elevated, i.e. made aware of a reality normally closed off to him. In effect, John's consciousness was used as a conduit for direct communication between the metaphysical reality of God and the physical reality of man.

Once in the exalted state John immediately encountered the exalted Christ. Though he describes Jesus, ' "like a son of man,"' the image is not that of the humble human John knew personally while on earth (Rev 1:13). "His head and hair were white like wool, as white as snow, and his eyes were like blazing fire. His feet were like bronze glowing in a furnace, and his voice was like the sound of rushing waters" (Rev 1:14-15). John encountered the glorified, DIVINE Christ who identified himself as such. "I am the First and the Last. I am the Living One; I was dead, and behold I am alive forever and ever! (Rev 1:17,18)."

Christ's immediate purpose in revealing Himself (and future events) to John was to rebuke, commend, instruct and encourage seven actual churches in Asia Minor. He dictated the contents of letters to each of the seven, (see Rev 1:11 and Chapters 2-3). False teachings had already crept into many local churches and there was widespread persecution of Christian believers throughout the Roman Empire. The young church, expanding dramatically in numbers, was in need of direction and support.

Many consider the seven named churches as also symbolic of the worldwide community of Christian believers as it moves through history. The church as a whole will continue to be threatened from within and without; and the words of Christ delivered by John to the seven churches in Asia Minor will continue to provide direction and support. Likewise, the revelations given to John about "what will take place later" provided great comfort and encouragement to the early church as it does today (Rev 1:19).

Time Out: On Timing and Time

Revelation, as noted in the above discussion of what John meant by "now," requires the reader to have a good sense of both timing and time. The distinction is not merely a play on words. "Timing" has more to do with historical reference; it is the manner in which we humans normally experience time. When we say "timing is everything," we allude to the importance we place on the sequential positioning of events relative to one another. Timing is extremely important in enabling us to organize conceptually. It enables us to measure change such as the passage of a day from sunrise to sunset and the passage of a year from season to season. On a larger scale we use it to measure the formation and development of the earth, and even the unwinding of the universe.

Timing, then, is a phenomenal experience—each individual's personal experience of time. In Kantian terms one could say that timing is the individual's phenomenal experience of the noumenal reality of time.[40] We experience time as an "object" of our subjective conscious awareness—a process that limits the reality of the experience. Until recently there was almost universal agreement that time as everyone experienced it was a "constant" of physical reality, i.e. unchanging regardless of where or by whom it was experienced.

People experience physical reality from within the bounds of what scientists refer to as a "reference frame"; this is simply a means of specifying the extant physical conditions under which observations are made. The reference frame for all individuals on earth is essentially the same, and it is primarily for this reason that the constancy of time could be so widely accepted for so long. It should be noted that human consciousness is also essential for making meaningful observations about the physical universe. However, even though consciousness is "bound" to the physical bodies of humans while they are on earth, it is not an integral part of the reference frame.

The speed of light was also considered to be a constant of the physical world, and scientific experiments continued to support that conclusion. But the constancy of time began to be challenged, and a young patent clerk by the name of Albert Einstein put forth a provocative theory that the actual flow or passage of time changes depending on the reference frame of the observer. In his Theory of Special Relativity Einstein first made a connection between the "dilation" or slowing of time and the relative speed of the observer. As the observer accelerates time begins to slow in a non-linear fashion. The slowing process becomes much more prominent until the speed of light is reached where it becomes zero. Einstein later concluded in his Theory of General Relativity that time is also slowed by gravity. Physical bodies with great mass can have the same effect as accelerating the reference frame to the speed of light.

Predictions based on Einstein's theories withstood the rigors of scientific testing. Nevertheless, the everyday, phenomenal experience of time impresses us as an absolute reality. We still experience it as extremely real and unchanging. It seems counterintuitive that our actual experience of time could be fundamentally different depending on where we are in the universe and how fast we are moving. If time is not constant within the physical universe, what are the implications for that phenomenon (or noumenon) in metaphysical reality? It may be completely different experientially or it may not exist.

In conceptualizing the relativity of time Einstein imagined it as inseparable from space. Time in this sense is not a separate constant of physical reality; it is integral with space. Obviously a fourth co-ordinate and fourth spatial dimension cannot be graphically depicted very well in the three-dimensional spatial reference frame we experience most clearly and with such realism. To overcome this inability to adequately represent his ideas pictorially, Einstein developed mathematical models—pure symbolic abstractions of what he was attempting to explain. The abstractions, it turns out, are almost certainly a more accurate representation of physical reality than the uninformed experiences provided by human consciousness operating in the "normal," earthly reference frame.

The physical reality Einstein expresses mathematically could lie closer to Kant's vision of noumenal reality. As earthlings we cannot experience it directly. Phenomenal observations, however, can be made that lead us to postulate about four-dimensional space-time without being able to fully experience the expected result. For example, we can calculate that time comes to a standstill for an observer traveling at the speed of light, but it may be physically impossible for the observer to be accelerated to that speed. Though we may never be able to achieve the stated conditions of the calculations (actually attaining the speed of light) does not mean that the calculations are incorrect.

Incidentally, even if the stated conditions could be reached, we would still only be experiencing phenomenal reality, albeit an enhanced one. Our consciousness within any reference frame in this universe will always be limited by our sensate receptors and limited cognitive function.[41] This limitation is the crux of Kant's insight into the power—and restricted scope—of empirical science. His *Critique* does not preclude metaphysical reality, merely the scientific proof of it.

What are the implications of timing and time for the Christian belief system? Since the Creator is the definer of reality, we may infer that He exists "apart" or "outside" anything He has created. Thus, the Creator is not bound by any particular reference frame within His creation, and cannot be contained by dimensionalities of His creation. We should also recognize that our own reference frame causes us to experience time as we normally do, i.e. as a sequential chain of events rather than a fourth spatial dimension.

The great probability that time is not a constant and can diminish to zero in certain reference frames should give us pause when we consider it in a moral context. For example, the comfort that some take in assuming their own moral standards is usually based on the presumption that there is no accountability "after" this life. If our ordinary perception of time is not accurate, there may be no such thing as a period of time called "after," but there may well be a four (or more) dimensional existence.

When *Revelation* speaks of "a new heaven and a new earth" we have obviously passed from the physical to the metaphysical (Rev 21:1). It is always fun to imagine what role time will play in the new universe which Christ promises. When we enter there will we immediately grasp the spatial significance of the fourth dimension? Will we become "timeless" at that point, and if so, exactly what does that mean experientially? Will there be other spatial dimensions about which we currently have no clue?

Observational techniques as we know them today can only take us near the periphery of our own universe, and is blind to anything beyond it. But even our current reference frame provides clues of what life (and consciousness) with the Creator may be like. Consider once again that impressive though unintelligent machine, the computer.

Early in its history the computer was a clunky contraption of little computational power. As people grew more adept at telling it what to do and how to do it, they became startled at a consistent trend. The computer processed more and more information in less and less time: ninety *thousand* instructions per second (IPS) in 1971, fifty-four *million* IPS in 1992, zooming to fifty-nine million instructions per *millisecond* in 2008[42].

Interestingly, the only limitations on the machine seem be physical ones such as the speed of light (energy), resistance of materials and distance. Absent those limitations there seems to be no reason that the computer could not process infinite instructions in zero time. That, of course, is where we transition from the physical to the metaphysical. It is where we move from a concept of what man's limited intelligence, aided by his machines, can know about reality—to a very rudimentary concept of the power of *unassisted* omniscient consciousness.

Segue From John's "Now" Into the Future

In chapter four of *Revelation* John attempts to describe the reality of God in basically visual terms. Having translated the wonder of metaphysical reality, he then moves on in chapter five to confirm the unique stature of Christ ("the Lamb") to reveal the future about His creation. In dealing with "the future" we need to bear in mind that it is a time bound concept that is not impervious to Christ as it is to man in his physical reference frame. God and His Son have full knowledge of what the future will bring because they define what Kant refers to as noumenal reality. In effect, they *are* reality and can define any reality they create as they WILL.

There before John, "was a door standing open in heaven," and he heard a voice say, " 'Come up here, and I will show you what must take place after this'" (Rev 4:1). Clearly this is language using a description of physical change in position to get across the idea of transition out of the physical into another realm. At once John was "in the Spirit," meaning that his awareness was not diminished but increased, and that the "environment" he was experiencing had simultaneously and dramatically changed.

Human language has difficulty depicting a transition such as John experienced because it is constructed largely to communicate physical characteristics of sensate phenomena, particularly things we experience visually. Not surprisingly, John immediately fell back upon visual imagery in an effort to relate the eternal state of heaven and the presence of God.

He describes a "throne," symbolic of regal power, and "the one who sat there" (Rev 4:2,3). Interestingly, John makes little attempt to anthropomorphize God at this point; instead he describes God as appearing like the precious stones jasper (possibly diamond) and carnelian. Most likely he is not speaking of stones *per se*, but rather the brilliant light they refract and reflect. Additional light, "…A rainbow, resembling an emerald, encircled the throne" (Rev 4:3). Perhaps the brightness of the light coming from and surrounding the throne obscured any clear form of the One on the throne. Giving emphasis to the perfect spiritual nature of God, John saw seven lamps blazing before the throne. "These are the seven spirits [or the sevenfold Spirit] of God" (Rev 4:5).

Power emanates from the throne of God. John experienced this as flashes of lightning and the rumblings of thunder. God, the source of power, is not alone in heaven; He is surrounded by created beings. In the center, closest to the throne, John saw four living creatures with the appearance of animals, each having six wings and covered with eyes. These creatures are usually interpreted as representing a high order of angelic beings (cherubim). They are of particular interest not only for the power and wisdom symbolized by their appearance, but also because they, like man, are creations of God on the throne. John sees them in relation to God in heaven but certainly not as His equal.

This emphasis on the supremacy of God is repeated in John's witness that the four living creatures never stop saying: ' "Holy, holy, holy is the Lord God Almighty, who was, and is, and is to come"' (Rev 4:8). In other words, the most powerful of created spirits give constant recognition of their relation to God. He is separate from them (holy), all-powerful and uncreated; they are separate from Him and brought into His presence through His power. Constant recognition of the subordination of creature to Creator is shared by all creatures in heaven and is a key characteristic of relationship with the DIVINE. Those in God's presence say: ' "You are worthy, our Lord and God…for you created all things, and by your will they were created and have their being"' (Rev 4:11).

Then John did see something more human in form,

"the right hand of him who sat on the throne," and it held a scroll with writing on both sides and sealed with seven seals (Rev 5:1). Are there really such material things as scrolls in heaven? And why would God use such a primitive form of communication to reveal anything to John? There could be something akin to physical scrolls in heaven, but it seems more likely that God is using the imagery to impress information on John's mind in a manner that was familiar and recognizable to him. Scrolls were a part of John's everyday, earthly life.

Coming from God the scroll obviously had tremendous significance, but its contents remained sealed to John and all mankind. John wept because, "no one in heaven or on earth or under the earth could open the scroll or even look inside it" (Rev 5:3). "No one" in this context has the meaning of no created being. God on the throne, who had possession of the scroll, must have originated it and had full knowledge of its contents. One of the elders in God's presence then comforted John not to weep because, "the Lion of the tribe of Judah, the Root of David has triumphed," and is able to reveal the contents of the scroll (Rev 5:5). Lion of Judah and Root of David are Messianic titles referring to Jesus, and the strong implication is that Jesus' power is beyond that of created beings. Furthermore, because Jesus has "triumphed," it is most appropriate for Him to break the seals and inform John.

Shockingly, John's next image is that of a lamb, "looking as if it had been slain, standing in the center of the throne…" (Rev 5:6). But this was no ordinary lamb. It "had seven horns and seven eyes, which are the seven spirits [or the sevenfold Spirit] of God sent out into all the earth" (Rev 5:6). John often uses the lamb image as symbolic of the atoning personage of Christ. He writes of his heavenly experience, however, that he actually *saw* a lamb, one that bore the marks of being slain. In other words, he did not see Christ the man with whom he was most familiar on earth, but actually had the visual impression of a lamb in his consciousness. The lamb being slain is indicative of the crucifixion of Jesus the man.

This particular revelation of Christ to John is one of the most forceful, and at the same time, one of the most easily missed exposes of Jesus' DIVINITY and His union within the Trinity. Undoubtedly the Lamb shared in the complete power and knowledge of God, as symbolized by the seven horns and seven eyes. And not only was the Lamb alive, it was *standing* in the center of the throne. It had effectively taken the same position in the center of power as that occupied by the Father. The power and knowledge of Jesus in that position are the same "seven spirits" (or sevenfold Spirit), i.e. the Holy Spirit sent by the Father to continue the work of the Son on earth. All three personages are one, and all three *are* the center of power.

Shepherd at Nazareth Village, Nazareth

The remainder of *Revelation* chapter five is a beautiful paean to Christ the Lamb, the DIVINE Son who renewed relationship with mankind. Because of His status as man's redeemer, the Trinity revealed man's future and eternal destiny through Him. "He [the Lamb] came and took the scroll from the right hand of him who sat on the throne" (Rev 5:7). Immediately all created beings in heaven, represented by the four living creatures and the twenty-four elders, fell down and gave praise to the Lamb.

Their "new song" was a song of salvation. It rejoiced at the mighty work of deliverance and ATONEMENT achieved by the DIVINE Lamb who was slain. "You are worthy," the multitudes sang "to take the scroll and to open its seals, because you were slain and with your blood you purchased men for God…"(Rev 5:9). Then John heard *every* creature, those in heaven and on earth, sing of the power and glory of the one God: "To him who sits on the throne and to the Lamb be praise and honor and glory and power for ever and ever!" (Rev 5:13).

CHAPTER SIXTEEN

THE SEALS

Lion seal on manhole cover, Old City Jerusalem

Background: Revelation and Judgment—Physical and Spiritual Death

In the future times that chapters six through eighteen of *Revelation* describe, the separation between believers and non-believes in Christ becomes increasingly more distinct. Non-believers are afflicted with a series of "judgments"—encounters with physical destruction and death—and they grow ever more hostile toward believers. Most people today are uncomfortable with the idea of judgment. It has even become fashionable to be "non-judgmental" under the false assumption that any kind of judgment, good or bad, somehow opposes tolerance. But judgment is a necessary feature of human existence, and it is one of the primary themes of *Revelation.* In large part the seal, trumpet, and bowl judgments give *Revelation* its apocalyptic character.

"Judgment," in the moral sense, is somewhat simpler to define than it is to rationalize to human consciousness. Morality deals with thought and acting out conscious thought, specifically whether we *should* or *should not* entertain certain thoughts and act upon them. The inertial guidance system we use in deciding what we should or should not think about and do is integral to individual consciousness. Moral judgment is the exercise of that inertial guidance system.

Christianity considers God to be the ultimate source of moral guidance. The WILL of God Himself is the best guide in determining what to bring into consciousness (i.e. what to think about) and how to act. Given that God has full knowledge of all reality, it makes perfect sense to strive to emulate the Creator of reality. No one ever has a more optimal or beneficial answer to any questions that humans face than does God. God's answers are always the best and should always be followed. To the extent that we willfully ignore or directly oppose the optimal answer—what God would WILL us to do—we are disobedient and offensive to Him.

Disobedience to God is what Christians call "sin," basically nothing more than willful mistakes concerning moral issues. Sins are mistakes in the sense that sinners are capable of better moral choices. It seems ironic but man's ability to sin is largely a result of him being made in the image of the Creator. God created man's consciousness in His image but not equal to His own.

God, being all-powerful and all-knowing, cannot make mistakes in the exercise of His free WILL. He cannot violate His own nature and, in effect, sin against Himself.

Man was created with free will, but because he was created subordinate to God, it is possible for him to err in the exercise of his free will. This is not to argue that because man possesses free will that he *must* err, only that he must have the *option* to err. Our progenitors, Adam and Eve, for example, had the ability to always obey God, and they also had the option to disobey. If man were not capable of erring he would either: (1) be God, which he is not because he is created; or (2) not possess free will, which makes no sense if he was created in the image of God.

Once we recognize that man has the ability to exercise the gift of free will and that he can sin in the process, the question of *why* he would do so comes to the fore. Again, it seems a bit ironic, but it is most likely a function of his being created in the image of the Creator. It is very easy to seriously underestimate the enormous power of free will. Because it is so powerful, the self-consciousness of that power can lead to the misuse of it, which can lead to extreme distortions and illusions. Specifically, simply experiencing the power of free will often leads to the false presumption—and the false internalization within consciousness—that man's WILL is *the same as* that of the Creator (rather than dependent upon it). The tendency to make this presumption became so great since the time of our progenitors (Adam and Eve) that it may be accurately described as unavoidable. Man can resist and avoid sin but not completely.

We all lack the power, by sheer force of human WILL, to harmonize perfectly with the WILL of the Creator. This state of affairs is particularly troubling when we consider that God's judgment regarding *any* sin is that it is deserving of *death*, physical death and spiritual death (or death of consciousness). That seems especially harsh if it is true that sin cannot be completely avoided. Many argue that such a set of conditions is inherently unjust, inconsistent with the nature of God, and, therefore, untenable.

The Christian rebuttal is not only tenable; it is merciful and revealing of God's character. The ability of human consciousness to be totally in sync with that of the Creator was lost by our progenitors, and cannot be recovered by us at the exercise of our will. Since this condition applies to all humans, we may conclude that *physical* death is like a portal through which we must all pass or transition we must all make. It is God's judgment—which we can think of as a moral decision on His part—that we must all undergo this very negative experience. In effect, the will of the Creator is unmistakably signaling its absolute supremacy to the will of His creation.

Thankfully, the Creator's justice extends beyond physical death, which is best viewed as a temporary or first death. Physical death was God's judgment on *mankind as a group*. It is a result of the disobedience of our progenitors that resulted in a defect of spirit. And that defect of spirit was passed down to us, much as physical defects are passed genetically to succeeding generations. Each *individual* person is given the choice—and can exercise his or her individual will—whether or not to accept Christ and eternal life.

As described above, individual people operating in the reference frame of time, have the "opportunity" of witnessing the very negative effects of disobedience, i.e. temporal death. They experience its destructive effects first hand. As individuals, however, they need not suffer the most dire consequences of disobedience. The choice to seek salvation from the worst consequences of sin is made by individual people. It is also made in the reference frame of time, and its consequences go beyond time into eternity.

In summary, we may conclude that as a result of the sin of our progenitors we must leave a reference frame that is temporal—we must die. But it is *each individual's unforgiven sin* that results in the horrible consequences of the second death, HELL. That tragic condition can be thought of as having to leave the Creator's reference frame, and surrendering the (partial) sharing of consciousness with Him. Incidentally, the negative consequences of our progenitors' sinful act of will could not be *reversed* at their will. The same holds true for our own individual sin. Only an act of DIVINE WILL—DIVINE forgiveness or ATONEMENT—can eliminate the consequences.

When contemplating the judgments laid out in *Revelation* and the seeming unfairness, injustice and cruelty of the end times, bear in mind the end of the story. For some, physical death is the first judgment, followed by evaluation of their lives on earth and eternal sharing with the Creator. For others the first judgment is followed by a second judgment at the Great White Throne and a second, spiritual death resulting in the elimination of relationship with the Creator. The difference between the two is the *personal* acceptance of forgiveness of the DIVINE personage of Jesus.

The "Future" As Experienced by John

John devotes more than half of *Revelation* (chapters 6-18) to that period of time between the receipt of his prophecy and the SECOND COMING of Christ to earth. It is within this time frame that the sharpest differences between historicist and futurist interpretations arise. Historicists consider much of what is described to have already taken place, whereas futurists focus on these events as eschatological, or dealing with the future end times of earth's history. For example, historicists often view the travails of Christ's church under the domination of Roman Catholicism to have fulfilled most or all of John's revelations for this period.

Befitting Christ's warning that it is not for man to know the exact timing of key events such as His return to earth (see Mk 13:32-33), many of the physical signs predicting them can be interpreted various ways. There is also reason to believe, as is true of much Biblical prophecy, that they may be fulfilled in more than one time period. John's prophecies in chapters 6-18 become problematic only if one concludes that they have been *completely* fulfilled. As will be discussed shortly, there is an end-times aspect of these chapters that is inescapable and that has not yet occurred.

Revelation, Chapter Six: The Lamb Opens the First Six Seals of the Scroll

Prior to Christ's return John foresees seven judgments that befall mankind. He describes them metaphorically as "seals" which protect the contents of the scroll handed by the One on the throne to the Lamb. The seals must be opened or broken by the Lamb before the outcome of God's creation can be revealed. In other words, the seals are events that must take place in the space-time universe before its purpose plays out and it comes to its end.

The events that the seals describe are actions initiated by the Creator as a result of His judgment upon His creation. Thus, the seals are referred to as "judgments." The seventh seal contains seven "trumpet" judgments, and the seventh trumpet contains seven "bowl" judgments. As an eschatological device the seven seals may be viewed as a continuous stream of judgmental actions that God brings about before the return of His Son to earth. The period of time during which the judgments described in the seven seals take place is referred to as the Tribulation.

Most interpreters consider the Tribulation to be a period of fixed duration initiated at a fixed point in time. Probably the single most important Scripture for establishing the duration of the Tribulation was prophesied by Daniel at the instruction of the angel Gabriel regarding the "seventy sevens" decreed for the Israelites (see Da 9:20-27). The last of the seventy sevens is usually taken to mean the seven year period preceding the return of the "Anointed One," i.e. the Jewish Messiah recognized by Christians as Jesus Christ. Daniel distinguished between the first and second halves of the final seven-year period:

> "The saints will be handed over to him [Antichrist] for a time [one year] times [two years] and half a time [six months]'"... "He will confirm a covenant with many for one 'seven.' In the middle of the 'seven' he will put an end of sacrifice and offering" (Da 7:25, 9:27).

John also confirms the length of rule by Antichrist (or the "beast") at three and one half years, (see Rev 11:2-3, 12:6, 12:14, and 13:5) and he fixes Christ's return at the conclusion of the second half of the Tribulation, which is also known as the Great Tribulation (see Rev 19:1,11).

Jesus, of course, did not specify exactly *when* he would return to earth, but he did establish the *manner* of his SECOND COMING—apparent to anyone with their eyes open. " 'For as lightning that comes from the east is visible even in the west, so will be the coming of the Son of Man. Wherever there is a carcass, there the vultures will gather'" (Mt 24:27-28). Since it is clear to the great majority of observers that Jesus has not returned as he said he would, we can conclude that the Great Tribulation has not occurred. Most also conclude that the full seven year period of Tribulation has not yet commenced.

Chapter six begins to make it clear that judgment is not something arbitrary, capricious or peevish on God's part. The reader begins to realize that it is something integral to creation—something critical to the whole enterprise. God's creation, which we usually think of and experience as the physical universe, is not a random occurrence. It did not happen by chance nor did it produce itself from nothingness. The universe is the handiwork of the Creator and, as such, it exhibits the purpose of its Creator in bringing it into being. Purpose or objective implies an evaluation of its fulfillment at some point by the one establishing the purpose. In this sense the "seals" that the Lamb opens telegraph God's evaluation of His purpose to the reader of *Revelation*.

If it is true that man is the only moral agent that was brought into being with the physical universe, does an apocalyptic ending to the universe make any sense? Physical creation, including physical man, is finite in all its dimensions. Sooner or later, it could be argued, the universe will come to its "natural" end. There would be no need for the trauma described in the seven seals, and at that point each person's spirit (consciousness) could best be judged.

This kind of analysis misses the point that creation is *sustained and empowered* by the WILL of the Creator. The metaphysical reigns over the physical and not the other way around as often conceived by man. In this sense the "natural" end of the universe must, of necessity, actually be a "supernatural" one—as was its beginning. In other words, nature as experienced by man was purposely caused by a supernatural power, and its purpose must be resolved by the same power. As we read of God's interventions in the first six seals it becomes apparent that His purpose, for the most part, has not been satisfied. God takes retribution against His own creation as He opens the seals.

"Judgment" in the normal sense of judicious decision making takes on the much narrower meaning of decision enactment—tribulation, destruction and death—in chapter six. It portrays actions stemming from God's perspective, unbounded by time, on what His creation has become in time. In effect, John sees into the future and writes about what God knows. Judgment in the "end time" periods (including the defeat of opposition following the millennium) is essentially God's concluding evaluation of the time-bound part of His creation (the universe). It should be added that Christ's ATONEMENT and the Great White Throne judgment are God's evaluation concerning the eternal aspects of His creation (man's consciousness and spirit).

God's judgmental actions—in the end times and historically—usually prompt a very important (and troubling) question from people who attempt to relate to Him: how is it even *possible* that the all-knowing, all-powerful Creator could produce something that He would decide is "unsatisfactory" and deserving of judgment? The most difficult admission for people to make in regards to this question is that *the only* part of our universe that could lead to God's dissatisfaction is humankind itself.

As far as we know, humans are the only part of the physical universe capable of moral distinctions and responsibility—the only part that has the WILL to resist His WILL. Thus, the "judgments" of God described in *Revelation* pertain solely to the exercise of the free will of man. The particular form that they take pertains solely to the free will of God. That their form may seem so "unfair" stems from a misconception of the Creator's perfection relative to the potential moral depravity of man.

John does not devote a great deal of narrative to the first six seals. The first four gained literary fame as the four horsemen of the apocalypse, and the imagery of horses of various colors is taken from Zechariah. Symbolizing conquest, most likely conquest without war, John first sees a white horse with its rider holding a bow. Most often this seal is viewed as a period of peace, i.e. false peace established by the rider who is often personified as the Antichrist. A second horse is of fiery red color and its rider was, "given power to take peace from the earth and to make men slay each other" (Rev 6:4). The initial period of false peace is followed by a period of violent revolt and warfare.

Black and gray (pale, ashen-green) horses and their riders are then revealed as the Lamb opens the third and forth seals. These are symbolic of famine and the pallor of death. The pale horse and its rider were given the power to kill one quarter of the earth's population—loss of human life on a much greater scale than that unleashed by the two "world" wars of modern times. The manner in which these first four judgments are enforced seems so commonplace in human history that they could hardly define the "end times." It will likely be their sheer magnitude that qualify them as DIVINE judgment.

Seal number five momentarily changes the focus of God's judgment. Caught up in the maelstrom of end-times judgment are people who come to accept Christ. When the Lamb opened the fifth seal John indicates that he saw, "the souls of those who had been slain because of the word of God and the testimony they had maintained" (Rev 6:9). The "souls" (spirits) of those martyred for their belief in Christ—possibly the martyrs of all time—manifested to John who was also "in the spirit."

John translates this metaphysical experience of sharing in the spirit of the martyrs as physically seeing and hearing them. They cry out for God to avenge their unjust earthly deaths. God's judgmental action in this instance is one of approval. He clearly distinguishes the martyrs from those receiving earthly judgment. Those whose physical lives were taken because of their belief in Christ are set apart. Each is given a "white robe," symbolic of the purity necessary to enter eternal relationship with Christ. Their eternal lives are secured. Justice has been achieved for them by their unyielding acceptance of Christ's ATONEMENT. Christ will determine their individual eternal rewards for their steadfast devotion. Justice (or vengeance) for their unrepentant murderers will be physical *and* spiritual death.

The martyrs' cry is an apt reminder of the connection between justice and judgment in God's consciousness. By His WILL one fourth of those remaining on earth at the start of the Tribulation are slain, and more destruction follows. Justice, the quality of being right or correct as determined by God, not man, is the outcome He desires. At the opening of the fifth seal, *injustice*, including the continued martyring of those who come to believe in Christ, prevails on earth. But in time (and beyond time), and according to His WILL, God will judge creation and achieve true justice.

Seal number six continues God's direct intervention in the judgment of His universe. On the timeline of eschatological events it occurs at the start of the second half of the Tribulation, marking the beginning of the Great Tribulation. The physical destruction that John witnesses is unprecedented and fearsome to the point of debilitating. Almost at a loss to capture its enormity, he speaks of phenomena such as the sky receding like a scroll, and "every mountain and island [being] removed from its place" (Rev 6:14). Earth's entire population seeks refuge from the terror. For the first time since the start of God's judgment there is widespread recognition that what is happening on earth has gone beyond the natural. People ranging from kings to slaves realize they are facing the "great day of their wrath…the wrath of the Lamb" (Rev 6:17,16).

Revelation, Chapter Seven: Looking Ahead to the End of the Great Tribulation

Prior to the opening of the last seal John provides an interlude in the story of justice come to earth. Having described the horrors of the first six seals, he seems to be providing the reader encouragement and assurance that the justice of God is true justice. John momentarily projects ahead to the completion of the Great Tribulation. His facility in being able to shift between various points in the future suggests the tremendous fluidity of time in the reality he experienced. The fascinating detail of the multitudes of people brought out of the Great Tribulation to share the joyful reality of the Creator warms the heart.

John is made aware that the judgments of the seventh seal must be held back until the "seal of the living God" is put on the foreheads of 144,000 servants of God (Rev 7:2). The servants are identified as twelve groups of 12,000 "from all the tribes of Israel" (Rev 7:4). "Seal" in this instance has the same meaning as the seven seals on the scroll, except here it represents God's protection for the individuals who bear it on their foreheads.

There has always been debate about whether the 144,000 represent actual descendents of Israel or, more generically, all believers who live during the Great Tribulation. Those who conclude that believers in Christ are removed ("raptured") from earth prior to the start of the Tribulation usually hold to the more literal interpretation. In this view the 144,000 are Jews who have accepted Christ and remain on earth as His missionaries. Their role as witnesses to Christ would fulfill the original commission of the Israelites, bringing the message of the Messiah to mankind.

The 144,000 servants of God are linked with those "who have come out of the great tribulation" (Rev 7:14).

John envisions the latter group as, “a great multitude that no one could count, from every nation, tribe, people and language, standing before the throne and in front of the Lamb” (Rev 7:9). They, like the martyrs revealed in the fifth seal, wear white robes, and they join with the angels, elders and the “four living creatures” in giving praise to God. Context strongly suggests that the efforts of the 144,000 helped lead the great multitude in white robes to commit to Christ. Obviously they have died and passed from earth, but their presence before the Lamb on the throne speaks gloriously of their eternal salvation.

Chapter seven concludes with another testimony to the pivotal role of Christ as the DIVINE Lamb who shares the power of God and extends eternal life to mankind. “For the Lamb at the center of the throne will be their shepherd; he will lead them to springs of living water. And God will wipe away every tear from their eyes” (Rev 7:17). These are words spoken by one of the elders in God’s heavenly presence to John, who was taken “in the spirit” to join in God’s presence. He uses the double metaphor of Christ as the Lamb-shepherd, where “Lamb” signifies God’s special role as ambassador to man, and “shepherd” is an ancient title for king. Both are at the DIVINE center of the throne.

The assurance John gives in Chapter seven that “multitudes” will be brought into God’s presence from the extreme stress of the end times raises an interesting question. Why would great numbers of people previously disinterested in Christ come to believe in Him under such torturous conditions? In one sense the end times are simply an intensification of all time that has passed on earth. Like other periods, the end times can be seen as periods in history when intelligent, conscious human beings make important moral choices. Christianity posits the basic choice as being between the deceptively attractive forces of evil (Satan and Antichrist) and the truly attractive, though non-compulsive force of good (the Creator and Christ).

Presumably, under the conditions of the end times the decision to follow Christ will be made more difficult than in prior times. In effect, conditions will grow so extreme that everyone will be compelled to decide for or against Christ within a short time span. The power—even "miracle" working power of the evil forces—will be almost completely uninhibited and very impressive. And the countervailing power of judgment against those siding with the evil forces will be confusing and terrorizing. This countervailing power should be helpful to those who have not yet chosen Christ since it belies the power of Satan. It will remain as evidence that he does not have ultimate control of the universe.

Into the confusing mix of the end times will come witnesses for the truth of Christ. They will continue to faithfully convey His message even under extraordinary conditions. The world's population will be pushed to its physical and psychological limits—facing the threat of death in God's judgment or at the hands of those being judged. Procrastination will fade as an option. And the powerful witness to Christ's word, in combination with the urgent conditions of judgment, will produce amazing results. The simple choice between Christ and his opponents will become patently clear, physical death looming as the stark outcome of *either* choice. John sees beyond this extremely unpleasant period of Great Tribulation in chapter seven. It (along with the millennium that follows) serves as a final test of those who WILL to be with Christ and those who reject His continuing offer of relationship.

CHAPTER SEVENTEEN

THE TRUMPETS

Revelation, Chapters Eight and Nine: Destruction Intensifies

Relief of the destruction of Jerusalem in A.D. 70; Diaspora Museum (Beit Hatfutsot), Tel Aviv University

Chapter eight begins with the opening of the seventh seal, the entree into a second series of judgments heralded by angels with trumpets. For what seems like "about half an hour" there was silence in heaven (Rev 8:1). This is a curious observation on John's part given that he was "in the spirit" and experiencing metaphysical reality directly. He seems to be using the time reference, i.e. the dramatic lengthy pause, as an attempt to convey the intensity of the reality he is experiencing to his readers. If so, the pause functions as a means of emphasizing the gravity of the additional judgments to follow rather than as an actual gauge of the flow of time. As suggested earlier, attempting to recount the metaphysical in physical terms is a daunting task. John's liberal use of the comparative qualifier "like" throughout *Revelation* hints at the difficulty he encountered in translating his impressions from one reality into the other.

Before the seven angels with trumpets announced their judgments from God another angel bearing a censer appeared. The angel offered incense "with the prayers of all the saints" before the throne of God (Rev 8:3). This action is indicative of communication between God and His creation, as is the angel's next act. Taking the censer filled with fire, the angel hurled it on the earth, "and there came peals of thunder, rumblings, flashes of lightning and an earthquake" (Rev 8:5). The angel's actions make it obvious that God interacts with His creation in both the metaphysical and physical realms. Only on rare occasions is man given a third-person view of this interaction. As witnessed here by John, God receives the prayers of His creation and also judges it.

The first four trumpet judgments impact mankind's physical *environment*—the earth, its solar system and the cosmos. With the sounding of the first trumpet, hail and fire mixed with blood were hurled upon the earth. One third of the earth's land mass was engulfed in fire.

Trumpet two unleashed more physical destruction. Something like a huge burning mountain, possibly an asteroid, was thrown into the sea. One third of the "sea," i.e. the oceans, turned blood red and became lifeless, and a third of the ships at sea were destroyed.

John saw the world's supply of fresh water partially destroyed in the third trumpet judgment. It resulted in a great "star" falling to earth, disintegrating, and turning one third of all rivers and springs "bitter." Extra-terrestrial creation was affected by the fourth trumpet judgment. A third of the sun, moon and stars, "was struck…so that a third of them turned dark" (Rev 8:12). This language may indicate that heavenly bodies will lose one third of their radiant intensity in this period.

Chapter nine of *Revelation* is a continuation of the trumpet judgments, the last three of which involve the demonic physical destruction of earth's *inhabitants*. As the fifth trumpet sounded John saw a "star" that fell from the sky to earth. This star is not a heavenly body but an animate, divine agent, probably an angel. The star opened the "Abyss," which is from the Greek *abussos* meaning bottomless or very deep. In taking this action the angel was releasing demonic spirits from containment, effectively neutralizing their separation from the physical and allowing them to interact with it. The Abyss (*Sheol* in Hebrew) is distinguished from HELL, which is a condition of eternal separation from the Creator.

Demonic spirits from the Abyss took the form of locusts and were given the power to torture humans with scorpion-like stings, but not to kill them. They were permitted to inflict pain for a period of five months on those without the seal of God on their foreheads. This is the only end-times judgment with a defined time span. Because they were sealed, the 144,000 "servants of God" were immune from the stings of these creatures. Presumably, those brought to Christ through their ministry would also be protected.

John provides a fairly detailed description of the netherworldly appearance and sound of the locust-demons. Unlike normal locusts that swarm with no apparent leadership or direction, these had a "king" over them, "the angel of the Abyss, whose name in Hebrew is Abaddon, and in Greek, Apollyon" (Rev 9:11). "Abaddon" translates as "destroyer," and this spirit's position as king suggests elevated status in the demonic realm. Some interpret Abaddon to be Satan, though the latter's name translates as "accuser."

The sixth angel with a trumpet released more demonic forces upon recalcitrant mankind. Four " 'angels…bound at the great river Euphrates'" were loosed to kill a third of the remaining population (Rev 9:14). Since heavenly angels are never spoken of as "bound," these must be interpreted as demonic spirits employed in the service of God. But the four angels do not do the killing themselves. They are apparently the leaders of an enormous number of mounted troops, also demonic spirits. John heard the number of these troops to be two hundred million, and he describes them in some detail. Grotesque in appearance like the locust-demons, they inflict death upon humanity with their mouths and tails.

At the completion of their gruesome slaughter more than half of humanity that entered the Great Tribulation will have been killed. "The rest of mankind that were not killed by these plagues," John grieves "still did not repent…" (Rev 9:20). The power of the WILL of man to resist God and continue in the pursuit of his own desires is borne out under the horrendous conditions of the trumpet judgments. We do have the solace of knowing that when John speaks of the "rest of mankind" not repenting, he is speaking of that condition remaining applicable to mankind as a whole at that time, not until the very end. Many, in fact "multitudes" we have been told, will be saved from the Great Tribulation—even from its last days.

An Aside: Destruction and Hell

Apollyon, the destroyer angel of the Abyss, takes its name from the Greek verb *apolloomee* meaning to destroy fully or to bring to complete ruin. Actions of the destroyer do not bring about annihilation or extinction, but result in total degradation, devaluation and loss of well-being. Destruction in this sense is the opposite of *construction*, which denotes the application of form and addition of value or meaning through a building process. Construction is similar to creation in the theological sense because it is formative, but creation has the much larger and more specific meaning of production and formation from nothing (*ex nihilo*). Only God is capable of true creation or annihilation; spirits that He empowers are only capable of constructive or destructive acts.

The primary motive behind earthly idolatry and apostasy is the inclination of human WILL to abrogate and replace the WILL of its Creator. This becomes a contest of wills in which people erroneously *assume* superiority. Such assumptions are a virulent form of narcissism that result in a completely distorted conclusion: nothing is greater than me. Narcissism at this level refuses the recognition of the individual's source of power and being as external to himself or herself.

By disowning relationship to its Creator, narcissistic WILL is left to its own devices and standards. Obviously this disowning of or distancing from the Creator can occur in various stages or degrees. Since the Creator's nature is to create, construct, and empower His creation, narcissistic WILL, which denies and opposes the Creator, progressively loses its ability to imitate His nature. It falls into rebellion and antipathy to creation and construction, and pursues this negative differentiation from the Creator.

One of the most fearsome aspects of demonic spirits is the destructive identity they have assumed through their exercise of WILL to separate themselves from their Creator. The internally generated impulse to break down, degrade and destroy characterizes their consciousness. Very possibly it also characterizes consciousness in the eternal state of HELL.

Revelation, Chapter Ten: The Angel and the Little Scroll

Chapter ten is the beginning of a major interlude that continues through the first half of chapter fifteen. Over this span of five and one half chapters John reveals a whole series of subplots that add remarkable depth and detail to the main plot of end-times judgment. His experience of metaphysical reality becomes both broader and sharper, and he moves back and forth in time as though it were inconsequential. John writes of an astounding string of experiences that paint a vivid and disturbing picture of the Great Tribulation. He encounters an angel with a little scroll; he is told of two mysterious witnesses; he observes wondrous signs and war in heaven; ominously, he sees vicious beasts rise from the sea and earth; and he experiences the Lamb and the 144,000 triumphant on Mount Zion.

Besides providing assurance and encouragement in the midst of judgment, chapter ten (as well as Rev 11-15:4) gives insight into the mystery of that judgment. Incidentally, the word "mystery" as used in the New Testament has a more specific meaning than it does in common usage. It refers to things that are obscure and kept secret, but has the added meaning that they can be made known to human consciousness *only* by DIVINE revelation.

John saw "another" mighty angel, not one of the seven sounding trumpets, come down from heaven to earth. The angel was holding a "little" scroll. Some assert that this scroll and the seven-sealed scroll in "the right hand of him who sat on the throne" are one and the same (Rev 5:7). Context and the special designation of this scroll as "little" argue against this interpretation.

John heard the mighty angel shout and "the voices of the seven thunders" spoke in reply (Rev 10:3). "Seven thunders" are indicative of DIVINE judgment and retribution. Apparently John was being given additional detail on the plight of those who continue in opposition to God. What is curious about this part of his revelatory experience, however, is that he was told *not* to write down what the seven thunders had spoken. It is possible that John gained insight into the eternal consequences of sin, i.e. some representation of HELL.

Then the mighty angel standing on earth took a solemn oath. " 'There will be no more delay! But in the days when the seventh angel is about to sound his trumpet, the mystery of God will be accomplished, just as he announced to his servants the prophets'" (Rev 10:7). The angel's oath taking speaks of the absolute certainty with which God's purpose—hidden in mystery but revealed in time through his prophets and His Son—will be fulfilled. A central part of that purpose is the judgment of mankind.

At this point John received what seem to be very strange instructions from the voice from heaven. " 'Go, take the scroll that lies open in the hand of the angel…Take it and eat it'" (Rev 10:8,9). In the physical world the angel's directions seem almost silly, but as part of John's "in the spirit" experience they are profound. This language commands John to fully assimilate into his human consciousness the truth, purpose and WILL of DIVINE consciousness. The content of the little scroll was weighty and "mysterious." John was required to absorb it completely so that he could prophesy "again about many peoples, nations, languages and kings" (Rev 10:11).

The precise meaning transmitted via the little scroll is not recorded. Given the context that "the mystery of God will be accomplished" in the last days, however, much can be inferred from John's reaction to what he learned (Rev 10:7). He took the little scroll from the angel's hand and ate it. "It tasted as sweet as honey in my [John's] mouth, but when I had eaten it, my stomach turned sour" (Rev 10:10). One has to ask how knowledge being revealed by God can be both sweet and sour to a devout believer in His Son. If one accepts the truth as spoken by Christ, it would seem that *any* further revelation about Him and His Father would be "sweet" and joyous.

Furthermore, if judgment is in fact the just consequence of God's righteousness, why isn't every believer's reaction to it a totally "sweet" experience? From the DIVINE perspective justice, judgment and love are integral. They are perfectly consistent in the mind of the DIVINE. Reward and the sweetness that accompany acceptance of the DIVINE WILL are attractive to human consciousness and easy to accept. It is only the retribution or punishment of those in opposition to the DIVINE WILL that seems unfair and "sour" from the human perspective. This sense of unfairness is a function of human WILL and cannot be completely avoided.

John's experience with the little scroll points to a critical aspect of the relationship between God and man. It is the exercise of human WILL vis-à-vis the DIVINE WILL that results in misunderstanding about the co-existence of love, justice and judgment in the consciousness of the Creator. Judgment and the resultant punishment may seem harsh and unjust to human consciousness. It usually considers them contradictory to God's love and mercy. But these thoughts and feelings are reflective of human consciousness, not the DIVINE. They are the indignant response of WILL that is capable of sub-optimal, erroneous choices and the stubborn, persistent defense of such choices.

Though "in the spirit" John retained the consciousness of a created human being. His—and all human consciousness that recognizes its own fallibility—still has a bittersweet reaction to DIVINE judgment. It is incapable of fully comprehending the perfect integration, consistency and simplicity of DIVINE consciousness. But it can acknowledge that it is faulty and that the DIVINE WILL is sovereign and perfect. With this acknowledgement comes the sweet sense of being forgiven of one's mistakes. Human WILL that rejects its own fallibility rejects the need for Christ's forgiveness. In doing so it usurps the position of DIVINE consciousness, persisting in its error and decrying the injustice of the infallible, perfect WILL.

This sense of injustice, in other words, is a product of the *projection* of error onto uncreated, perfect consciousness by created, imperfect human consciousness. In this manner imperfect WILL staunchly and desperately defends its own imperfection while it assumes the perfection of God. DIVINE judgment and punishment is just and consistent with a perfect, loving God. Humankind's narcissistic attempts to supplant God condemn it physically and place individual people in eternal jeopardy.

Revelation, Chapter Eleven: God's Two Witnesses and the Seventh Trumpet

Chapter eleven continues the interlude begun in chapter ten, and provides some fascinating detail concerning prophecy during the Great Tribulation. John was given a measuring rod and told to measure the temple of God and the altar. Bear in mind that the temple that existed in Christ's time had been destroyed. Also, keep in mind that John received directions from heaven to measure

Foundation stones of the western wall of the Temple Mount as viewed in the western wall tunnel. The foundation stretches eastward underground from the exposed Western ("Wailing") Wall or Hakotel.

the temple while he was "in the spirit." Obviously the temple he was told to measure did not exist in the physical, but was real enough in John's consciousness that he could actually measure it. This is another interesting example of his transitioning between the physical and metaphysical.

The direction to take a measure (a physical property) is a strong indication that the temple will have physical representation at some future time. And the following direction to not measure the outer court because it would be given to the Gentiles who, "will trample on the holy city for 42 months" establishes that time (Rev 11:2). It will be in the latter half of the tribulation period. The reference to "holy" city points to Jerusalem as the site of the temple. "Gentiles" in this context has its historical meaning, i.e. non-Jewish. But here it has the additional meaning of those who continue to oppose Christ and his message of salvation.

John was then given a verbal description and apparently some visual images of "two witnesses" who will "prophesy for 1,260 days," the same period during which the Gentiles will trample the holy city (Rev 11:3).

The two witnesses are interpreted numerous ways including more abstractly as the Spirit and Word of God, or more literally as prophetic archetypes such as Moses and Elijah or Moses and Enoch. Given the fairly large amount of personal detail about them in chapter eleven, the latter view of them as incarnate human beings seems more likely.

Throughout the Old Testament a minimum of two witnesses was required to validate or discredit another individual's testimony. These two are special in that they will not only bear witness to Christ, but they will also prophesy (or expound) upon what they have witnessed. They will also posses power over physical phenomena to help persuade belief in their prophecy.

Their power to cause extended drought will be similar to that of Elijah, and their power to strike the earth with all kinds of plagues will be like that of Moses. Their witness will allow the light of spiritual revival to shine forth in the moral darkness of the Great Tribulation. They are likened to "the two olive trees and the two lampstands that stand before the Lord of the earth" (Rev 11:4). Olive oil was the primary fuel used in lamps to produce light. During their period of witness they will be physically invincible, breathing fire on anyone who seeks to harm them.

Having learned of the work of the two special witnesses, John is told of their demise. The Antichrist or "beast," mentioned for the first time in *Revelation* at 11:7, will be loosed from the Abyss and will attack and kill them. Opponents of the two witnesses will show their great disdain by leaving their bodies unburied. The bodies will lie in the street of the great city, "where also their Lord was crucified"—a good indication of the location of their witness and the temple, i.e. Jerusalem (Rev 11:8).

"Inhabitants of the earth," a synonymous phrase for unbelievers, "from every people, tribe, language and nation" will rejoice at the death of the two witnesses (Rev 11:10,9). Their prophecy and actions will be as torment to unbelievers and their influence will be enormous. But even in the face of the powerful works of the two witnesses many will follow the lead of the Antichrist. Many will reject the pleadings and demonstrated power of the special witnesses provided by Christ. Unbelievers will continue to exercise their individual WILL to follow the beast.

The euphoria at the death of the two witnesses will continue for three and one half days. Then, writes John, "a breath of life from God entered them and they stood on their feet" (Rev 11:11). Of note here once again is the use of the past tense ("entered" and "stood") speaking of an event to occur in the future as though it has already taken place. It indicates the certainty of the event occurring in space-time. God completely understands His creation irrespective of space and time as we experience them. John shares in and bears witness to that metaphysical reality.

As discussed earlier, God uses physical resurrection as a *nearly* irresistible display of power to persuade belief. Those who will see the two witnesses raised to life will be struck with terror. But God's demonstration of power to unbelievers will not end with the resurrection of the two witnesses. He will raise them up to heaven as their "enemies" look on, and "at that very hour" a severe earthquake will rock the holy city killing thousands (Rev 11:12,13). The combined effect of these dramatic displays will result in many of the "survivors," hitherto implacable resistors of God's grace and mercy, to change their hearts and minds. They "were terrified and gave glory to the God of heaven" (Rev 11:13). This wording strongly suggests unbelievers' conversion and acceptance of God's WILL rather than some sort of tactical submission. Perhaps most astounding about the story of the two witnesses is the level of persuasion some will require to recognize the Creator.

With the partial destruction of the holy city the "second woe" (the sixth trumpet judgment) passed (Rev 11:14). John then heard loud voices in heaven and the seventh angel sounded a trumpet. Here the narrative flow gets a bit confusing because what John hears about has to do with world conditions *following* the Great Tribulation. In other words, he again projects ahead to a later point in the main plot. The sounding of the seventh trumpet, like the seventh seal, is an entrée into another series of DIVINE judgmental actions (the seven bowl judgments) that pick up in chapter fifteen. John's reference to "flashes of lightning, rumblings, peals of thunder, an earthquake and a great hailstorm" at 11:19 anticipates the conclusion of the bowl judgments at 16:21.

The loud voices in heaven spoke to John of a time when the kingdom of Christ will come to the world. John again envisioned heavenly reality and received a short recapitulation of end-time events. Verses 15-19 summarize the SECOND COMING of Christ, the final rebellion against Him, the Great White Throne judgment, and transition into perfect covenantal relationship with God as *faits accomplis*.

Of particular interest is John's description of the relationship with the Creator in heaven. "Then God's temple in heaven was opened and within his temple was seen the ark of his covenant" (Rev 11:19). This is an obvious allusion to God openly and fully relating to all those in covenant with Him—a condition that those who are earthbound have yet to experience.

John did not perceive God directly. What his consciousness was able to grasp was a symbolic representation of God's relationship with mankind, the ark of His covenant. It is clear that the ark that he saw was not the earthly copy made of acacia wood. More likely it was a non-physical representation of covenantal relationship discernable to John's spirit (consciousness) but not dependent on space-time for its existence or meaning. Like God Himself it could simply "be" apart from the created universe. One could conclude that John was given a vibrant awareness of perfected covenant with the Creator by being elevated "in the spirit" to the consciousness of the Creator.

An Aside: Heaven

The term "heaven" is used frequently in *Revelation* and has various shades of meaning. It is taken from the Greek *ooranos* the translation of which closely parallels the Hebrew *shawmeh.* Heaven was viewed by the ancients as including all existence not occupied by the terrestrial globe. Beginning on the earth's surface it was conceived of as expanding outward and upward in concentric spheres increasingly distant from earth. Thus, *shawmeh* could be used to signify the envelope of air in which men breathe and birds fly. It could also designate the space in which clouds float and, beyond that, the firmament that the stars traverse, i.e. the entire visible cosmos.

From his earthly perspective man saw heaven receding from himself in stages. The stage beyond the visible firmament or "vault of heaven" was conceived of as the "highest heaven" (see, for example Deut 10:14 and Ps 115:16), an expression representing the abode of God. Though contiguous with heaven conceptually—in the sense of higher or beyond the visible cosmos—the heaven of God was not conceived of as an extension of His created, physical universe. God's realm was defined by His presence and was not dependent on anything visible or conceivable by man to define its existence. God was and is the absolute reality.

Given this background it becomes fairly obvious that "going to heaven" implied a journey of sorts, but not a physical journey to an unimaginably distant place. Though moving away from the earth physically is suggestive of the transition to the "highest heaven," it cannot completely describe that ineffable change. The human spirit completes the journey by joining that of the Creator in a reality unbounded by the physical dimensions with which we are so familiar. This passage from earth to be with God in heaven is the one spoken of in Hebrews and Ephesians when Christ ascended following His resurrection. He "passed through the heavens" (Heb 4:14), "ascended higher than all the heavens" (Eph 4:10), and was "made higher than the heavens" (Heb 7:26, KJV).

From man's vantage point on earth's surface any movement *downward* was away from heaven and distinctly negative. *Shehole* (Hebrew) and *Hades* (Greek) are terms that describe the subterranean abode of the dead. But *shehole* was never understood to be a place of punishment, and is usually understood in Christian theology as a condition that all humans must experience.

The eternal counterpart to the heaven of God is not some place extremely deep in the earth. We are told that in the end times the earth and heaven "passed away," strongly suggesting that they will no longer exist (Rev 21:1). "Hell" derives from the Greek *ghehennah* and, like God's heaven, may be best understood in terms other than physical space and time. It is the *antithesis* of heaven—an eternal condition devoid of relationship with God.[43]

Revelation, Chapter Twelve: The Woman and the Dragon

As the scenes in chapter twelve unfold, it becomes obvious to the reader that John's view into metaphysical reality has expanded almost beyond comprehension. He begins experiencing a series of "signs," i.e. symbolic spectacles and events that have meaning beyond their own occurrence. The first sign that appeared in heaven was "a woman clothed with the sun, with the moon under her feet and a crown of twelve stars on her head" (Rev 12:1). Several symbolic women appear in *Revelation*. The twelve stars (suggestive of Israel's twelve tribes) along with subsequent description disclose this woman as a symbol of Israel.

Another sign immediately appeared to John in heaven—"an enormous red dragon with seven heads and ten horns and seven crowns on his heads" (Rev 12:3). Dragons are used symbolically and metaphorically in the Old Testament to depict the enemies of God and Israel, and that is the likely meaning of this apparition. The next verse (Rev 12:4) confirms that this dragon is the rebellious Satan who "swept a third of the stars [angels] out of the sky and flung them to the earth." Much is often made of the dragon's seven heads and ten horns, but the symbolism is actually fairly straightforward. They are indicative of earthly (and Satanic) dominion and power, with the heads usually interpreted as past worldly kingdoms and the horns as components of a future worldly kingdom.

Verse 12:5 jumps from the past when a child (usually interpreted as Jesus) was born, to the future beyond the Great Tribulation when the child will rule with an iron scepter. Mention is then made that the "child was snatched up to God and to his throne," a reference to Jesus' ascension to the Father following his crucifixion, death and resurrection (Rev 12:5). In making this observation John again bears witness to Jesus' DIVINITY. Christ raised Himself to heaven to be with God on "his throne," i.e. back to His position of DIVINE authority. Then, again looking to the future, John notes that the woman fled to a place in the desert "where she might be taken care of for 1,260 days," the second and most intense half of the seven-year period of tribulation.

The incredible expanse of John's view into metaphysical reality then becomes more apparent. He witnesses "war in heaven" (Rev 12:7). In other words he experiences conflict between spiritual beings, and the conflict is spoken of as contemporaneous with the "1,260 days" just mentioned. War erupts between angels led by Michael the archangel and angels led by Satan "the dragon." This scene is beyond comprehension and almost beyond imagination. It seems to be the stuff of some of the most phantasmagoric fairy tales of all time—and yet Jesus' beloved apostle reveals it as absolute truth. Satan and his forces are defeated: "He was hurled to the earth, and his angels with him" (Rev 12:9). This defeat is almost never interpreted as Satan's original, failed rebellion against God. It is usually construed as that point in time when his ability to accuse mankind before God is eliminated.

Following Satan's defeat John again projects ahead at 12:10 to a scene similar but not quite identical to the one described at 11:15. In heaven the emphasis is one of gratitude for Michael's defeat of Satan: " ' For the accuser of our brothers, who accuses them before our God day and night, has been hurled down [to earth]' " (Rev 12:10). At this point in the woman-and-the-dragon subplot Satan has not been completely defeated on earth. Heaven rejoices at his ultimate defeat, but the "loud voice in heaven" warns John and the reader that increased destruction and tribulation are to follow (Rev 12:10). Satan has been cast to the earth and he " 'is filled with fury, because he knows that his time is short' " (Rev 12:12).

Confined to earth, Satan (the dragon) pursues the symbolic woman, Israel. This is not an amorous pursuit in any sense but one spurred by rage and jealousy. Satan, God's opponent and the accuser of His creation, seeks to destroy any human who is or may become a confidant of his opponent. The text becomes even more laden with symbol as Israel is given "the two wings of a great eagle." She is taken to a place of protection during the days of the Great Tribulation, "for a time, times and half a time out of the serpent's [dragon's] reach" (Rev 12:14). Unable to harm Israel, Satan prepares to "make war against the rest of her offspring." John identifies her offspring as, "those who obey God's commandments and hold to the testimony of Jesus" (Rev 12:17).

Why might Satan be so enraged at people in relationship with the Messiah? We have all experienced jealousy to one degree or another. And it appears that jealousy in its full-blown, most vicious form motivates Satan's great animosity. The "woman" and believers in Christ have the promise of something that Satan, by an act of his own WILL, has irreversibly forfeited—sharing in eternal reality with the Creator.

Revelation, Chapter Thirteen: the Beasts Out of the Sea and Earth

As chapter thirteen opens, Satan—the dragon cast down from heaven in chapter twelve—"stood on the shore of the sea" (Rev 13:1). This is a foreboding picture. Satan, a powerful and furious evil spirit, is loosed among the nations of the earth. From out of the "sea," symbolic of the abyss (as mentioned at 11:7 and 17:8), John saw a "beast" come forth. The connection between Satan and the beast seems fairly obvious. Satan, unrestrained from contact with earth, unleashes another evil spirit to assist him in his malevolence.

John spoke of the "beast" earlier as the one who would attack and kill the two witnesses sent to testify about Christ during the Great Tribulation. It becomes clear as *Revelation* continues that the beast is a person vehemently and diametrically opposed to the teachings of Christ, one who attempts to displace Christ and assume His DIVINITY. His opposition is so complete that he is often referred to as the Antichrist. But the beast is more than a demon-possessed person; he is inseparable from the total world governance and apostate religion that he propounds.

"He [the beast] had ten horns and seven heads, with ten crowns on his horns, and on each head a blasphemous name" (Rev 13:1). The symbolism is very similar to that used to describe Satan the "dragon" at 12:3. An angel later interprets the meaning of John's symbolic vision in some detail (see Rev 17:8-14). The seven heads represent kings (and kingdoms), five past, one present (in John's time) and one future. Antichrist is an eighth king who "belongs to" the other seven, meaning that he will function as a secular ruler, but his greater purpose will be to "make war against the Lamb [Christ]" (Rev 17:11,14). The "ten horns" also represent kings; they have not yet come to power but will receive authority as kings for "one hour," i.e. for a short period of time (Rev 17:12). The purpose of the ten kings will be to give their power and authority to the beast.

Stacking symbol upon symbol, John notes: "One of the heads of the beast seemed to have had a fatal wound, but the fatal wound had been healed" (Rev 13:3). In the more generic sense this may simply be an indication of the tremendous recuperative power of the string of corrupt kingdoms, all seven of which are described as "blasphemous." Many, however, interpret the healing of a wound that "seemed" fatal to be the enactment of a deceptive scheme by Antichrist. Several later verses (see, for example Rev 13:12,14-15) suggest that Antichrist will attempt to win converts by staging his own fake death and resurrection.

Through trickery and the display of great power the "whole world was astonished and followed the beast" (Rev 13:3). Satan "gave" his power to Antichrist and men worshipped them both. People will become infatuated with the beast's power and will ask seemingly profound but rhetorical questions: "Who is like the beast? Who can make war against him?" (Rev 13:4). Questions such as these highlight a blatant misunderstanding of the origin and flow of power. *All* power originates with and flows from the Creator. The One who provides Satan and all his subordinates their power can easily war against them and defeat them.

John writes that Antichrist will be given great power and it will last for a specified time, the forty-two months of the Great Tribulation. Antichrist will have the power to "blaspheme God…and those who live in heaven…power to make war against the saints [on earth] and to conquer them" (Rev 13:6,7). Such power, especially the power to *conquer* the saints is somewhat puzzling. Why would God allow this condition?

In the end times, including the Great Tribulation and the Millenium, the bifurcation between those who accept and reject Christ will become more intense than at any time in history. By God's design the inhabitants of earth will be drawn with increasing power toward one of the two camps—toward Christ or Antichrist. The dichotomy between good and evil will be stark and the test for allegiance to either will be severe. Many of those choosing Christ will be required to give up their lives to validate that choice. And many of those siding with Antichrist will take the lives of Christ's saints as validation of their choice. All of these events will be empowered by the Creator, but with direct input from the WILL of individual men and women. *Revelation* 13:10 is a call for believers to acquiesce to the WILL of God: "If anyone is to go into captivity, into captivity he will go. If anyone is to be killed with the sword, with the sword he will be killed."

The split between those who will choose Christ and those who choose Antichrist has been known to God for all time. John equates those who will worship the beast with those whose names have *not* been written in the book of life "from the creation of the world" (Rev 13:8). Christ, the DIVINE Lamb, has known the outcome since he created the world. The choices of those in the end times, as in all time, are real and effective, but Christ knows them "before" they happen in space-time. This is a clear indication that Christ's reference frame, especially with respect to time, is not the same as that of man. He knows everything with certainty in the eternal present.

Satan and Antichrist will be joined by a second "beast," sometimes referred to as the third person of the "trinity of evil." John saw the second beast "coming out of the earth," where the word "earth" is probably another allusion to the abyss (Rev 13:11). The exact distinction John is attempting to draw between the first beast coming out of the sea and the second from the earth is not clear. He may be pointing to the earthly wisdom and appeal of the second beast as demonstrated by it having "two horns like a lamb" (Rev 13:11). Though he has the power and authority of Antichrist, the second beast will be deceptively gentle, attractive and persuasive.

Being lamb-like and a "beast" simultaneously is an obvious oxymoron that is used as a counter-figure to the Lamb of God. Lamb-like beast will use its power to perform "great and miraculous signs" to deceive the inhabitants of earth in the service of Antichrist (Rev 13:13). In other words, the second beast will use its power for the exact opposite purpose that Christ the Lamb used his power. He will purvey false religious belief in support of secular dominion instead of true teachings about Creator God.

Whether under the teaching of Christ the Lamb or the lamb-like beast people will still possess WILL power, the power to make meaningful moral choices. They will be able to accept or reject the displays of physical power—whether real or mere deception—as evidences of the true source of all power. And apparently these displays will be quite dramatic during the reign of the beasts. John writes: "He [the second beast] was given power to give breath to the image of the first beast, so that it could speak and cause all who refused to worship the image to be killed" (Rev

13:15).

Those who accept Antichrist and his "prophet" (the second, lamb-like beast) will be deceived in three ways: by sheer trickery; by failing to understand that the ultimate source of all power is God; and by failing to recognize that displays of physical power, of themselves, are insufficient evidence of DIVINITY worthy of worship. It is the complete message of the Lamb of Christ and His power to effect ATONEMENT that set Him apart from and in opposition to Satan and the two beasts. Displays of physical power demand the attention of man. But it is the "word" (as John refers to Christ) and the full assimilation of the word into human consciousness that offers eternal reward.

Even in the dire circumstances of the Great Tribulation there will remain the option of not worshipping Antichrist and rejecting the mark (or name) of the beast. The threat of physical death will not be sufficient to persuade everyone then living on earth to commit themselves to the spirit of the beasts and join in their distorted consciousness of reality. Some will submit to the power of the beasts and many will be martyred for refusing to do so. Given that physical human beings populate the earth *following* the SECOND COMING of Christ, some must refuse to accept Antichrist and escape death during the Great Tribulation. Incidentally, much has been written about how to interpret the "666" mark of the beast. Suffice it to say that whatever the locution of the beast's name may be, it is antithetical to Christ and His name.

Revelation, Chapter Fourteen: Previews of Mount Zion and the Second Coming

Following the revelations of deceit, suffering and destruction during the reign of Antichrist, John again sees images of great hope and promise. Before him were the

Lamb and the 144,000, "who had his name and his Father's name written on their foreheads," standing on Mount Zion (Rev 14:1). Some regard this scene as depicting the SECOND COMING of Christ to Jerusalem. Context, however, suggests that this is the Mount Zion mentioned in Hebrews 12:22, i.e. the eternal, heavenly Jerusalem. If so, Chapter fourteen begins with a leap beyond the end-times and final judgment into the new metaphysical reality of heaven. As mentioned previously, these shifts forward and then backward in time provide the reader with a sense of DIVINE control and certainty of outcome. John's narrative is more focused on relating the power and justice of the Creator than hewing strictly to a time line.

The heavenly throne scene of chapter fourteen is similar to that of chapter five. Salvation and its "new song" are again the theme, and in this instance there is special emphasis on "the 144,000 who had been redeemed from the earth" (Rev 14:3). The 144,000 are said to have "kept themselves pure" and to have been "offered as firstfruits to God and the Lamb" (Rev 14:4). "Firstfruits" can be variously interpreted depending on one's view of exactly who the 144,000 are and what role they play in end-time events.

John then experienced a series of three angelic visions that shift the scene back to the time near the end of the Great Tribulation. The first angel "flying in midair," i.e. visible to all, proclaimed the eternal Gospel to "every nation, tribe, language and people" on earth (Rev 14:6). In the midst of tribulation God will continue to shout out the basic message of salvation. " 'Fear God [and the DIVINE Lamb] and give him glory…Worship him who made the heavens, the earth, the sea and the springs of water'" (Rev 14:7). The Creator's urgent plea will be to join Him and reject the Antichrist.

A second angel then announced: " 'Fallen! Fallen is

Babylon the Great, which made all the nations drink the maddening wine of her adulteries'" (Rev 14:8). "Babylon the Great," symbolic of the world political-economic-religious system, (and perhaps an actual restored city representing its center of operations), collapsed. The time of tribulation was nearly complete. World order, such as it will be under the influence of the "beasts," will apparently slip into complete chaos as a result of the excesses encouraged by the system.

Specific consequences of yielding to Antichrist were then revealed to John by a third angel. " 'If anyone worships the beast and his image and receives his mark…he, too, will drink of the wine of God's fury, which has been poured full strength into the cup of his wrath'" (Rev 14:9,10). God's full wrath—HELL—is then described in some detail. *Revelation* speaks unequivocally of the existence of HELL, a condition that seems totally illogical to many non-believers. It is another paradox that will be dealt with separately, but at least two important inferences can be drawn here: it is an eternal reality; and those who commit to Antichrist will share in that reality.

The opposite of committing to Antichrist (and the world system) will be "patient endurance on the part of the saints." "Endurance" or perseverance, John explains, requires Christ's followers to "obey God's commandments and remain faithful to Jesus" (Rev 14:12). In other words, the continuing exercise of human WILL to follow Christ is required for salvation. It is not sufficient, but it is required even under extreme conditions such as will exist in the end times. The Spirit of God confirmed to John that those who die in the Lord (i.e. remain obedient to His WILL), "'will rest from their labor, for their deeds will follow them'" (Rev 14:13).

John's next vision previews the SECOND COMING that all earthbound Christians patiently await. There before him "was a white cloud, and seated on the cloud was one 'like a son of man' with a crown of gold on his head and a sharp sickle in his hand" (Rev 14:14). This is an unmistakable reference to Daniel's vision of the Messiah (see Dan 7:13). The "crown" or victory wreath is symbolic of the achievement of Christ's purpose and the defeat of His enemies. Given this context, one could conclude that the Messiah's following action speaks of the destruction of those on earth who oppose Him. "So he who was seated on the cloud swung his sickle over the earth, and the earth was harvested" (Rev 14:16). This interpretation seems a bit forced, however, since the harvest metaphor is not normally used in a destructive sense. Usually it represents an ingathering of bounty and may well have the meaning here of the assemblage of believers at the return of Christ.

There is little doubt that the grapes-winepress images John next envisions do speak of the elimination of earthly opposition. Two angels, one bearing a "sharp sickle" and another "who had charge of the fire" came forth (Rev 14: 17,18). The one in charge of the "fire"—symbolic of judgment—instructed the other to, " 'gather the clusters of grapes from the earth's vine, because its grapes are ripe' " (Rev 14:18). Then the angel swung his sickle and gathered the grapes into "the great winepress of God's wrath" (Rev 14:19). Lest anyone be confused about the grapes-winepress metaphor indicating physical slaughter, John completes the picture. "They were trampled in the winepress outside the city, and blood flowed out of the press, rising as high as the horses' bridles for a distance of 1,600 stadia [approx. 180 miles]" (Rev 14:20).

CHAPTER EIGHTEEN

THE BOWLS

Revelation, Chapter Fifteen: The Sign of Seven Angels with Seven Plagues

This brief chapter transitions the reader back to the main storyline of *Revelation* and is the entrée into the final series of seven "bowl" judgments. It is noteworthy in its own right for reinforcing and repeating three basic sub-themes: (1) the relevance of time on earth versus its apparent irrelevance in heaven; (2) communication between God and His creation; and (3) direct interaction between the metaphysical (God) and physical.

Chapter fifteen opens with John seeing another "sign" in heaven—"seven angels with the seven last plagues" (Rev 15:1). Presumably what he saw is symbolic because he knew that the angels represented additional tribulation without actually seeing the "plagues" at that time. Somehow he also knew that they represented the "last" of the tribulation. John's characterization of the plagues in this manner provides a good peg-point for eschatological sequencing. They are the "last, because with them God's wrath is completed" (Rev 15:1).

Given the context of the bowl judgments occurring

after the rise to power of the beasts out of the sea and earth (Rev 13:1,11) and before the return of Christ (Rev 19:11-16), along with the knowledge that Antichrist will be empowered for a period of forty-two months (Rev 13:5), some fairly precise inferences can be made. God's wrath will be completed during the reign of Antichrist in the three and one half year period preceding Jesus' SECOND COMING. The one variable that cannot be known with any precision by man is purposely kept that way by God: the exact timing of His Son's return to earth.

By this point in one's study of *Revelation* it should be apparent that time and timing do not have the same relevance in heaven that they do on earth. After having just fixed the time of the Great Tribulation on earth, John again envisioned a heavenly throne room scene. It anticipates the earth's future but he uses the past tense to describe the reality of heaven. "And I saw what looked like a sea of glass mixed with fire and, standing beside the sea, those who had been victorious over the beast..." (Rev 15:2) This scene is similar to those envisioned at 4:6 and 14:1-3 and, like those, seems completely disconnected from the flow of time on earth. In heaven there was celebration of victory over the beast, but on earth Antichrist had not even appeared—and has yet to appear almost two thousand years *after* John's vision.

As in the other heavenly throne room scenes there was also communication (i.e. sharing of consciousness) between God and His creation. Those victorious over the beast recognized and gave thanks for their deliverance. They sang the song of Moses who delivered his people from physical bondage and "the song of the Lamb" who delivered His saints from spiritual bondage. Their song *of* the Lamb attests to His DIVINITY because they sing *to* the Lamb and *about* the Lamb. They praise Him as "Lord God Almighty...King of the ages...For you alone are holy" (Rev 15:3,4).

The final verses of chapter fifteen speak of the opening of the "temple" of heaven and the emergence of seven angels—seven agents of God's final wrath upon the earth (Rev 15:5,6). These agents are not described as some impersonal force of nature but as creatures of God, "dressed in clean, shining linen and [wearing] golden sashes around their chests" (Rev 15:6). They were given "seven golden bowls filled with the wrath of God, who lives for ever and ever" (Rev 15:7). God, the highest conscious power, in other words, unleashed other conscious power from His realm to exert His WILL on the consciousness of men. As with all of the end-time judgments, God's involvement is personal and intentional. Interaction between Him and His creation seems as direct and intense as possible, without completely crushing the WILL of individual people.

Revelation, Chapter Sixteen: The Great Showdown Between Godly and Satanic Power

Monument at Yad VaShem Memorial and Holocaust Museum, west Jerusalem

"Then I [John] heard a loud voice from the temple saying to the seven angels, 'Go, pour out the seven bowls of God's wrath on the earth'" (Rev 16:1). This is the culmination of the seventh seal and seventh trumpet, the pouring out of God's wrathful power as though from bowls upon the earth. The judgments are horrific and seem to follow in quick succession one upon the other. Their injurious and deadly impact is aimed at those, "who had the mark of the beast and worshipped his image" (Rev 16:2).

It is worth a moment for the reader to contemplate God's seven final acts of judgment. Those in allegiance with Antichrist will suffer ugly and painful sores. The seas and rivers will become blood-like and unable to sustain life. Searing heat from the sun will become intense enough to "scorch" the flesh of Christ's opponents. Darkness will cover the kingdom of Antichrist, compounding the misery of his followers. The river Euphrates will be dried up in preparation for an assault by the kings from the East. And finally, the earth will be physically shaken and pummeled as it never has been in its entire history. The means of destruction will not be new ones, but the intensity and extent of God's judgment will have reached a climactic peak.

God's awesome display of destruction in chapter sixteen can be described as the ultimate "showdown" of power between Christ and Antichrist. Christ's power is complete and undeniable, and the power of Antichrist—absent the power that Christ allows him—is shown to be non-existent. It is not an "ultimate" contest of power in terms of sheer might. For example, the total destruction of opposition by "the sword that came out of the mouth of the rider on the horse [Christ]" is more impressive in that regard (Rev 19:21). It is ultimate in the sense of being a final opportunity for human WILL to choose between the power of God and the power of Satan. At this point in time (and at the end of the Millenium) the limitless power of God will be juxtaposed with the impotence of Satan. The correct choice would seem to be a simple one.

Perhaps the most remarkable knowledge revealed in chapter sixteen is the total devotion of those who choose to follow Antichrist. It is unshakeable and, based on John's description, comparable to those who choose Christ. And it is all the more remarkable given that the "showdown" of power is so totally one-sided. Christ has complete control and Antichrist is helpless to come to the aid of his followers or compete with God. Under these circumstances how is it possible for Antichrist's followers to be so completely duped, and so adamant in the defense of their obviously bad choices? And how does the DIVINE power over Satan's followers differ from the power Antichrist was given, "to make war against the saints and to conquer them" (Rev 13:7)?

Steadfast devotion on the part of the followers of Christ and Antichrist traces back to human WILL. It becomes obvious in chapter sixteen that Antichrist's followers use their WILL to deny their powerlessness, a powerlessness which they recognize for: "they cursed the name of God, who had control over these plagues, but they refused to repent and glorify him" (Rev 16:9). Antichrist demanded worship and that his image be worshipped. But Antichrist himself was not sufficiently powerful to *force* people to follow him, i.e. compel their consciousness to yield to his. Unlike God, he could not overwhelm their WILL.

Satan and Antichrist are, after all, nothing more than consciousness that has separated itself from its Creator and assumed its own superiority. By aligning with Satan (and his subordinate, Antichrist) people simply repeat the error of Satan—declaring themselves totally self-sufficient. The perversity and culpability of such people in the final days of the Tribulation is that they will become fully aware of their powerlessness, and yet continue to exercise their WILL to deny that fact and to continue assuming supremacy.

Christ's saints being under the power of Antichrist and Antichrist's followers being under judgment will be in similar, desperate straits. Both groups will suffer physical destruction as a result of their commitments. Both will also become aware of the greater power of God. But the saints will accept this reality while Antichrist's followers will consciously reject it—even cursing the superior power. The WILLful error of Antichrist's followers will thus be exposed by God's judgment. And the WILLful obedience of Christ's saints will be made clear by Antichrist's persecution.

Prior to the pouring out of the seventh bowl judgment John again saw further into the future. He envisioned demonic spirits being released and going out "to the kings of the whole world, to gather them for the battle on the great day of God Almighty" (Rev 16:14). The kings were being drawn to Armageddon from the "whole world," and special mention is given those coming "from the East" beyond the Euphrates (Rev 16:12). John combines the "great day of God Almighty" (the battle of Armageddon) with Christ's warning in the following verse that he will, "come like a thief"—a direct reference to His SECOND COMING (Rev 16:14,15). Armageddon and Christ's return exhibit the singular purpose of a singular God. The return of Christ will be thief-like in the sense that it will be totally unexpected, but it will also be unmistakably public.

God's wrath poured from the seventh bowl bringing the greatest cataclysm ever experienced by man on earth. The most powerful earthquake of all time split "the great city [Jerusalem]" into three parts and collapsed "the cities of the nations." Mountains and islands disappeared, and hailstones weighing nearly a hundred pounds each fell upon men (Rev 16:19,20,21). And from the temple in heaven "came a loud voice from the throne [of God], saying, 'It is done!'" (Rev 16:17). Judgment of man preceding the return of the Son of Man was completed. As *Revelation* makes clear, however, mankind will be given additional opportunity for salvation *after* the SECOND

COMING—and additional opportunity to rebel against the Creator.

Revelation, Chapter Seventeen: Antichrist's Rise to Power

At this stage in the narrative John recapitulates Antichrist's consolidation of political-economic-religious power, and gives insights into how that will be accomplished. Chapter seventeen begins with one of the angels who had the seven bowls describing the punishment of "the great prostitute who sits on the many waters" (Rev 17:1). Later in the text the angel explains that the "waters" are, "peoples, multitudes, nations and languages" (Rev 17:15). In other words the prostitute "sits" on or has authority over the world's population. This raises the question of what kind of authority or power she may have since the next verse reads that, "the kings of the earth [indicating political and economic power] committed adultery" with her (Rev 17:2).

John was then carried away "in the Spirit into a desert" suggesting a shift away from the throne scene in heaven to provide a special, negative emphasis. In the desert he saw the prostitute sitting on a scarlet beast, much as a horseman would sit on his mount. Joining the prostitute and beast in this manner is an obvious allusion that the two were working together for some purpose. The beast was none other than the one that rose from the sea in chapter thirteen, i.e. Antichrist. It was "covered with blasphemous names and had seven heads and ten horns" (Rev 17:3).

The prostitute was richly adorned and, as was common for prostitutes in the Roman Empire, bore an identifying band on her forehead. She was: "Babylon the Great, the Mother of Prostitutes and of the Abominations of the Earth" (Rev 17:5). It becomes clear from the next verse that this prostitute-Babylon was not the ancient city (which still existed in John's day), but a religious-philosophical system in opposition to Christ. "I [John] saw that the woman was drunk with the blood of the saints, the blood of those who bore testimony to Jesus" (Rev 17:6). The "wine of her adulteries" with which she intoxicated herself and the kings and inhabitants of the earth was the physical destruction or "blood of the saints" opposing her.

Nothing more is said of the prostitute herself until the end of chapter seventeen. Instead, the angel with John focused next on explaining the beast on which she sat. The angel provides two very similar but not identical descriptions of the beast in Rev 17:8. First the angel said that the " 'beast which you [John] saw, once was, now is not, and will come up out of the Abyss and go to his destruction.'" This wording is imitative of descriptions of God (see, for example, Rev 4:8) and may be intended to emphasize the spirit nature of the beast. Given that the time references are relative to when John had the vision of the beast, we may infer that as of that time the beast had not yet been released from the Abyss nor gone to its destruction.

In the second description (or second part of the description) of the beast the angel spoke in the future tense (relative to the time of John's vision) and noted that those, " 'whose names have not been written in the book of life…will be astonished when they see the beast because he once was, now is not, and yet will come'" (Rev 17:8). For those people the beast's release from the Abyss will have occurred but will not be apparent to them. Their "astonishment" (as described here and previously at Rev 13:3) will result from his "fatal wound" having been healed. They will be impressed by a physical occurrence: in their time they will experience that he "once was" (was alive), "now is not" (will appear to die), and "yet will come" (will appear to come back to life).

If the above interpretations of the beast's descriptions are correct, we can draw the following conclusions. Antichrist will be a demonic spirit released from the Abyss that will inhabit a human body and simulate a "resurrection" of that body. His simulated resurrection will be the antithesis of the real resurrection of Christ from earthly death to eternal life. There will be no actual resurrection and Antichrist will be condemned to eternal death.

Believers in Christ, whose names have been written in the book of life, cannot be impressed by the false resurrection of the beast because they will be knowledgeable of the true resurrection of Christ. In effect, for them the beast's resurrection will be too little and too late to be convincing evidence of DIVINE power. Believers will be on the lookout for the glorious, unmistakable return of Jesus as He described it (see Mt 24:27-30).

Much of the angel's remaining explanation of the beast (verses 9-14) has already been covered in the discussion of chapter thirteen. It should be added here, however, that the king who "has not yet come," represented by the seventh head of the beast from the sea, is most likely the physical person inhabited by the demonic spirit of the beast, i.e. the "eighth king" (Rev 17:10,11). This joining of the seventh and eighth kings is consistent with the angel's two-part description of the beast's physical/demonic makeup.

Toward the end of the chapter the angel concludes the explanation of relationship between the great prostitute, the beast and the ten horns (leaders in collusion with the beast). The prostitute will influence and have some control over the world's population. This is power and control to which the beast and his subordinate kings will also aspire. They "will hate the prostitute...[and] will bring her to ruin" (Rev 17:16). The beast will completely assume her power and that of the ten horns.

The angel also reiterates the absolute certainty of the outcome of the battle between Christ and Antichrist. The Lamb's (Christ's) victory is certain because his power is DIVINE or, as the angel puts it, " 'because he is Lord of lords and King of kings'" (Rev 17:14). Chapter seventeen concludes with an interesting lead-in to the following chapter, describing the "woman" (the great prostitute) as " 'the great city that rules over the kings of the earth'" (Rev 17:18). Having just disposed of her as a separate religious-moral force, John indicates that she (like the beast) will manifest physically. Babylon the *city* will come to represent the physical center of Antichrist's earthly power.

Revelation, Chapter Eighteen: Destruction of Antichrist's Earthly Realm

Chapter eighteen of *Revelation* is as transparent in its content as chapter seventeen is mysterious. John provides a detailed account of the enormous sense of material loss that accompanies the fulfillment of the final bowl judgment. Again, the destruction of Babylon is described with the certainty of a *fait accompli*. " 'Fallen! Fallen is Babylon the Great'" was the shout of the mighty angel from heaven (Rev 18:2). As suggested above, "Babylon the Great" likely has a composite meaning—a specific city representing the capital of a world federation, other cities across the globe, and the economic-political-religious rule of Antichrist.

A voice from heaven recognized the justice of God's full measure of retribution for the unrepentant. " 'Give back to her [Babylon] as she has given; pay her back double for what she has done'" (Rev 18:6). Her great error is that: " 'In her heart she boasts, "I sit as queen; I am not a widow and I will never mourn"'" (Rev 18:7). The essence of the Babylonian world system is defiant, arrogant self-sufficiency. It defines a monarch (queen) who boasts that she cannot be brought to the lowly dependence of a widow even under the desolate conditions of the Tribulation. Interestingly, the heavenly voice calls out to " 'my people'" under these same conditions to " 'come out of her [Babylon]'" to avoid her sins and judgment (Rev 18:4). This plea is confirmation that some of earth's inhabitants will physically survive the Tribulation without succumbing to Antichrist and Babylon.

All references to Babylon the "city" in chapter eighteen are in the singular, despite the quote from chapter sixteen that "the cities of the nations collapsed" as a result of the seventh bowl judgment (Rev 16:19). John uses the singular to focus on the center of power in the world system, its epitome of excess and moral corruption. Across the globe those enamored with the luxuries of Babylon—especially the "kings" and "merchants"—will mourn their great material losses (Rev 18:9,11). And they will be terrified that the destruction is accomplished so quickly.

Verse twenty-one is a particularly explicit depiction of interaction between the metaphysical and physical during the Great Tribulation.

> Then a mighty angel picked up a boulder the size of a large millstone and threw it into the sea, and said: "With such violence the great city of Babylon will be thrown down, never to be found again."

In this scene an angel (universally recognized as a non-physical being) employs a huge boulder (an obviously physical object) to exert great physical violence upon the earth. John then lists a series of activities that will cease in Babylon as a result of the destruction, another good indication that it is an actual city.

An Aside: Deism—Mankind's Attempt to Ignore the Creator

Interactions between the metaphysical and physical are not rare in Scripture. Those such as the angel hurling a huge boulder into the sea are dramatic reminders that God can and does deal directly with His creation. In less dramatic fashion they may occur on a more frequent basis in everyday life. Unexplained "miraculous" cures and numerous other events interpreted as "answers to prayer," for example, may be the result of such interaction.

Establishing an observable link between metaphysical cause and physical effect, however, is impossible. Since the demand is for an "observable" link, one reducible to sensate verification, the causal side of the interaction always remains murky at best. As suggested earlier, this inability of human consciousness to perceive the linkage between the metaphysical and physical in sensate terms, i.e. as data reducible to sensate perception, is what allows even the most dramatic of miracles to be deemed tricks or flukes.

The insistence that all reality be reducible to sensate phenomena within the specified range of man's consciousness is closely tied to *deism*. This is a belief system that allows for the existence of a Creator God, but disallows the revelation of truth from God and any possible interaction He may have with His creation. Deism assumes that man's only means of becoming aware of reality is through his sensate abilities to perceive it, and through his rational abilities to process the sensate data. Many consider such notable latter-day scientists as Charles Darwin, Albert Einstein and Stephen Hawking to qualify as deists.

In effect deism is a convenient means of separating God from His creation. It pays lip service to the probability that the universe did have a beginning and did not come about by mere chance. At the same time it provides man the license of pursuing the truth of reality based solely on a consciousness constrained to sensation and reason. The impetus to do this is reasonable in itself. It makes sense for man to want to understand and control his own reality. But from the larger perspective, i.e. from the perspective of aiming to rationalize *all* of reality, deism is inherently self-contradictory and self-defeating.

The argument that God set His creation apart from Himself *at some point in time* misses the point that time itself is part of the creation—one of its dimensions. Man's experience of time is affected by his being defined within that dimension. It is impossible for man to have an unbiased and comprehensive understanding of time because it is an integral part of the reference frame from which he makes observations and draws conclusions about reality.

In Kantian terms one would argue that man's reference frame may be real in the noumenal sense, but his experience of it (and the reality it reveals) are restricted to phenomenal observation. Such observations are the product of the observer and cannot copy underlying reality with complete accuracy.[44] Man's perspective from "within" and as part of creation remains inadequate for him to distinguish when (and therefore if) God separated Himself from His creation. Mankind simply does not have the clear "overview" of creation (afforded by a perspective outside of it) that God has. As a result, man is not able to venture in any credible fashion what God may or may not have done.

In other words, mankind operates within a reality that he did not define. To conclude that there was a time when his reality included God and another when it did not is nothing more than WILLful speculation. Time is part of the reality that man has to deal with, but simply because it has particular significance to him (stemming from his limited perspective) is no basis for presuming the discontinuance (a time-defined concept) of relationship between Creator and creation.

Recognizing a Creator extraneous to the universe, as deism does, places man in the correct, subordinate position to God. In doing so it also precludes the possibility of man determining with any certainty that God has terminated that subordination. God and man are inextricably related and cannot be pulled apart for the convenience of mankind—a part of the creation. God Himself could, of course, end the relationship but there is no convincing evidence that has happened. It only makes sense to conclude that the relationship persists—whether or not man, guided by his own self-interests, desires to set it aside and redefine reality as "deistic."

Relationship between Creator and creation is the concern of religion and of Christianity in particular. The teachings of Christ and the Judaism that preceded Him are chock full of the revelations of God to man that are disallowed by deism. Christianity unlike deism, however, places no artificial constraints on how mankind relates to its Creator. It makes no assumption that the relationship is one-way from man to God and dependent upon mankind's limited capabilities to define its scope. Rather, Christianity teaches that mankind should avail itself of all means of relationship with its Creator. These would include all powers of consciousness bestowed by the Creator, and especially the communications of the Creator.

CHAPTER NINETEEN:

THE SECOND COMING, THE MILLENNIUM, AND FINAL JUDGMENT

Revelation, Chapter Nineteen: Hallelujah for the Second Coming!

Having been removed from the heavenly throne scene in chapter seventeen, John returns there in chapter nineteen. On the timeline of earthly events Babylon has been destroyed and the Great Tribulation is complete. In heaven a "great multitude" sang praise to the Lord—Hallelujah—for the justice and salvation He wrought (Rev 19:1). John witnessed a massive group of individual spirits, including the "twenty-four elders and the four living creatures," in joyous communication with their Creator (Rev 19:4). This image of heaven and heavenly praise is striking. It is the polar opposite of that sometimes portrayed in the popular media where bored angels tirelessly strum their harps.

John then invokes the very personal and intimate imagery of a wedding couple—the Lamb and His bride—

to describe whom among creation will share in eternal relationship with the Creator. " 'For our Lord God Almighty reigns...Let us rejoice...For the wedding of the Lamb has come and his bride has made herself ready'" (Rev 19:6,7). Here the Lamb figure, which is used extensively by John as a sacrificial symbol of Christ, is praised as the omnipotent Yahweh of Judaism and the triumphant redeemer of mankind coming to claim his "bride." He is Christ the DIVINE, transitioning for a second time from the metaphysical to the physical. The heavenly multitude is joyous that this time He will reign on earth with His communion of believers, His "bride" or "church."

Significantly, it is then revealed that there are those *outside* the church who will join in eternal relationship with the Lamb. John quotes God Himself via an angel: " ' "Blessed are those who are invited to the wedding supper of the Lamb!"'" (Rev 19:9). If Christ's church represents the bride at the initiation of eternal relationship (following the wedding feast), whom do the "invited" guests represent? Like the bride they are persons saved by faith, but unlike the bride they have not had direct exposure to the message of Christ. The distinction, however, seems significant only from an earthly perspective where timing is an important factor.

As the angel concludes in verse ten, " 'the testimony of Jesus is the spirit of prophecy'" (Rev 19:10). All people of all time will *not* have had witness to that testimony. Some, such as Old Testament saints, will avoid judgment and be saved by their faith in God and His gracious recognition of it. Even though they will not have known Christ in earth-time, it is the saving grace of His ATONEMENT that will qualify their faith for eternal relationship with Him.

John's image of Christ then shifts from that of the Lamb to a rider on a white horse. The shift is a dramatic recasting of the character of the DIVINE Christ for more complete comprehension by human consciousness. It is one of the very few truly pivotal moments in creation's history—the re-emergence of the Creator Himself into His creation. The event is so profound that John makes three separate attempts at describing the nature of the rider on the horse and His purpose in coming to earth.

He first describes the rider as the one who "is called Faithful and True" (Rev 19:11). In the DIVINE sense these descriptors denote much more than steadfastness (Faithful) and accuracy (True). The character of the rider is that He *is* truth, i.e. synonymous with it—an apparition of ultimate reality. John's experience is as much a noumenal sharing of DIVINE consciousness as it is the phenomenal experience of the incarnate Christ. Chillingly, the rider's purpose is to bring real justice and make war upon His enemies.

John also writes that the rider on the white horse "has a name written on him that no one knows but he himself" (Rev 19:12). "Name" (*onomah* in the Greek) is used here in its fullest sense, meaning all of the essential characteristics that a name implies. The rider's name is "the Word of God" where "Word" denotes ideation, i.e. projection of the non-physical Spirit of God into the cognitive consciousness of man.

In describing Christ the rider as the DIVINE Word or Spirit of God who no one knows but God Himself, John places believers (His "bride" and the invited guests) on notice regarding a fundamental aspect of their relationship. The groom fully understands and has complete consciousness of believers, but the believers do not and can never share the full consciousness of the groom. John is pointing out that eternal relationship will exist between Creator and creation, but that it is not a relationship between equals.

In order to emphasize the distinction between the

nature of the rider and that of the kingdom (His subjects) He is coming to establish, John writes of another "name." "On his robe and on his thigh he has this name written: King of Kings and Lord of Lords" (Rev 19:16). This is a clear statement of the absolute sovereignty and DIVINITY of the rider. Thus, John symbolizes Christ as a Lamb and as a rider on a white horse—comforting and powerful images of a savior who is coming to initiate eternal relationship with His creation. But His creation must be aware that He is "like" them and not literally one of them; He remains their absolute, holy (separate) ruler.

The remainder of chapter nineteen (19:17-21) picks up from chapter 16:15-16, which previews the SECOND COMING of Christ and the resulting Battle of Armageddon. Though there are several Old Testament references to this great battle (see, for example, Is 66:15,16; Joel 3:12-21; Eze 39:1-4, 17-20), Rev 16:16 is the only instance where it is actually named.

Some would argue that Mount Megiddo (or *Har Mageddon* in Hebrew, from which Armageddon takes its name) and its surrounding plains is not a physical, geographical reference. This argument holds that the Battle of Armageddon stands only as a symbol of Christ's defeat of earthly opposition. The context of the great battle in *Revelation*, however, points to physical conflict at an actual location. Verse 16:16, for example, refers to Armageddon as a "place," and 19:17-21 put heavy emphasis on the physical destruction of Christ's opponents.

John reuses the meal-taking metaphor to create a shocking and sobering contrast between the believers in Christ and his enemies. Instead of a wedding feast culminating in eternal relationship, the battle with Christ's opponents is described in terms of " 'the great supper of God'" (Rev 19:17). At this meal the birds of the earth are invited to feed on the flesh of all those committed to "the beast." Such earthly destruction is effected by the word of the Creator Himself—by "the sword that came out of the mouth of the rider on the horse" (Rev 19:21). Rather than initiating eternal relationship, the imagery of the Battle of Armageddon as a great supper suggests the beginning of an eternal divorce and separation.

Notably the beast and his false prophet meet their eternal doom following the Battle of Armageddon. They were "thrown alive into the fiery lake of burning sulphur," a common Biblical depiction of HELL (Rev 19:20). Their followers are "killed," meaning that they meet their earthly demise at Armageddon (Rev 19:21).

Eternal judgment of the beast's followers is apparently deferred to the end of time, when all who have consciously opposed Christ will be judged. "Deferment" of judgment for those who have passed from physical reality reflects the perspective of those still bound by that reality, those still alive on earth. In the absence of the time dimension one can think of eternal judgment and reward as *de facto* upon earthly death.

Revelation, Chapter Twenty: The Thousand Years and the Great White Throne

Chapter twenty of *Revelation* speaks of a thousand year period (millennium) when Christ reigns on earth. As with the other parts of this astounding piece of apocalyptic literature, the notion of a millennium on earth ruled by Christ has various interpretations. Most of them can be categorized as "premillennial," "postmillennial" or "amillennial."

The premillennial view considers the thousand years to be a well-defined period of time that can be fixed along the timeline of history. Specifically, it fits near the end of the Tribulation-SecondComing-Armageddon-Millennium-Final Judgment scenario that a fairly straightforward interpretation of John's experience yields. In contrast, the amillennial view holds that the millennium is actually an indeterminate length of time that has been underway since Christ's ascension. The postmillennial view is similar to the amillennial in that it does not consider the SECOND COMING as a precursor to the thousand years. Postmillenial interpretations hold that the thousand years refers to a long period of time that will ensue once the earth has been Christianized.

As noted earlier, throughout *Revelation* John sequences specific events along a timeline that is readily understandable to his earthbound readers. For example, when he first touches on the subject of "a thousand years" he indicates that those who did not receive the mark of the beast and were martyred, "because of their testimony for Jesus" will reign with Jesus during the millennium (Rev 20:4). The context and syntax support the conclusions that: (1) the Tribulation period is completed prior to the millennium, and (2) that Christ will be present to reign with the martyrs. It is established in the second half of chapter nineteen that Christ will physically manifest on earth prior to the millennium. Amillennial and postmillennial interpretations pay little heed to John's careful sequencing of specific events such as these.

Also in support of the premillennial view of chapter twenty is the use of specific numbers in combination with the word "year" or "years." In Scripture they are always combined literally, not symbolically. Thus, when chapter twenty speaks of "a thousand years," it is reasonable to assume the literal meaning. Christ's own descriptions of the SECOND COMING and millennium comport well with John's portrayal of specific events occurring at specific times (see, for example, Lk 17:22-24; Mt 19:28; Mt 24:42-44).

In describing the Tribulation martyrs who will reign with Christ in the millennium John writes that he "saw" their souls (Rev 20:4). Apparently he became consciously aware (i.e. had a visual impression of) their disembodied spirits. Assuming that his description is accurate, an obvious interaction between the physical and metaphysical had taken place. He then uses the interesting phraseology that they "came to life" to reign with Christ (Rev 20:4). Coming to life denotes resurrection and John qualifies this instance as "the first resurrection" (Rev 20:5).

But "coming to life" is more than a synonym for resurrection. John seems to be using the phrase exegetically—to expose more clearly what resurrection entails. Souls of the martyred saints "came to life," or "journeyed back to life" on earth—life that involved corporeal form. Those in the first resurrection are described as taking on some manner of physical representation. Their spirits transitioned back into space-

Inscription (Eze 37:14) at entrance to Yad VaShem Memorial and Holocaust Museum

time (came back to earth life) to reawaken the consciousness of prior space-time existence and become physically manifest. That resurrected beings could appear in the physical does not imply that their essential nature is physical. Such manifestations of spirit were described earlier as "spirit bodies."

Chapter twenty specifically mentions only the Tribulation martyrs taking part in the "first resurrection" and reigning with Christ during the thousand years (see Rev 20:4-5). The "rest of the dead" could then be interpreted as everyone except the martyrs; and they would, "not come to life until the thousand years were ended" (Rev 20:5). Other Scripture, however, strongly suggests that the group reigning with Christ will be much more inclusive than the Tribulation martyrs. For example, John indicates that the "armies of heaven" followed Christ on his return to earth (Rev 19:14). This is likely a reference to angelic beings, but may have been intended to include believers of all time.

Perhaps most revealing with respect to whom is resurrected when is Paul's teaching on the subject to the Corinthians. He provides a clear sequencing in the context of the end times.

> "For as in Adam all die, so in Christ all will be made alive. But each in his own turn: Christ, the firstfruits; then, when he comes, those who belong to him. Then the end will come, when he hands over the kingdom to God the Father after he has destroyed all dominion, authority and power" (1Cor 15:22-24).

Paul undoubtedly knew that Christ spoke of a separate resurrection for His followers, a "resurrection of the righteous" (Lk 14:14). John's "first resurrection" is most likely synonymous with Christ's "resurrection of the righteous" and "those who belong to him" being made alive as described by Paul.

It is in connection with the "first" resurrection that John speaks of the "second" death. As he explains at the end of chapter twenty, the second death is "the lake of fire," also known as HELL and perdition (Rev 20:14). The second death has no power over those who take part in the first resurrection; they will not experience HELL. There is the clear and ominous implication, however, that others will be resurrected and subject to death for a second time, the death of HELL. The second death, like the first, physical death, is a transition. What makes it so ominous is that it is a transition to a permanent condition.

During the millennium Satan is prevented from influencing the affairs of men on earth. John "saw" Satan bound in the Abyss (Rev 20:1-3). This is noteworthy because it implies that the DIVINE Christ and the resurrected saints will be the only "extraneous" moral influence on those who have not experienced the first (physical) death. Presumably those who have not died would be survivors of the Tribulation and their descendants. In other words, it appears that during the millennium the single inducement to immorality and rebellion against Christ will be man's own consciousness, specifically his own WILL. Nevertheless, under these ideal circumstances—perhaps even more ideal than existed in the Garden of Eden—mankind will develop antipathy toward God.

John indicates that when Satan is released after the thousand years he will go to the "four corners of the earth" to gather the nations for battle against God's people (Rev 20:8). How could this be possible? Earlier chapters of *Revelation* describe the elimination of earthly opposition to God during the Tribulation—a task personally completed by Christ at the Battle of Armageddon. Christ will then reign with His saints on earth for a thousand years. And yet, seemingly with little effort, Satan is able to stir up large numbers of people into rebellion.

Absent two critical factors—the enormous grace of God and the surprising power of the human WILL given by God—this unlikely chain of events makes no sense. One almost has to conclude that those gathered by Satan will need little or no proselytizing. Their hearts and minds will likely be opposed to Christ before Satan is released from the Abyss. If this is so, it speaks volumes about the power of the human WILL to set itself against the manifest presence of the Creator of the universe. That *any* level of opposition would be tolerated for a thousand years speaks volumes of the mercy and patience of the Creator. It also points to the Creator's purpose in providing the thousand-year period. As with the extreme conditions during the Tribulation, the extreme conditions during the millennium will present conspicuous opportunities for man to declare himself in unison with or in opposition to his Creator.

Looking a thousand years beyond Christ's SECOND COMING John speaks with certainty. Fire came down from heaven and devoured Satan's followers, those who "surrounded the camp of God's people, the city he loves" (Rev 20:9). Earthly opposition to God finally ceased, and Satan suffered the second death. This end-time event demonstrates commonalities between man and Satan. God created both; both exercise their WILL in opposition to their Creator; and both are subject to His judgment.

What follows Satan's spiritual demise in chapter twenty is the grand finale of the creation story. As God's creation had a beginning and a purpose, John now gives a brief and startling revelation of its end and the Creator's final evaluation of it. In a single, declarative sentence John prophesies the end of creation and the physical dimensionalities as we know them. Time and place vanish. "Earth and sky fled from his [God seated on the great white throne] presence, and there was no place for them" (Rev 20:11). This is not the only Scripture describing "un-creation" (see Mt 24:35; 2Pet 3:10; and Rev 21:1, 4-5), but it is the one that relates it most clearly to the reference frame (space-time) on which humans rely so heavily for their view of reality. John is speaking of the passage into a new, metaphysical reality undefined by the place and time that provide such comfort—and illusion—to human consciousness.

Christ and his saints, extant as essentially spiritual beings in their resurrected "bodies," would remain unaffected by what might be termed a "Reverse Big Bang." Similarly "the dead," who John saw resurrected and standing before the great white throne of God, continue to exist beyond the end of the universe (Rev 20:12). Exactly who "the dead" are is open to some question. Since Old and New Testament saints are said to have joined Christ in space-time during his millennial reign, the simplest conclusion is that "the dead" are those not alive in Christ at the cessation of time. Are we to understand, then, that "the dead" are all doomed to the second death for their opposition to Christ and their lack of faith?

Many do hold that *all* the dead who are judged at the great white throne are condemned to the lake of fire. But the context of the final judgment scene given by John does not support this view very well. When John says the dead were "judged" (Rev 20:12), the Greek *kreeno* is apparently being used with its most common meaning, i.e. to distinguish or choose and not in its much more restricted sense of condemnation. In other words, the context suggests that an actual DIVINE decision process is taking place.

John also notes that the judgment involves a review of what "they had done as recorded in the books," phrasing that the decision is dependent on the review (Rev 20:12). Conditionality is also strongly suggested at the very end of the chapter: "If anyone's name was not found written in the book of life, he was thrown into the lake of fire" (Rev 20:15). The implication of "if," of course, is that some of the names of those being judged may be in the book of life.

For which individuals might the final judgment at the great white throne be a judgment procedure in the normal sense? In what sense might the final judgment at the great white throne be something other than a summary condemnation? The most obvious cases that come to mind are those where individuals may have had no (or insufficient) exposure to Christ and His message. Their numbers could be huge, including those on earth before Christ, those who died while still young children or unborn, and those kept from receiving Christ's message. Only God would know the "sufficiency" of each individual's exposure to His Son's message and each individual's measure of faith.

An Aside: The Great White Throne Judgment and the End of Time

As suggested above, the great white throne judgment may seem even more foreign and mysterious than the end-time events that precede it in John's *Revelation*. The universe in all its dimensions has gone from existence and the reader is ushered into the reality of Christ as He judges people.

Time has ended as John attempts to describe the eternal reality in terms that make sense to people still alive on earth, i.e. his readers. In order to explain the great white throne judgment to space-time dwellers John translates God's certain knowledge about His Creation into a judgmental process involving time. But at the great white throne Christ operates outside the universe, and it becomes more apparent that time is irrelevant. Time cannot restrict the knowledge of the Creator of time; and there never existed a time when Christ the Creator was unaware of the outcome of His creation.

The great white throne judgment requires some appreciation of two distinct perspectives on reality, the temporal (earthly) and the eternal. For humans who have not yet died, a heavy dose of time references is helpful in making sense of the judgment scene. Thus, we talk of "final" judgment even though it occurs outside the universe. And John describes a deliberative process that can result in either redemption or condemnation. In effect, John's description is a sort of temporal best estimate of God's eternal reality. It yields a conscious awareness of what transpires, albeit an incomplete and somewhat illusory one.

Earthbound man's inability to fully grasp the eternal perspective is due, at least in part, to not being able to clearly conceptualize noumenal time—i.e., timelessness or time that is experientially different from earth time. The upshot of not being able to do so can be a seemingly contradictory conclusion: God knew everyone's eternal disposition *before* creating the universe, but will still be making decisions about their eternal existence *after* the universe has "fled from his presence" (Rev 20:11).

If one recognizes, however, that temporal reality is separate from and subordinate to God's greater, eternal reality, the apparent contradiction can be explained. What God knows only appears to contradict the *written translation* of John's experiences. The translation process necessarily reduced his metaphysical experiences to symbols (human language) derived totally from physical experience. In this manner John's metaphysical experiences could not avoid taking on the characteristics of our own earthly experiences, including our sense of time. But our space-time is only a "subset" of God's total reality. Experiences we have within our created subset seem real enough to us, but are not equivalent to the full reality of God. Our experience of reality is incomplete and subordinate to God's, and is often conceived as a "DIVINE experiment."

We also need to recognize that it is necessary to train our consciousness in the direction of the Creator's eternal perspective. With respect to the great white throne judgment this means understanding that Christ's perspective does not completely negate our own time bound perspective but, instead, greatly enhances it. We may conclude that God offers redemption "when" he chooses (our perspective) without rejecting the notion that He has "always" known who will and will not be saved (His perspective).

As we move outside the time dimension we will come closer to God's broad and true perspective. One might say that as time looses its hold on us by virtue of its own end we will share a truer perspective of the Creator's judgment. Our space-time reality will expand into that of the Creator; or, to use the "subset" framework, our subset will lose its boundaries and merge into the overall eternal set. This kind of thinking is particularly important when considering how our created WILL interacts with that of the Creator.

Curiously, death itself is judged at the great white throne and, along with the resurrected "dead" (or at least some of them), undergoes the second death of the lake of fire (see Rev 20:14). How is it possible for death to die? Or, more precisely, how is it possible for the first death to die the second death? Given that the second death is defined by separation from the Creator, the banishment of physical death to that state implies perfection of the saints in glory *with* their Creator. Their spirits (consciousness) become immune to any further negative experiences such as death. Conversely, negative experience would continue to exist in that state of consciousness having no relationship with the Creator—the state to which such experiences are banned. Imperfection (sin) would be possible only in HELL.

Revelation, Chapter Twenty-One: The New Jerusalem—The New Reality

Without question chapter twenty-one of the book of *Revelation* is one of the most intriguing and exciting in all of Scripture. It is nothing less than a peek behind the curtain into the new reality that we sometimes wistfully refer to as "heaven." As such it demands the utmost imagination, concentration and spiritual guidance to unveil its truths. At this point in his writing John has completely transitioned into the reality of the eternal state. "Then I saw a new heaven and a new earth, for the first heaven and the first earth had passed away..." (Rev 21:1). He employs every nuance of language to communicate about heaven to his fellow earth dwellers.

Missouri woods sunrise

John's first vision of the "new heaven," "Holy City," or "New Jerusalem" is, "as a bride beautifully dressed for her husband" (Rev 21:2). Once again he invokes the metaphor of a Jewish wedding ceremony in an attempt to articulate the ineffable. As before "bride" is symbolic of the faithful collection of believers in Christ—His church. But here the bride becomes a group of individual persons likened to a place, the new Holy City of Jerusalem. How is it possible that persons can constitute a place? In our more literal space-time reality it makes almost no sense; place and person are always distinct. John is obviously attempting to stretch our understanding of what is to be.

A loud voice from the throne of God, presumably God Himself, then tells John: " 'Now the dwelling of God is with men, and he will live with them. They will be his people, and God himself will be with them and be their God' " (Rev 21:3). The "dwelling" of God (the city and bride) has come into being, and God will live there. As John learns later, it is the personage of Christ, again symbolized as the Lamb, who will join in intimate relationship with the bride. Thus, Christ is coming to live with people who—at least metaphorically—comprise a great, newly created city. Pursuing this thought we might conclude that the New Jerusalem is "new" in that it is made suitable (i.e. perfected) for intimate co-habitation with Christ.

God, speaking from the throne, then confirms that he is making everything new (see Rev 21:5). He also confirms that he has the power to remake reality because he *is* the ultimate reality and defines all of reality. " 'I am the Alpha and Omega, the Beginning and the End' " (Rev 21:6). In other words, God is totally inclusive and contains all reality in all its possible dimensions, including time and space. " 'It is done' " God says, meaning that heaven, the New Jerusalem has been brought into being (Rev 21:6). Again, God's emphatic use of the past tense is confusing for time bound earth dwellers.

God delineates sharply between those who will be in the new Holy City and those who will transition to the "second death" reality of HELL. " 'He who overcomes will inherit all this [the new heaven], and I will be his God and he will be my son' " (Rev 21:7). The Greek gives a clearer meaning of two key words in this declaration. "Overcomes" (*nikaho*) denotes conquering or gaining

Mosaic of The Alpha and Omega in the Basilica of the Agony (Church of All Nations) on the Mount of Olives outside the eastern wall of Old City Jerusalem

victory, but its use in combination with "inherit" (*klayronomeho*) indicates that victory over the opposition will be handed down as a gift or inheritance from the Father. The gift is conditioned on faithfulness and obedience to the Father. Thus, the reality of heaven flows from interaction with God, but in no sense is payment for it. As in the earthly state, inheritances are not earnings in fulfillment of an obligation; they are gifts in recognition of relationship.

God Himself characterizes in detail those persons who will not dwell "in" the bride, New Jerusalem. " 'But the cowardly, the unbelieving, the vile, the murderers, the sexually immoral, those who practice magic arts, the idolaters and all liars—their place will be in the fiery lake of burning sulphur'" (Rev 21:8). It is noteworthy that God speaks of character traits, not specific actions. In other words what is abhorrent to God is that these persons have taken on the character—they have WILLfully drawn into their consciousness—the quality of prohibited behavior. They have willfully come to personify disobedience to their Creator.

Having distinguished between the saved and unsaved, i.e. between those who are and are not the bride, an angel reveals even more clearly the identity of the groom to John. The wedding metaphor is completed as the angel names the bride as the " 'wife of the Lamb'" (Rev 21:9). This particular reference to Christ "the Lamb" is one of the most elegant and unmistakable Biblical assertions of Christ's DIVINITY. Christ is the groom who will dwell with faithful mankind, the same one identified *by God* as, " 'God himself [who] will be with them and be their God'" at 21:3. Thus, the bride (or Holy City of believers) is made new and enters into intimate partnership (becomes the wife) of God (Christ). *This is what heaven is all about: close relationship with the Creator.*

The same angel who shows John "the wife" then reveals her beauty in glorious detail. She, "the Holy City, Jerusalem, coming down out of heaven from God" is said to shine brilliantly "with the glory of God" (Rev 21:10,11). God's own magnificent character and beauty stream forth from the city. Interestingly, John attempts to describe this experience in very material—one could even say hyper-material—terms. Walls, streets and gates are all of gargantuan size as measured by earthly standards; still, they are all made of precious materials. The great street of the city is pure gold but not the type man has treasured for millennia. It appeared as transparent glass to John.

Having described the New Jerusalem in material terms, John makes a critical observation: "I did not see a temple in the city…" (Rev 21:22). On earth the temple was a material structure used to define the physical locus for communication between spiritual God and physical man. In heaven, however, there is no temple, "because the Lord God Almighty and the Lamb are its temple" (Rev 21:22). In other words, God and Christ are spirit and need no physical representation in heaven. They can be present "in" the city and the city dwellers can be "in" the temple absent any material structures.

John continues his description of the non-material nature of the God-man relationship. "The city does not need the sun or the moon to shine on it for the glory of God gives it light, and the Lamb is its lamp" (Rev 21:23). To paraphrase we can say that the city (glorified people from the physical realm) does not need a sun or moon (which existed in the old physical realm) because the glory of God (obviously non-physical) gives it light (physical in the sense of photons, but non-physical in the sense of enlightened spirit or consciousness).

Is John's description of the New Jerusalem in both hyper-materialistic and spiritual terms a contradiction? Should we conclude that the New Jerusalem parallels the Old Jerusalem in both its physical nature and as a state of communion between God and man? *Revelation* 21:22 argues against this interpretation. It would be inconsistent for the New Jerusalem to manifest physically and the temple (its most important structure) and its Creator not to do so. Our own spatio-temporal inclinations pull us toward a view of Christ in heaven as a physical person placing Himself in the midst of a huge, jeweled metropolis filled with reincarnate believers. This view may well reflect the limits of language more than the nature of the new reality.

If we begin with the premise that the eternal does not rely on the physical expressions of reality with which we are most familiar, the Lamb-temple/bride-city imagery can be clearly interpreted. It speaks of the God-man relationship discussed by Jesus in his final discourse on Thursday of Passion Week. Jesus spoke about His relationship with the Trinity and His relationship with His followers. Habitation of Christ "in" the Trinity is analogous to that of Christ "in" the saints.

Individual people are "in" Christ as He is "in" the Father. Furthermore, Christ is in the bride/city, and by virtue of that relationship the bride/city is "in" the ultimate reality that is God. But neither space nor time is a requisite feature of these relationships. As John's failure to see the temple indicates, eternal reality does not depend on visual cues from physical objects. Still, the image of Christ dwelling in His temple within the city of His people gets across the basic idea of co-existence in close proximity. Where it falls a bit short is in communicating the very real, intense and intimate sharing of consciousness within the Trinity and between Christ and His creation.

Does this line of thinking mean that the streets of heaven will not be paved with pure gold and that its walls will not be made of pure diamond, sapphire and emerald? Obviously no one knows with certainty whether John's vision will be realized in a new material or hyper-material form. It may take such form but would not require it to realize the ineffable glory and fascination of shared consciousness with the Creator.

Revelation, Chapter Twenty-Two: Jesus Is Coming Soon

The final chapter of John's *Revelation* continues describing the reality of the New Jerusalem. "Water of

Golden Gate in the eastern wall of Old City Jerusalem

life" flows from the throne of God down the middle of the great street, and on either side stands the tree of life, bearing nourishing fruit and healing leaves. Again, the imagery is of substantive, physical "things" very familiar to earth dwellers—water and trees. In the context of the new reality of heaven, however, the life-giving water is of the type Jesus spoke about to the Samaritan woman at the well near Sychar (see Jn 4:13-14).

In the New Jerusalem it is the belief in Christ that provides ongoing access to and relationship with the

DIVINE spirit of Christ. The intimacy of relationship between man and God is captured by John's statement: "They will see his [God's] face, and his name will be on their foreheads" (Rev 22:4). The glorified saints will share the personal presence of God and God will claim them as His own—the exact antithesis of HELL.

As the saints share the presence of God, "they will reign [with Him] for ever and ever" (Rev 22:5). But John again makes it clear that the God-man co-regency in heaven is not one shared by equals. The angel showing John the New Jerusalem says: " 'The Lord, the God of the spirits of the prophets sent [me] to show his servants the things that must soon take place'" (Rev 22:6). Man and other created beings (e.g. angels) will be servant-kings in heaven, remaining subordinate to God but realizing their full potential and reigning with Him.

This condition in eternal reality has an interesting, inverse analogue in temporal reality. Christ the eternal DIVINE King temporarily subordinated Himself as the servant-king in order to redeem mankind. In heaven man will be eternally glorified to reign as servant-king with Christ.

Having experienced at least part of the reality of heaven, John is told by the angel to, "not seal up the words of the prophecy of this book..." (Rev 22:10). Apparently John was being encouraged to disseminate his astoundingly positive vision of the reality that awaits believers in Christ. This contrasts with the angel's earlier command to: " 'Seal up what the seven thunders have said and do not write it down'" (Rev 10:4). "Seven thunders" is indicative of divine judgment, specifically the judgment of those who reject Christ.

John hints at the role of human WILL in determining the righteous and unrighteous. "Let him who does wrong continue to do wrong; let him who is vile continue to be vile; let him who does right continue to do right; and let him who is holy continue to be holy" (Rev 22:11). This is not a suggestion that some *should* do "wrong" and others "right." John is simply noting that individuals will be saved or damned in accordance with what they *continue* to do. Implicit in the statement is that discontinuance (repentance) can lead to the opposite result.

Jesus re-enters directly into the narrative in verses seven and twelve, announcing: " 'Behold, I am coming soon!' " And He immediately reaffirms his DIVINITY. " 'I am the Alpha and the Omega, the First and the Last, the Beginning and the End' " (Rev 22:13). The word "soon" is a time reference for John and his readers, but the context suggests an absolute meaning derived from Christ's DIVINE, timeless perspective. Christ is speaking from heaven and John has been transported there in the spirit. Christ's repeated claims of being the Alpha and Omega (four times in *Revelation*), unaffected by time, also supports this absolutist interpretation of "soon."

What is the *absolute* meaning of an adverb that signifies a relatively short period of time to humans with an earthly perspective? In the absolute sense "soon" loses its temporal quality and takes on the quality of certainty. Christ's SECOND COMING is a function of His WILL which is not bounded by earthly time schedules. His repeated promise that He is "coming soon" indicates that, without question, he will again manifest on earth. The exact placement of that event on man's timeline, however, is indeterminate—definable, as all time is, by the WILL of the Alpha and Omega.

Jesus then makes another clear distinction between the saved and unsaved. Those who have the right of access to the tree of life may enter the New Jerusalem. Those who have not " 'wash[ed] their robes' " (Rev 22:14), i.e. have rejected Christ's forgiveness of their sins, must remain outside the city and Christ's presence. Verse 22:15 suggests that their immorality is ongoing eternally.

The key distinction between heaven and HELL is life-sustaining relationship with Jesus who is God. Significantly, Jesus' last recorded words in *Revelation* are bold statements that He is God, He became man, and He is coming soon. " 'I am the Root and the Offspring of David…Yes, I am coming soon' " (Rev 22:16,20). Jesus declares Himself as the DIVINE, life-giving source or "Root" of the great king David and also his human descendant or "Offspring." Jesus answered the question He had put to the Pharisees: " 'If then David calls him "Lord," how can he be his son?' " (Mt 22:45).

John completes his *Book of Revelation* with the somber warning that no one should add to or take away from it.

> If anyone adds anything to them [the words of prophecy], God will add to him the plagues described in this book. And if anyone takes words away from this book of prophecy, God will take away from him his share in the tree of life and in the holy city, which are described in this book (Rev 22:18-19).

The threats to those who would alter John's prophecy with the horrors of the Tribulation and the second death speak of its enormous consequence to believers. The *Book of Revelation* stands as the completion of scriptural canon—complete because it spans all of time from shortly after Christ's ascension, through the SECOND COMING, and beyond time into the New Jerusalem. Because it is complete, it is unique; it stands alone and needs no embellishments or deletions. And its status as revealed truth is attested to by Jesus, the DIVINE truth Himself: " 'I, Jesus, have sent my angel to give you this testimony for the churches' " (Rev 22:16).

ENDNOTES

[1] M. H. Shakir, trans., *The Qur'an*, 12th U.S. ed. (Elmhurst, N.Y.: Tahrike Tarsile Qur'an, Inc., 2001) 73.

[2] N. K. Sandars, trans., *The Epic of Gilgamesh* (London: Penguin Books, 1972).

[3] Martin Luther, *The Bondage of the Will*, trans. Henry Cole (Grand Rapids, Mich.: Baker Book House, 1976).

[4] James Strong, *The New Strong's Expanded Exhaustive Concordance of the Bible*, Red-Letter ed. (Nashville, Tenn.: Nelson, 2001). Word derivations from the Hebrew and Greek are also quoted from this source.

[5] Kenneth Barker, ed., *The NIV Study Bible: New international Version* (Grand Rapids, MI.: Zondervan, 1985).

[6] Charles Darwin, *On the Origin of Species* (New York: Sterling, 2008).

[7] Michael J. Behe, *Darwin's Black Box* (New York: The Free Press, 1996).

[8] Hopefully the logic of this conclusion is obvious to the reader. If Jesus was in fact God incarnate, He spoke truth with absolute knowledge and authority. One critical feature of His teaching is that belief in Him is the *singular* path to eternal life. Thus, the issue of which source of revealed truth is the correct one is settled, and all other paths become dead ends. The primary issue for Christians then becomes one of correctly interpreting what Christ revealed.

[9] *The NIV Study Bible*. Unless otherwise noted scriptural quotes are from this Bible.

[10] "Dionysius Exiguus." *Encyclopedia Britannica Online*. 8 May 2009 <http://www.britannica.com/EBchecked/topic/164239/Dionysius-Exiguus>.

[11] Synoptic Gospel writers Matthew, Mark and Luke were so-called because of their one or very similar view in describing the events of Jesus' ministry.

[12] Maps of Galilee show Capernaum at the northern end of the Sea of Galilee, i.e. "up" from Cana. However, Capernaum is "down" from Cana with respect to elevation. This latter use of "up" and "down" is common throughout Scripture.

[13] The Lockman Foundation, *The Amplified Bible*, (Grand Rapids, MI.:

Zondervan, 1987).

[14] *Holy Bible: Authorized King James Version*, (Nashville, Tenn.: Nelson, 1990).

[15] *The Amplified Bible.*

[16] *Ibid.*

[17] *King James Version.*

[18] *Ibid.*

[19] John MacArthur, *The MacArthur Bible Commentary* (Nashville, Tenn.: Nelson, 2005) 1216.

[20] MacArthur 1379.

[21] MacArthur 1382.

[22] MacArthur 1391.

[23] MacArthur 1231.

[24] Sir John Eccles, neurologist and Nobel Prize winner used this term in his book *Evolution of the Brain: Creation of the Self* (London: Routledge, 1989) 241. To quote Sir John: "I maintain that the human mystery is incredibly demeaned by reductionism, with its claim in promissory materialism to account eventually for all of the spiritual world in terms of patterns of neural activity. This belief must be classed as a superstition…We are spiritual beings with souls in a spiritual world, as well as material beings with bodies and brains existing in a material world."

[25] Dinesh D'Souza, *What's So Great About Christianity* (Washington, D.C.: Regnery, 2007) 239-249.

[26] Mario Beauregard & Denyse O'Leary, *The Spiritual Brain: A Neuroscientist's Case for the Existence of the Soul* (New York, N.Y.: HarperOne, 2007).

[27] Dr Francis Collins makes essentially this same argument for the inability of science, including Darwinian evolution, to prove or disprove the existence of God. Collins, a practicing Christian, headed the Human Genome Project which succeeded in mapping out the entire human DNA sequence. See: Francis S. Collins, *The Language of God* (New York, N.Y.: Free Press,

2006) 165-67.

[28] Edward Feser, *The Last Superstition: A Refutation of the New Atheism* (South Bend, Indiana: St. Augustine's Press, 2008).

[29] At the risk of belaboring the point, it should be noted that the notion of *absolute* randomness does *not* argue that natural selection occurs for no *apparent or discernible* reason. If it exists, absolute randomness must occur for *no reason (or cause) whatsoever*. Absent complete knowledge of *all* reality the case for absolute randomness cannot be made. And absolute randomness is the only alternative that can substitute for intentionality, i.e. the directed (purposeful) causative force that is antithetical to absolute randomness.

Incidentally, if the case for absolute randomness in nature *could* be made, the consciousness (mind) making it would replace God as the highest consciousness since it would know with certainty that a primary mover or cause (God) is not required for reality to exist. Such knowledge, however, is highly problematic for the "promissory" or "eliminative" materialist given that the mind that would know it could only be illusory and , therefore, no substitute for God after all.

[30] McArthur 1420, "Explaining Two Passovers."

[31] Ayn Rand developed and espoused a philosophy that she labeled "Objectivism." It champions laissez-faire capitalism and the preeminence of the individual, and is portrayed in her two best-selling novels, *The Fountainhead* and *Atlas Shrugged.* The basic ethic of Objectivism Rand terms "rational self interest," the notion that mankind's greatest moral purpose is the attainment of individual happiness. This purpose derives from and is justified entirely by man's existence as a sensate, conscious being.

Central to Rand's conclusion that selfishness (i.e. "selfishness" in the sense of rational pursuit of happiness by individuals) is the greatest virtue is the presumption that individual people have the greatest value of all extant beings. This line of thought ignores Christian concepts of reality. Like atheism, Objectivism places limits on reality that are a function of the human observer's abilities to perceive and think rather than from truly "objective" knowledge about its makeup. Obviously, it also ignores the possibility of a Creator God, and a moral system based on the metaphysical perspective of a supreme being.

[32] The meaning of "eternal" or "eternality" can be a difficult one for earthbound observers to grasp. Scriptural definitions often center around the notion of everlasting time or perpetuity, i.e. an unrestricted version of time as we experience it on earth. For a better understanding of the distinction between eternality and earth time it is helpful to examine scriptural

references such as Psalm 90:2: "Before the mountains were born or you brought forth the earth and the world, from everlasting to everlasting you are God." "Everlasting" (or "eternal") as used here is from the Hebrew *olawm* and means "at the very beginning."

In other words it describes the perspective of the Creator "before" He brought the universe into existence. Since the Hebrew God, Yahweh was considered "preexistent," His existence "before" the creation of space-time (wherein our whole notion of time arises) could more accurately be thought of as "outside" or "separate from" the universe. Thinking of God "at the very beginning" as meaning separate from His creation distinguishes two realities: an eternal reality unbounded by time in the manner we experience it on earth; and a created reality in which time is a defining dimension. The concept of eternal as separate or unrelated to time is consistent with most metaphysical definitions of the term. The *Oxford English Dictionary* (*Shorter* version, sixth edition, Oxford University Press, 2007) for example, defines "eternal" as: "not conditioned by time; not subject to time relations."

[33] "Pluto Not a Planet, Astronomers Rule." *National Geograpic News*. 2006. MasonInman.24August2006<http://news.nationalgeographic.com/news/2006/08/060824-pluto-planet.html.

[34] Thomas's exchange with the risen Christ gives additional support to the argument that Jesus' body was transformed upon resurrection. Obviously Thomas would not have been able to place his hand into the open wound of Christ's unchanged physical body.

[35] MacArthur 1446.

[36] MacArthur 1457.

[37] MacArthur 1462.

[38] For an insightful exposition of the theistic background and underpinnings of Darwinian theory read: *Darwin's God: Evolution and the Problem of Evil* by Cornelius G. Hunter (Grand Rapids, MI.: Brazos Press, 2001).

[39] Peter Russell, *From Science to God* (Novato, CA.: New World Library, 2003) 90.

[40] Immanuel Kant, *Critique of Pure Reason* (New York, NY: Barnes & Noble, 2004).

The reader of Kant will note that he attributes special qualities to space and time. In his view we know nothing about space and time apart from our subjective experience (or awareness) of them as necessary conditions for experiencing "external" and "internal" reality, i.e. reality outside and inside ourselves. They are not the objects of experience, but have the peculiar quality of being "necessary components" of *any* sensory experience. In Kant's terminology they are "empirically real" (we are aware of them) *and* "transcendentally ideal" (they are components of all cognition involving sensory input). Mankind's knowledge of space and time, he argues, exists *"a priori,"* i.e. absolutely independent of all sensory experience.

Einstein's theories of relativity, however, oppose this absolutist attribution of space and time; i.e. they are not fixed preconditions within the observer for experiencing physical existence, but rather dimensions of it. Our conceptions (knowledge) of space and time are affected by how we experience them. In Kantian terms we know of them *"a posteriori,"* rather than *"a priori"* as he reasoned. Thus, our knowledge of them derives at least partially from sensate experience.

But Kant's distinction between our *phenomenal* experience of physical existence (which in his nomenclature is always *a posteriori*) and *noumenal* physical existence still holds. Our intellectual constructs of physical existence are defined and limited by our sensory and cognitive capacities, as well as the physical nature of what we are experiencing. Einstein's work brought space and time into Kant's phenomenal realm and subject to the same critique of reason concerning what we are capable of knowing about them.

[41] This statement ignores the state of consciousness of Christ's saints who return to earth for the thousand-year period (or "millennium") spoken of in *The Book of Revelation.*

[42] "Timeline of instructions per second." *Wikipedia.* 6 December 2008 <http://en.wikipedia.org/wiki/instructions-per-second.

[43] For an interesting summary of the distinction between death (or the "abode of the dead") and hell see: McArthur 2037, "Key Word: Hades."

[44] For man's consciousness to "copy" or represent all of reality with perfect accuracy it would have to be omniscient, a condition which deism does not accept.

ABOUT THE AUTHOR

Douglas Michael Browning received his baccalaureate in Psychology from the University of Cincinnati. He served as a Russian linguist in the U.S. Air Force Security Service during the Vietnam War. Following military service he earned an MBA in Finance from Indiana University. Since retiring early from a career in finance and investing he has been a student of Biblical Scripture and comparative religion. As a Roman Catholic turned agnostic turned born-again evangelical, he argues that sharing in the consciousness of God as taught by Jesus Christ is open to all mankind.

www.ingramcontent.com/pod-product-compliance
Lightning Source LLC
LaVergne TN
LVHW050918080826
845145LV00001B/122

* 9 7 8 0 5 7 8 0 2 6 8 2 4 *